The Kids' Nature Book

The Kids' Nature Book

· · · · · · · · · · · · · ·

365 Indoor/Outdoor Activities and Experiences

Susan Milord

WILLIAMSON PUBLISHING
CHARLOTTE, VERMONT

**Library of Congress Cataloging-in-
Publication Data**

Milord, Susan.
   The kids' nature book.

   Bibliography: p.
   Includes index.
   Summary: Suggests activities, poems,
and stories to explore nature throughout
the year.
   1. Nature study—Juvenile literature.
2. Natural history—Outdoor books—
Juvenile literature.   [1. Nature study.
2. Natural history—Outdoor books] I.
Title.
QH51.M57 1989   508   89-14724
ISBN 0-913589-42-X

Cover design: Trezzo-Braren Studio
Book design: Susan Milord
Illustrations: Susan Milord, with selected
works from the Dover Pictorial Archival
Series
Typography: The Sant Bani Press,
Tilton, NH
Printing: Capital City Press

Williamson Publishing Co.
Charlotte, Vermont 05445

Manufactured in the United States of
America

10 9 8 7 6 5 4 3

Selected illustrations taken from the following books:

Animals: 1419 Copyright Free Illustrations of Mammals, Birds, Fish, Insects, etc.
Selected by Jim Harter (Dover Publications, Inc., 1979)

Beasts & Animals in Decorative Woodcuts of the Renaissance
Konrad Gesner (Dover, 1983)

1800 Woodcuts by Thomas Bewick and His School
Edited by Blanche Cirker (Dover, 1962)

Food and Drink: A Pictorial Archive from Nineteenth-Century Sources
Selected by Jim Harter (Dover, 1979)

Harter's Picture Archive for Collage and Illustration
Edited by Jim Harter (Dover, 1978)

Pictorial Archive of Printer's Ornaments from the Renaissance to the 20th Century
Selected by Carol Belanger Grafton (Dover, 1980)

Pictorial Archive of Quaint Woodcuts in the Chap Book Style by Joseph Crawhall
Selected and arranged by Theodore Menten (Dover, 1974)

Plant and Floral Woodcuts for Designers and Craftsmen: 419 Illustrations from the Renaissance Herbal of Clusius
Selected and arranged by Theodore Menten (Dover, 1974)

Read-to-Use Old-Fashioned Animal Cuts
Edited by Carol Belanger Grafton (Dover, 1987)

Silhouettes: A Pictorial Archive of Varied Illustrations
Edited by Carol Belanger Grafton (Dover, 1979)

Treasury of Art Nouveau Design and Ornament: A Pictorial Archive of 577 Illustrations
Selected by Carol Belanger Grafton (Dover, 1980)

Acknowledgements

For Angus

There are many people I would like to thank for making this book possible. I am especially indebted to Jack and Susan Williamson, who care a great deal not only about books, but about the people who write them. Their support throughout has been tremendous. My thanks to Bonnie Hughes for all she has done.

I would also like to thank the many people who offered suggestions, criticism and information that have made this a book kids will enjoy and learn from. Special thanks to Jerry Rasmussen, Steve Faccio and Kai Underwood of the Stamford Museum & Nature Center in Stamford, Connecticut. Thanks to Diane DeLuca and Zoë French of the Audubon Society of New Hampshire. Thanks to Connie Tobey of the Gale Memorial Library in Laconia, New Hampshire. Thanks also to Rick Glatz, Alan Pistorius, Larry Frates, Ellen Chandler, Richard Moore, Chuck Rogers, Nancy LaPlante and special friends Heidi Currier, Francesca Fay and Deb Stavin.

Finally, thanks to my mother, Anne Pitoniak Milord, for her special brand of wisdom; and to my husband, Skip Gorman, and our son, Angus, for encouraging me and enabling me to see this project through.

Contents

continued on the next page

Contents

Something for everyone

The world of nature beckons you! There are so many fun things to do to get to know nature, both indoors and out, every season of the year. *The Kids' Nature Book* is chock-full of ideas and projects that will take you from the first day of January to the last day of December. There's something you can do every day!

Are you looking for some great ways to spend time outdoors during the winter months? Look no further. Would you like to make a rain gauge? Or learn what clues to look for to tell how fast the wind is blowing? Would you like to make your own snow cream? It's all here!

How do you find what you're looking for? Well, there are a couple of ways to use this book. Take a minute and flip through the pages. You'll notice the year (and the book) is divided into weekly sections. Every week centers around a theme, such as watching birds in flight, or exploring in and around water.

You can use this book like a calendar, following the suggestions day by day. Everyday there's a suggestion for an outing, or for a project you can complete all by yourself. There are plenty of ideas for crafting with materials you find in nature; and simple experiments to conduct that will help you understand the natural world. There are even games you can play with all your friends, and suggestions for stories and poems to read when you're in the mood for something quiet.

Just keep in mind that even though the suggestions are as closely tied to seasonal happenings as can be, you'll have to make allowances for what is actually happening in nature at any given time. You'll also have to take into account where you live, and the busy life you lead. Not everybody can spend time down at the beach in July, for example. It hasn't rained at all this April? Skip over those weeks and turn to some others that make more sense for you.

You can also use the book selectively. Let's say you want to know about counting the rings on a tree stump. Flip to the index and look under *Trees, rings*. That entry will direct you to page 31. On that page, you'll see "Count the rings on a tree stump" right on February 10. Would you like to know more about trees? Maybe you'd like to plant a tree on Arbor Day this year, or learn more about those trees that shed their leaves in the fall. The index will tell you exactly where to go.

Get it together!

Luckily, you don't need much in the way of equipment to enjoy nature. You already have the most important tools there are—your eyes, ears, nose and hands! (Taste, the fifth sense, isn't as important here as the other four senses are.) You can, and will, venture out-of-doors empty-handed much of the time. But there are a few small items that will help you make the most of your nature discoveries.

The following list includes those items that may prove useful throughout the year. It is a fairly basic list, and does not include the materials you'll need to construct such things as a wormery, bird house or kite. What you'll need to complete those projects will be listed with the instructions on those particular days.

All the items listed here are readily available, but you can make substitutions in many cases. A small paring knife (with some sort of protective sheath) can go in your backpack instead of a pocket knife. You can also rig some of your own equipment. Make your own nets (the instructions for a basic net are on June 24). You don't have a yardstick? Just mark off inches on a long, straight stick. It works just as well!

How to use this book

For viewing
Magnifier (folding field lens is handiest—5x or 10x magnification)
Binoculars (7 × 35 is a good choice for all-round viewing)
Camera

For collecting
Small net for aquatic life
Large net for insects
Trowel
Pocket knife
Hammer and chisel
Jars, pails, boxes and other containers

For recording
Tape measure
Yardstick
Thermometer
Small notebook
Plaster of Paris

Tape recorder
Compass

For keeping
Aquarium
Pet carrying case
Wire cages
Cardboard boxes

Miscellaneous
Backpack
Insect repellent
First aid kit
Field guides
Reference books

Don't forget that many containers for collecting and keeping can be made from recycled boxes, jars and plastic containers. For more on recycling containers for your nature studies, see *Wait, don't throw that away!* on page 20.

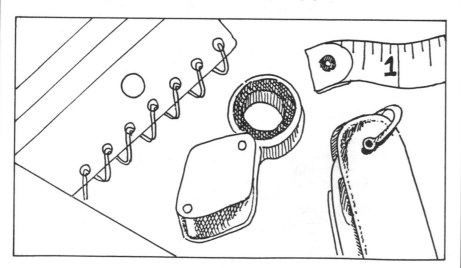

Rules of the road

Nature is all around you, whether you live deep in the country or in the heart of a bustling city! In most places, you don't have to go far to touch a tree, or listen to crickets chirping, or to collect rock samples.

There are a few things you should keep in mind when exploring outdoors. First, you must respect any property you venture on. Much seemingly wild property actually belongs to someone. Always ask permission before you wander onto someone else's land (especially if it is posted with signs that say KEEP OFF). A lot of people who tack these signs on their property feel much the same as you do about nature. Most are simply trying to protect their land from misuse. Who knows? You may make some new friends!

When you are on public property (be it a park in your town or a national forest) remember not to pick any plants or tamper with nature in any way that would disturb the beauty and serenity that is there for all to discover.

Secondly, show respect for wildlife by treating all habitats with care. Don't go turning over rocks, or poking sticks into holes. Animals live in these places! In every habitat, there's a delicate balance between the plants and animals that live there. While swatting a mosquito that lands on your arm will make little difference one way or another, disturbing nesting sites or pulling up clumps of grass is disruptive.

That goes for picking plants, such as wildflowers, too. When you find wildflowers that are free for the taking, don't be greedy. Many wildflowers are annual plants that need to set seeds (and distribute them) so that there will be more plants the following year. A general rule of thumb—take only a few of any one kind of plant, and only if there are lots to choose from. Don't pull plants up by

their roots. Instead, cut the stems cleanly with a knife or a pair of scissors. Cut branching stems whenever possible. Remember, don't pick any plants that are endangered. You can find out what plants these are by contacting a local nature center or your state's department of natural resources.

What about animals? Is it all right to capture them, even for just an overnight stay? Well, this is a harder question to answer. Many animals are protected by law against handling. You can understand why this is. Who's to make sure animals don't suffer at the hand of man unless we do?

You should certainly only capture an animal if you can do so without harming the animal (and yourself) in any way. You should ask yourself if you will truly benefit from studying the animal at such close range. You can learn so much more by watching animals in their natural habitats, where they can go about their daily business.

. . . .

Saltwater wetlands are often found in sheltered areas between shoreline and dry land further inland. They are valuable breeding grounds and storm buffers, and as you might suspect, are teeming with life. Conservationists are trying hard to preserve these important areas whenever possible.

Try attracting wildlife to your property with food and shelter. You can get all sorts of animals from birds to butterflies to make themselves at home in your yard. You can set up a blind on your property to hide behind, or just look out your windows!

Room and board

If you would like to observe some animals up close, keep in mind that some animals take to captivity better than others. Insects are among the easiest to capture and care for; reptiles and amphibians do well in captivity, too. Shrews, on the other hand, fare poorly in cages. These animals eat round the clock. Without the proper food to sustain it, a shrew will die within hours.

You don't need any fancy lodging for most animals that you bring home for an overnight stay. Just make sure your cage is escape-proof! Wire cages or large aquariums are the best bet for many animals (put some screen over the top of an aquarium, and weight it down with a board). Rodents (mice and their kin) will gnaw their way out of cardboard or wooden cages.

For a longer stay (say a week or so), make the cage as comfortable as possible for your animal guest. For a snake, that will mean adding a low-wattage bulb to keep the animal warm. For a frog, that will mean water

deep enough to submerge in. Try to offer conditions that are similar to the natural habitats these animals live in.

A longer stay also means that you'll have to provide food for your guests (many animals can go overnight without food if you have nothing suitable on hand). Every animal's diet is different, but you can try offering some food that is easy to come by. Animals that eat insects can be given small pieces of meat or fish, or even cheese. If you want to raise your own mealworms, these are much appreciated by a number of animals, from birds to toads (see *June 27* to learn how to raise your own). Overripe fruit will satisfy the hunger of various ani-

mals, such as many insects. Mice and voles will happily gnaw on grains and seeds. Hazelnuts in the shell are a real treat for these creatures. Watch them nibble right through the hard shell to get at the nuts!

. . . .

Some birds will happily nest in an old kettle or jug in the grass, or one securely placed in the fork of a tree. Hang up a hollowed-out coconut that has an entrance hole and see if anybody moves in.

Can we keep it?

It's hard not to fall in love with many of the animals that you find and bring home. But should you keep any of them as pets?

Very few wild animals make suitable pets. Many require too much room, or their food needs are too hard to meet. Snakes fall into this category. They need live food such as mice and rats and frogs. Some animals are just too unpredictable (especially when they become adults) to be trusted. Playful raccoon babies turn into mischievous adults that can tear apart a room in no time.

Remember, these are wild ani-

mals, and they don't possess some of the characteristics that have been bred into domesticated animals over the centuries. Keep this in mind when approaching and handling any wild creature.

The animals that can be cared for with some success include various wild mice, rats and voles; toads, frogs and salamanders; turtles and lizards. Make sure that you have the proper cage for each, and that you provide the right kinds of food. None of these animals is affectionate the way dogs and cats are, but you can develop a very special relationship with them.

How to use this book

Catch as catch can

So how do you go about capturing those wild animals that you plan to observe and learn from? It depends on the animal, of course, but the following ideas for trapping live animals work for many amateur naturalists, so give them a try.

Both ants and earthworms (for populating your ant farm and wormery) can be dug up with a spade or trowel (taking care to shield them from the light which can harm earthworms, especially). Ants should be put into a plastic bag that you can tie shut. Place the bag in the refrigerator for an hour—this slows the ants down so that you can transfer them to the ant farm easily.

Other ground-dwelling insects can be captured in glass jars sunk into the ground (with the rims at ground level). You can bait these traps with meat, cheese or bits of overripe fruit, although many types of insects will fall into your traps quite by accident. Cover your pitfall traps, as they are called, with a flat rock or a piece of wood set on top of several small

stones, leaving just a fraction of an inch of space. This will keep both the rain and any insect-eating animals from entering your traps. The insects themselves will not be able to escape because the sides of the jar are too slippery. Because many ground-dwelling insects come out at night, you should set your traps one day and check them the next morning.

Other insects that live in meadows, for instance, can be swept up during the day with a net. A large sweep net is traditionally used for this purpose, but a sturdy butterfly net works just as well. (See *June 24* for a basic net you can make yourself.) For capturing insects that live in tall grass, sweep the net to and fro as you walk along, checking it after every two or three sweeps. For flying insects, chase after your quarry with the net, twist-

ing the handle once you've caught something so that it cannot escape. Nocturnal fliers can also be caught with a net, but you'll have better luck if you first attract them with light. Hang a sheet outdoors and light it with a flashlight. All sorts of insects will appear, and flutter around the sheet.

You can also catch insects with something known as a beating tray. This is simply a piece of fabric stretched over a wooden frame and held under a tree branch or bush. Hit the branch with a stick (give it a good whack!) and all sorts of insects will drop into the tray. An upturned umbrella works just as well.

Some of these same methods can be used for capturing other animals. Pitfall traps will work for many small mammals, provided the jar is deep

enough and the cover is set above the trap an inch or two. Humane traps, such as those manufactured by several companies, are also ideal. They come in a full range of sizes, from small enough for mice to large enough to hold a bobcat. These traps should be baited, and it is also best to place them near an area you think wild animals frequent. You can also rig your own traps from sturdy cardboard (or wood), making a closing door that will fall shut once the animal is inside the trap. (Place the food well away from the entrance, and fix a stick or string that the animal will bump into, causing the trap to drop.) A makeshift trap may not hold the larger more boisterous animals, but you may have luck capturing a meadow mouse or other small creature.

Amphibians and reptiles don't seem to take to this kind of trap, especially in the case of amphibians living in or near water. A net is your best bet for capturing frogs and fish in ponds, although you can use your hands if you're fast enough! Grasp the animals gently but firmly around their entire bodies. Even snakes can be caught with your hands, but you should have on gloves, as they may bite in self-defense. Snakes can be transported home inside a pillowcase, which solves the problem of their slithering about, and serves to calm them somewhat.

Which brings us to a final reminder. While some animals (notably many insects) can be easily captured without a fight, many animals will strive to break free. Who can blame them? Animals have all sorts of defense tactics that they will resort to. Toads secrete a substance that is toxic to animals attempting to eat them (but you needn't worry about getting it on your hands—just wash them well); many sharp-toothed animals will bite; many with claws will lash out. It is important that you be properly dressed when you are searching for animals to bring home. Wear sturdy shoes or boots (waterproof ones if you are down by the water), and put on a pair of thick leather gloves to protect your hands. Remember, too, to give up the chase if you sense the animal may come to harm. Leave the creature be, and go on your way. **Note:** It is very important that you return any animals you've captured to the VERY spot where you found them. If only twenty-four hours have passed, or if a whole summer has gone by, you should remember to do this. Most animals will be able to continue with their lives, as they are meant to live them, if they are released in their original habitat.

Nibble with care

Throughout this book, there are a number of suggestions for sampling plants that can be found growing wild. This isn't such a strange idea—after all, all the plants now cultivated for human consumption were once wild plants gathered in fields and forests. It's a lot of fun to make your own maple syrup, or gather up nuts before the squirrels get them! There are delicious berries that you can pick right when they're plump and juicy; there are leaves you can harvest to add to salads; there are even roots you can dig from the ground to eat like potatoes.

There's a surprising number of edible plants. But some are better than others, and some you should avoid altogether. How can you tell what's tasty and what to steer clear of?

Luckily, most edible plants are easy to identify. With the help of a good identification guide, you can pick out such plants as cattails, dandelions, and elderberries to feast on. But there are several edible plants that have look-alike cousins that are downright poisonous. Queen Anne's Lace, for example has a fleshy root that is edible (in fact, this plant is related to the garden carrot), but it is too easily confused with poison hemlock. Sev-

. . . .

Early settlers learned about making maple syrup from the Indians.

eral delicious mushrooms also closely resemble poisonous fungi—too close to make it safe to eat these mushrooms without an expert's okay.

Play it safe. Before you take even the smallest nibble of a leaf or berry or mushroom, make *absolutely* sure you know what you're eating. Use a field guide to help you identify the plants that aren't readily mistaken for others. Join up with experienced foragers to learn what little things to look for to help you distinguish some of the look-alike goodies. And if you have *any* doubts, leave the plants for other animals to enjoy.

. . . .

Wild garlic is a lovely plant that smells of onions. The Winnebago Indians called it Shi-ka-ko. That's where Chicago gets its name.

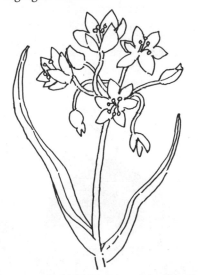

How to use this book

Have a question? Find the answer!

As you spend time observing the natural world, there are bound to be times when you are puzzled by something, or would like to know more about some aspect of nature. Maybe you would like more information about the changes that take place as a tadpole grows. Perhaps you are interested in organic gardening. Maybe you're having a hard time identifying some wildflowers. Where can you turn for help?

One of the best places to look for answers is the library. In both the children's and adult's sections of the library, there are hundreds of books on nature. There are field guides for identifying everything from animal tracks to the stars in the sky. There are books that will help you care for orphaned animals; books full of ideas for conserving our natural resources. You'll find books that show you how to craft all sorts of objects with things you find outdoors. There are exciting books written by eminent naturalists about their adventures in the wilds.

Have a librarian help you find what you're looking for. Just ask for any books that cover the subject you're interested in. Or ask for several books by name. You'll find a good selection of both children's and adult's books in the Appendix under *Other books you might enjoy reading*.

Don't forget to look for information in an encyclopedia, as well. Your library probably has current editions of several encyclopedias in its reference section.

Is there a question you just can't find the answer to in books? Then call or visit a nature center or science museum near you. Don't be shy—the people working at nature centers are there to help teach the rest of us about the natural world. They are always happy to answer questions, or tell you where to go for more information.

For keeps

At some point, you'll probably wish you had some field guides or reference books of your own. There are so many to choose from! How do you know what would be best for you?

Well, you have to take into account a number of factors. First of all, would you like just one book that has most of what you need to know in it? There are lots of wonderful books that include a little bit of everything in them. But they do have some drawbacks. For one, they can be expensive! For another, many are too heavy to carry with you when you are hiking out in the wilds. But there are ways of getting around these problems. Do you have a birthday coming up? Put in a request for one of these fat books! Use the book at home (or close to home). You can train yourself to observe insects and mammals so

that you can identify many from memory.

Field guides you can take with you into the "field" are great fun to use, too. Nothing could be handier than whipping out the guide to identify that bird that won't sit still for long. Or those rocks that are too heavy to bring home. Luckily, there are lots of pocket field guides that don't cost much, and that will literally fit into your pocket! The nice thing, too, is that you can buy only those guides for subjects that interest you, such as wildflowers or insects. Collect other volumes as you need them.

Before you buy any books, however, it might be a good idea to check at your library to see what they have. You can try out various books to see which ones you like best. There's something to recommend all of them.

The writer's gift

You'll notice that throughout the year in *The Kids' Nature Book* there are several lists of stories and poems to read, that celebrate various aspects of nature. Many writers have a strong love for nature—this is evident in their stories and poetry.

The stories listed can all be found in books bearing those same names. Look for them in the children's section of your library or bookstore.

The poems, with few exceptions, can all be found in one of two books. You may be familiar with *Read-Aloud Rhymes For the Very Young,* selected by Jack Prelutsky (Alfred A. Knopf, 1986), and *The Random House Book of Poetry for Children,* also selected by Jack Prelutsky (Random House, 1983). These books are bursting with all sorts of poems that you are sure to enjoy. They can also be found in both libraries and bookstores.

A word to parents

If you've ever watched your kids exploring on their own outdoors, you know how excited they are by every little thing they discover. Kids find delight in the way jewelweeds magically send their seeds flying at the slightest touch; they are amazed by the strength and determination of tiny ants struggling with heavy loads. Kids find beauty in both rainbows and rocks. And you know how quickly their pockets become filled with treasures!

The natural world *is* full of wonders, and what better way to let your children discover the ways of nature than to encourage them to explore. *The Kids' Nature Book* will introduce your children to the wonders of nature both indoors and out; in your backyard and halfway across the world. They'll meet some of the animals we share this planet with; they'll learn what brings winter weather; and

how important trees are in nature. They'll discover creatures that live beneath the soil, and stars that shine overhead.

The Kids' Nature Book is full of ideas for outings and projects that appeal to children of all ages. Each and every one of the suggestions is written in simple terms so that older children can have the satisfaction of doing things on their own. But don't let that keep you from joining in many of the activities. You may not be sure of the name of a single wildflower, or you may be a confirmed amateur naturalist familiar with all sorts of plants and animals. Even an interest in gardening or crafts makes you the perfect partner for many of the activities suggested in this book. You can share both your knowledge and your enthusiasm with your children. Taking walks in the woods, putting out food for the birds, and flying kites are great ways for families to spend time together.

Younger kids will get just as much out of this book with a little help from you. You can round up any materials that are needed, and bring home books from the library that would interest your children. And even older kids are advised to seek

not only their parents' permission but their help when using sharp tools or the stove, and any other potentially dangerous items. Help them find where they can screw in hooks to hold hanging plants. Be ready for all the living animals your children bring home!

Take some time to experience nature with your children. There's so much we all can learn.

18

January

January brings the snow,
Makes our feet and fingers glow.

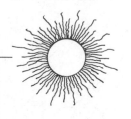

1

Create an area to display nature treasures.

Start the New Year by setting aside a spot to house and show off your nature treasures and projects. This needn't be elaborate. While a table that can remain set up with your collections would be nice, a windowsill can easily be turned into an ever-changing exhibit space. A bulletin board is ideal for tacking up pictures and information, but the refrigerator works just as well with a good supply of strong magnets. Explore the possibilities of using pegboard or a free-standing oversized box to tape things on, or even a piece of string stretched taut from which items can be hung.

It's fun to collect things that you find when you are out on walks, and, within the bounds of nature etiquette (only take what you really need, and leave plenty of flowers to reseed themselves, et cetera), you can bring home some of what you find. You may discover that you have to design some creative storage solutions for everything you save!

2

Design some display and storage boxes.

With a little imagination and tape and glue, you can turn all sorts of ordinary boxes into display cases and storage bins. Look around for containers that can be sectioned off to hold small items (such as rocks and insects); larger boxes can serve as filing cabinets or even temporary cages for small animals. Use interlocking strips of cardboard to divide the boxes into smaller specimen sections, or just mark the boxes with ruled lines if your collections will be glued in place.

Save yogurt or sour cream containers for protecting individual specimens, and for planting seedlings and windowsill gardens.

Wait, don't throw that away!

There is plenty of free stuff for the taking that can make your nature studies easy on your piggy-bank. Save paper and plastic goods (especially the boxes and containers that food, clothing, and shoes come wrapped in), and turn them into storage and display units. Look through the mail for pictures you can cut out.

Consider buying the ends of newsprint rolls which newspapers sell for only a few dollars. The width and continuous length are perfect for murals. (Used, continuous, computer print-out paper also works well.) This paper can also be shredded as bedding for small animals.

Be on the lookout for these and other items that can be used and re-used. Recycling begins at home!

Shoe boxes
Berry boxes and baskets
Plastic bags
Jars, large and small
Cardboard boxes of various sizes
Catalogues and magazines
Film canisters
Styrofoam butcher's trays
Egg cartons
Coffee cans
Deli containers
Plastic soda bottles
Yogurt and cottage cheese containers
Margarine tubs

3

See how the earth's tilt brings winter.

You probably know that winter weather differs greatly around the country and throughout the world. The cold often associated with winter occurs when the portion of the earth where we live is tilted farthest from the sun, as the earth makes its year-long journey around the sun.

A globe that is tilted on its stand (check your library if you don't have a globe like this at home) shows how this happens. Or try this trick: Turn on a lamp (one where the bulb faces downward) and let it warm up. This is the sun. Using your hand as the earth (you might even draw the outline of the United States on your hand!), move the "earth" around the "sun," rotating it as you go. Do you feel the warmth of the "sun" on that part of your hand where you live?

When it's winter in the United States (and other places in the northern hemisphere), people in Australia (in the southern hemisphere) are enjoying their summer! What about a place like Florida? It stays warm year-round because it is near the equator. The middle section of the earth doesn't have such extremes in temperature, although they do have their winter. Several other factors, such as the prevailing winds and ocean currents, also contribute to Florida's mild climate.

4

Think of some winter words.

Word games are a good way to become familiar with language in general, not to mention the words or terminology that are part and parcel of nature studies.

Conjure up all the synonyms you can for cold (such as freezing, frigid, numbing, arctic, teeth-shattering); find rhyming words for winter conditions (nice ice, snow show, and sleet treat are just a few); think of the colors associated with winter (white, grays and black, thought of as "cool" neutrals). Make up some winter-sounding words of your own.

This is one activity that can be done in the comfort of your home, when you find it positively toe-chilling outdoors!

. . . .

The blackest month of all the year
Is the month of Janiveer.

5

See how people stay warm in winter.

We humans have come up with some ingenious ways of dealing with the cold, often by changing our surroundings to suit us rather than adapting to the environment as most other animals do. While we have borrowed many ideas from nature, we have gone one step farther in many cases.

We insulate our homes, just like squirrels do their nests, but we also heat them artificially. Place thermometers both inside and out to see what a difference this makes.

We also dress for the weather, since we have lost much of the fur that once covered our bodies, in order to be active year-round. Step outside for a minute on a chilly day with little on, and then bundle up and go back outside. You're more comfortable, aren't you? You'll also notice that you don't feel quite as cold if you are wearing a hat. It's a fact that you lose a lot of body heat right out the top of your head! So keep it covered on a cold day. If you dress in layers, you can add or shed clothing as the temperature climbs or dips. (For more on warm clothing, see *December 11*.)

. . . .

Think of the birds fluffing up their down feathers when you slip on your down jacket!

6

Look at some of the ways animals keep warm.

You may wonder how animals stay warm without the benefits of clothing and heated homes. Animals have some creative solutions for keeping warm, many of which people have borrowed!

Many animals migrate to warmer areas (just as your grandparents may choose to spend the winter in Florida!). Others hibernate or are simply dormant, having created insulated havens much like your own house. (See *January 17* for the differences between hibernation and dormancy.)

Some animals remain active even in very cold regions, and those are the ones you can look for. Watch how the birds at your feeder fluff up their feathers, trapping body heat in their soft downy feathers. Stroke the thickened fur of a dog or horse, and you'll see these animals also "wear more clothing" in winter! And if you've found evidence of mice in your larder (see *December 15*), you can see how some creatures share the shelters we have built for ourselves, as well.

7

See how plants withstand cold.

Just like animals, plants have ways to deal with the cold and frozen precipitation that envelop them this time of year.

A lot of them may *look* dead, but only the annual plants have actually died. These are the low-growing plants that you can pull up easily, roots and all. They die after producing and scattering their seeds. Some plants take two years before their seeds mature, and these are known as biennials.

Many plants live for more than two years. These are the perennials. Trees are the most visible members of this group. Because little moisture is available to them (it's frozen!), these plants halt their growth, and shed the leaves that normally transpire a lot of water. At least the broad-leaved trees and bushes do this. Evergreens can keep their leaves (or needles as we call them), because they have a protective waxy coating. It's a bit like the hand lotion you use to protect your hands in winter!

Some plants are sensitive to changes in temperature. Have you ever noticed how rhododendron leaves curl up tightly (they almost look like cigars!) when it's very cold outside? They relax and unfurl when it's warmer. Do you think you might be able to gauge the temperature by watching these plants?

January

The Eskimo language has more than 50 words for snow, from *ganik* ("snow that is still falling") to *pukaq* ("crusty snow") and *masak* ("mushy snow").

8

Watch for snow.

When the temperature at cloud level is at freezing or below, and the moisture-filled clouds can hold back no longer, be on the lookout for snow. (See *April 1* for more on clouds that produce precipitation.)

If the air close to the ground is warm enough, the precipitation that started out as snow may turn to rain by the time you see it falling. (Snow, however, is not frozen rain, which is properly known as sleet.) The same principle determines whether the snow will be "wet" (good for making snowballs and snowpeople) or "dry" (light and flaky). "Wet" snow forms when slightly warmer temperatures cause the falling flakes to bunch together in clumps; "dry" snow forms when the air temperature is very low (cold), and the resulting flakes are smaller and harder.

All snowflakes are six-sided crystals of ice, forming in one of seven basic shapes. It is said that no two snowflakes are alike. Could that be? Well, considering the average snowflake contains 10^{18} molecules of water (that's $10 \times 10 \times 10$, 18 times!), the number of different combinations those molecules can make is mind-staggering.

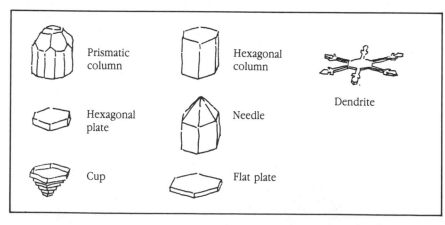

Prismatic column

Hexagonal column

Hexagonal plate

Needle

Dendrite

Cup

Flat plate

The greatest single day's snowfall was recorded in Silver Lake, Colorado in April, 1921. An astounding 75.8″ fell during those twenty-four hours!

9

Catch some snowflakes.

Because snowflakes melt so quickly when they land on a warm surface, catching them requires some planning. Chill a dark sheet of construction paper outdoors or in the freezer. Examine single flakes with a magnifying glass as they land on the paper (before they melt!).

Permanent impressions of snowflakes can be made by catching falling flakes on a chilled pane of glass which has been sprayed with chilled hair spray or artist's fixative. (Both the glass and the spray can be stored in the freezer to await use.) Keeping the prepared glass as cold as possible, take it outdoors and allow some flakes to settle on it. When you have collected enough, take the glass indoors and let it dry at room temperature for about 15 minutes. You'll have a permanent record of some of nature's most amazing designs!

In 1880, Wilson Bentley of Vermont began a study of snowflakes that occupied him for nearly fifty years. He photographed thousands of snowflakes, giving him the nickname—you guessed it—Snowflake Bentley.

10

Cut some snowflakes from paper.

To create super-sized snowflakes to decorate windows or hang from thread, fold paper circles (trace around a plate) in half, then in thirds, and then in half again before snipping. The resulting snowflakes will have the requisite six sides. By altering the little cuts from one snowflake to the next, your snowflakes will be as varied as those found in nature!

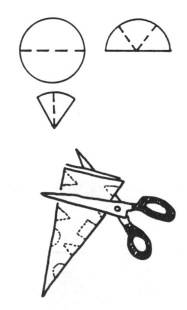

Ten inches of snow are roughly equal to one inch of rain.

January

11

Read a story or poem about snow.

There is something magical about snow, the way it blankets fields, and rests on tree branches; the way it softens a landscape, and quiets a city.

The Big Snow
Berta and Elmer Hader (*story*)

First Snow
Marie Louise Allen (*poem*)

It Fell in the City
Eve Merriam (*poem*)

Snow
Karla Kuskin (*poem*)

The Snowy Day
Ezra Jack Keats (*story*)

Stopping by Woods on a Snowy Evening
Robert Frost (*poem*)

When All the World Is Full of Snow
N.M. Bodecker (*poem*)

12

Make a snow gauge.

You can measure the amount of snowfall with a homemade gauge made from any container that you can mark off in inches or centimeters. A simple but effective gauge can be made from the bottom half of a clear plastic soda bottle, marked with an indelible laundry marker on the outside. Though less reliable because of the way snow drifts, you can also measure snowfall with a yardstick. Compare your findings with the forecasted amount.

Put several gauges outdoors—near a tree, out in the open, on your front steps—and see if they all measure the same. Are you surprised?

Only the sky knows for sure

Because winter sports are big business, and inadequate snowfall might be the ruin of an area that attracts skiers and other snow enthusiasts, man-made snow is commonly made to get the season off to a good start. (It is sometimes made throughout the entire winter.)

Most machine-made snow, as it's called, is made when compressed air and compressed water are combined to create a very dry ice crystal. This "snow" is blown and pushed and packed into place from early November until mid-March at some locations. The machine-made snow is very durable, and while it cannot be made unless the air temperature is at freezing or below, an unexpected rain will not melt it, but instead will soak right down through it.

Do you think you can feel the difference between real and machine-made snow? Do you think that machine-made snow is cold?

13

Melt some snow indoors.

Scoop up a cupful of snow in a container, record the level, and then allow it to melt. Are you surprised at the change in volume? The greater amount of snow melts to a lesser amount of water. The air trapped within the flakes accounts for the difference, of course.

The amount of air depends on the conditions when the snow fell. "Dry" snow traps more air than "wet" snow that clumps together. Faced with a driveway full of snow to shovel, you would probably hope for "dry" snow, because it weighs a lot less! Conditions being equal, "dry" snow will also melt more readily than the "wet" stuff. If you are hoping to build a snow fort, "wet" is best.

14

Draw or paint a snow scene.

A simple way of doing this is to use white chalk or paint on colored paper. While it takes some practice to visualize in reverse, as it were, this technique is very effective. A textured painting can be made by brushing slightly watered-down white glue on your paper, and then sprinkling it with white cornmeal or powdered laundry soap.

You can also make a three-dimensional floating snow scene, much like those you can buy. Glue small plastic figures (trees, animals or people) to the inside lid of a small jar such as baby foods come in. You need to use a waterproof glue, like epoxy (have your parents help you with the gluing). Fill the jar with water and a tablespoon or so of white glitter. Screw the lid on tightly. When shaken gently, the "snow" will appear to be falling on the scene you have created.

January

15

Look for animal tracks in the snow.

Tracks are often well defined in shallow snow, so after examining your own tracks look for those made by other animals that are winter-active in your area. You may only find prints left by neighborhood dogs and cats, but check for those made by birds and, in areas that support these animals, those left by squirrels, rabbits, raccoons and deer, to mention just a few.

Follow any tracks you come across, and try to piece together something about the animal's activities. You may find evidence of a wild chase, or even a kill, or tracks that lead from a food source to an animal's den. Many general field guides include diagrams of tracks along with their descriptions of animals.

16

Look for signs left by foraging animals.

Animals that remain active during the colder months basically like to eat the same types of food that are available to them at other times. There are usually far fewer choices, however, and heavy snow-cover makes for difficulties. Some animals are capable of storing fat, which not only sustains them during lean times but keeps them warmer. Other animals continue to need to eat daily (deer and rabbits, for instance, eat all the time!), and where they once ate the fresh leaves of trees and shrubs, they turn to nibbling on buds and soft twigs.

Be on the lookout for the signs left behind by animals that have been foraging for food. Examine the bark torn from tree trunks and branches, as it offers some clues to the presence of animals. (This can be done year-round, of course.) Wild cats, like their domestic counterparts, leave shredded bark on trees, a result of sharpening their claws. Porcupines nibble on patches of bark high up in trees; small toothmarks may even be evident. Freshly nipped buds may mean that deer have feasted recently. You may also come across blood-stained snow, for although the carnivores don't need to kill but every so often, they must continue to occasionally do so to survive.

17

Name some changes that occur during hibernation.

Some of the animals that stay in cold regions prefer to sleep away the winter! They find themselves a cozy place to hole up in (safe from freezing temperatures) and undergo some changes that enable them to go for a long, long stretch without food.

True hibernators include reptiles, amphibians and insects (all cold-blooded creatures) plus a handful of mammals. The best-known hibernating mammal is the woodchuck (or groundhog, see *February 2*). After fattening himself during the later summer months, the woodchuck grows languid and settles down to spend the next six months asleep. A woodchuck's body temperature which is normally 96.8°F (very close to your own) drops to as low as 37.4°F! Its heart rate slows from 160 beats per minute (tap these out) to as few as four beats per minute. Breathing decreases to as little as one breath every minute. Other mammals that hibernate include the brown bat and the jumping mouse.

Animals that are merely dormant include the chipmunk, raccoon, skunk, and bear, much to many people's surprise. These animals are relatively inactive and their metabolisms are slowed considerably, but it is not uncommon for them to rouse themselves when the weather is kindly to either eat their stored food or even emerge from their cozy dens for brief spells.

18

Continue to feed the birds.

Once you decide to put out food for the birds, you should continue to do so. You can't possibly hope to provide for all (luckily, feeding birds is one of the most popular ways to attract wildlife, so many people do it), but the birds will come to rely on the seed, suet and water you provide.

For the pleasure birds give, it's not asking much that they be helped out during the cruelest months of the year. Make sure the snow is cleared from their food, and break the ice on their water dish as it forms. (Feeding wild birds is discussed at length during the week of *September 30* to *October 6.*)

The coldest recorded temperature was −128.6°F, chillingly measured in Vostok, Antarctica.

19

Look for snow fleas.

If the day is sunny and relatively warm, you might find a sprinkling of tiny insects at the base of trees. Check the south facing side where the sun's warmth is greater. What appears to be a dense sprinkling of pepper is, in fact, a gathering of one of the few winter-active insects, the snow flea.

These insects are not actually fleas, but an even more primitive insect. Look closely and you'll see the minuscule specks jump into the air as high as three or four inches. Tucking their tails beneath their bodies propels them upwards, giving these creatures their other common name, springtail.

20

See how animal fur changes in winter.

Some winter-active animals not only grow extra fur to keep them warm (see *January 6*), but they also grow more fur on their feet, as the snowshoe hare does! This makes it easier for the animal to get around on the snow. (See *January 27* for some snowshoes you can try out.)

The snowshoe hare, also known as the varying hare, and both the ermine and weasel, change their fur color to white for the winter, as a means of camouflage. You can see how this works by dropping a piece of white paper on the snow. It's hard to see, isn't it? Many animals that live in permanently snow-covered regions are also permanently white, such as the polar bear and the snowy owl.

How do these animals know when it is time to change the color of their fur? It seems the decreasing daylight hours of late autumn triggers these physical changes. An unexpected early snowfall often finds these animals vulnerable, if they have not made their transformation from dark fur to white fur, yet. That's easy to see, isn't it?

21

Think of some of the ways snow affects nature.

While people can usually carry on with few setbacks in snowy weather, snow has a great impact on nature. The benefits of snow include its insulating properties, which make the underground burrows of animals warmer (you can test this inside a snow fort), and also protects the roots of plants from damaging temperature extremes. Animals are sometimes safer from their predators, as the snow hinders the hunters' movements, but, of course, the hunted cannot escape as easily either. Snow, when it eventually melts in the spring, provides both plants and animals with life-giving moisture.

On the negative side, even a shallow snow can make finding adequate food difficult for many animals, especially if the snow falls earlier than usual. Some animals take advantage of deeper snow, standing on it to feed higher up on twigs and buds that they normally can't reach. Some, however, starve to death or are so weakened as to be easy prey to predators and disease. Small animals are sometimes trapped beneath deep drifts blown by the wind.

Snow is simply a fact of life in nature. In what ways do you find it a help? And a hindrance?

All dressed in white

Winter is an excellent time to be out-of-doors, experiencing nature during one of the quieter seasons. Without the distraction of birds and insects and greenery, you can concentrate on what is on display. Dress warmly and arm yourself with ideas for exploring, many of which can be found in these fine books.

The Cold Weather Catalog
edited by Robert Levine and Nancy Bruning *(adult)*

A Guide to Nature in Winter
Donald W. Stokes *(adult)*

Exploring Winter
Sandra Markle *(juvenile)*

Into Winter: Discovering a Season
William P. Nestor *(juvenile)*

Winter Book
Harriet Webster *(juvenile)*

January

22

Build a snow structure.

The Eskimos use the word igloo to mean any type of house, but we usually think of igloos as fashioned from snow. These are rarely built by the Eskimos these days, but references to them still abound. Try your hand at constructing a shelter made from "bricks" of packed snow. The Eskimos actually cut their blocks from solidly packed snow, but you probably don't have that kind where you live. Make your "bricks" using a mold such as a bread pan or a heavy plastic container.

"Wet" snow works best, but "dry" snow can be moistened with water to help bind it together. Make a sturdy structure by overlapping the bricks and gradually doming the top, or simply by building straight walls and anchoring a tarpaulin over the top as a roof.

Cave-like openings can be carved out of piled-up snow, perhaps where snow has been pushed into a heap by plows (but take care that you are never in the cave on days when the plows are out, and keep clear of heaps that cars may drive through). An older, well-compacted pile works best, as it will hold its shape better when you scoop out the inside.

23

Make angels in the snow.

Besides making your own tracks in the snow, make angels, trees and other shapes using your whole body. Dress warmly (preferably in waterproof clothing) and then, go to it!

Gaze up at the winter sky when lying on the snow, and let the flakes gently fall on you if it is still snowing. Listen carefully for the "sound" of falling snow. What do you hear?

Winter Olympics

Flopping around in the snow is just one way to have a good time during the winter! You can also ski, skate or go sledding. But what kind of fun can you have right in your own backyard? Here are some ideas!

"Fox and Geese" is one game that you may know. Playing it in winter works well because the circle and paths really stand out in the snow. Make a circle large enough to run around easily. Divide it into six segments by means of paths that meet in the middle (like a pie). One player is the fox and all the others geese. The fox, naturally, chases after the geese who are safe only when standing on the center spot. Run for your lives!

Another good game is an adaptation of an Iroquois Indian game known as "Snow Snake." This game calls for some advance preparation, for you need to make snow snakes for everyone who wants to play. Find some straight branches that have fallen (at least four feet long) or use quarter-round molding from a lumberyard.

Sand the wood well and anchor some washers at the front end with wood screws to make eyes (these serve to weight the front end of the stick). To play the game, prepare a track by dragging a log through the snow and then packing the snow down firmly, making a lip along the sides so that the snakes won't fly off the track. Each snake is sent slithering down the track one at a time, and the one that travels farthest wins. Do you think it might be better to "go last" in this game? Better draw straws!

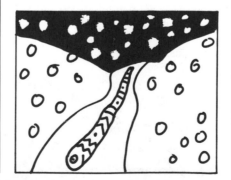

24

Whip up some snow cream.

Who can resist eating some new fallen snow? You can concoct a tasty treat from snow called, logically enough, snow cream! Two recipes follow, the first using snow as the main ingredient, the other using it as the freezing agent.

Snow Cream #1
Into a bowl of clean snow, sprinkle some granulated sugar and some vanilla extract and a bit of milk or cream to make a slushy treat. Eat it with a spoon or sip it through a straw as it melts.

Snow Cream #2
Into an aluminum can or bowl, mix together ½ cup milk, 1 tablespoon sugar, and 1 tablespoon condensed milk. Flavor it with a little vanilla extract or cocoa powder. Place the can inside a larger container that has a layer of salt in it. Add snow (or crushed ice), alternating with layers of more salt, until the inner can is completely nestled in snow up its sides. With a wooden popsicle stick or spoon, continually scrape the freezing snow cream away from the sides of the can, allowing more of the mixture to freeze on contact with the cold metal. In ten minutes or so you should have a thick slush. Enjoy!

25

Dress a snowperson with treats for the birds.

A snowperson can double as a bird feeder, laden with all sorts of goodies for our fine, feathered friends to enjoy. Try using dates for the eyes and nose, a row of raisins for the smile. Pinecones slathered with peanut butter make fine buttons, and strung cranberries can be hung like a loose belt. Popcorn garlands can be wound around a cap or hat.

Don't forget to use some sturdy branches for arms, so that the birds have a place to perch.

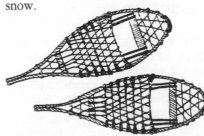

26

Measure some snow drifts.

The wind blowing unchecked over light snow can cause impressive drifts to build up, obscuring roads and blocking passage. Notice how snow fences are put up to trap snow. Some people run several yards of fencing on one side of their driveway, so that they don't have to spend all their time shoveling their way out!

With a ruler or yardstick, measure some drifts and compare their depth to the depth of the surrounding snow. Push a board into some solid snow and see if the snow builds up along one side. Can you tell which way the wind is blowing?

27

Try out some snowshoes.

Have you ever tried to walk through snow, only to sink knee-deep in binding drifts? Snowshoes are designed to make walking easier by dispersing your weight, so you won't fall through the snow's crust. (The snowshoe hare grows extra fur for this very reason, see *January 20*.) With practice, a person wearing snowshoes can travel through snow with relative ease, moving as fast as 3 to 4 miles per hour.

Borrow, rent, or even make your own homemade snowshoes from coniferous boughs. A branch that is naturally forked can be bent back to form a rounded toe and tied with heavy twine. Shorter branches can be arranged crosswise to support your weight, and then tied in place. The shoes themselves can be lashed to your boots with more twine or slightly thicker rope.

The trick to successfully maneuvering on your snowshoes is to lift your toes. This may seem obvious, but the front edge of a snowshoe extends so far beyond your own foot, that it sometimes gets caught in the snow.

28

Make a pair of snow goggles.

Have you ever run outside to play in the snow on a sunny day and been momentarily blinded by the glare? The sunlight reflecting off the bright white snow can actually harm your eyes, but not if you're wearing sunglasses or snow goggles.

Snow goggles are worn by Eskimos and other people who live in snow-covered regions. You can easily make your own from some sturdy tagboard. Cut out an eye mask very much like the kind that are sold at Halloween (use a Halloween mask for a pattern if you have one handy). Instead of round eye holes, however, cut narrow slits, which will shield your eyes from the glare but still let you see where you're going. The goggles are even more effective if they are black (blacken around the inner rims of the slits, too). Staple a piece of elastic to the outside edges to hold the goggles in place.

Do the goggles help? Why do you think the slits work better than holes?

January

29

Look for icicles.

Icicles are awe-inspiring creations, formed when water freezes as it's dripping. You can find icicles cascading over rocky outcrops, hanging from tree branches, and along most rooflines. The heat from buildings and the warmth from the sun are enough to melt snow that may have clung to the roofs, but the air temperature is cold enough to refreeze the water quickly as it drips.

Watch out for icicles hanging over entry ways. Too much warming sun will loosen their hold on buildings. Grab one for a hand-held icy treat before knocking the others off.

Snap, crackle, mmmmm

If you look closely at trees after a winter storm, you may notice small icicles hanging from the ends of branches that were broken by the strong winds. If these trees are in the maple family, you should venture out when the storm is over to sample one of these icicles. The icicles are actually frozen sap that has dripped from the broken branches. They are delicious, and some compensation for any damage done to your trees.

30

Make your own icicles.

Make your own icicles! All you need is a container you can puncture a very small hole in (make sure you'll be able to hang it, too), and some water.

Poke a hole in the bottom of the container, just big enough to allow the water to drip out very slowly. The success of this experiment depends greatly on the freeze/thaw cycle, so don't be disappointed if your man-made attempts don't work at first. Try changing the size of the hole, or hang the container in another location, to speed up or slow down the process as you see fit.

. . . .

The Arctic is not a continent (unlike Antarctica which is a solid land mass), but a region comprised of ice that moves and shifts with the wind and water.

31

Stomp through frozen puddles.

Puddle-stomping is always fun, but the crunch of frozen-topped puddles is even better! The shallow depressions that collect water year-round, forming puddles, do so in winter, too, but the water quickly freezes when it's cold.

Have you ever wondered why frozen puddles are hollow? The cap of ice serves to insulate the puddle, allowing what little water remains to be soaked up by the ground. Try stepping lightly onto some puddles, stomping hard on others. Does it make a difference?

February brings the rain,
Thaws the frozen lake again.

Since 1887, members of the Punxsutawney Groundhog Club in Punxsutawney, Pennsylvania have made quite a to-do over the emergence of the groundhog on February 2. Look for his picture in your newspaper that day or the next.

February

1

Explore a frozen pond or lake.

It may not look like much is happening on and around a frozen pond or lake, but there's a lot going on beneath the insulating layer of ice. If the pond is covered with the clear ice commonly called black ice (or if you chisel a small hole in the ice—with your parents' permission), you can actually see fish swimming around! Look closely and you might catch a glimpse of the water-borne insects that make up their diet. It's not uncommon to find some of these creatures "suspended" in ice.

What you can't see are the animals that bury themselves at the bottom of the pond. Frogs and turtles hibernate there until the spring thaw brings much needed oxygen to the water (see *March 18*). Even those fish that remain active are in a relative stupor, but that doesn't stop the so-called ice fishermen from boring holes in the ice and dropping their lines!

A note: You should NEVER walk on ponds, lakes or rivers that appear to be frozen, without your parents' approval. The water usually freezes first around the edges, and the ice farther out may not be as thick. The reverse is true in the spring, when the ice close to shore is the first to melt. There's a wise saying that warns, "If you don't know the depth of the ice, stay away from it." Not bad advice, considering.

2

Groundhog Day!

This much ballyhooed event traces its origins to Europe where centuries ago the Germans sought to predict the final stages of winter by keeping an eye out for badgers. In this country we watch for the groundhog, hoping that when it leaves its burrow it won't see its shadow. This supposedly will send it scurrying for shelter to wait out the long weeks of winter sure to follow.

Where do you suppose this idea came from? Go outside and see if you can see your own shadow. Take your dog or cat with you—does he seem to notice his? Just imagine how the reclusive groundhog might feel thinking there was someone out there besides himself. It *might* give him a start!

The groundhog, incidentally, is just another name for the woodchuck. Few mammals truly hibernate (see *January 17*), but the woodchuck is one of them, sleeping soundly from late September until April. Its emergence in early February is as unlikely as its ability to predict weather.

3

Use sand, instead of salt, on icy surfaces.

There's no question that icy roads and sidewalks can be dangerously slippery. You've probably noticed how both sand and salt are used to combat the ice. You've probably also noticed how salt leaves a white stain on roads and walkways (and your boots, too), eventually washing away. Where does it go? Unfortunately, the salt usually ends up leaching into the soil alongside roads and sidewalks, making the soil inhospitable for most plants. Many fine old trees are lost each year because of the salt.

Luckily, many communities are now turning to sand (where it can be used safely) and planting salt-tolerant species that they hope will be able to withstand the dissolved salts. While salt actually melts ice, sand simply adds grit to the slick surface, providing some traction but not hastening the melting much. You can see how this works by sprinkling some table salt on an ice cube and dusting another cube with sand. Which melts first?

At your own home, use sand wherever possible, which is better for your property, and much kinder, too, on your car, and your shoes and boots.

4

See if salt water freezes in winter.

Have you ever wondered why the ocean doesn't freeze in winter? Well, it does, of course, but the heavy concentration of salt means that a lower temperature is needed for ice to form. The constant movement of the waves also discourages ice from taking hold. Only in the far north (and the far south, of course) does salt water freeze with any regularity.

In fact, approximately 10 percent of the earth is covered with glaciers, huge masses of ice that are so thick they never melt. Icebergs, which are chunks of glaciers that have broken off and float at will, sometimes melt if they make it to warmer waters, although they also sometimes adhere to other bergs and actually increase their size.

The amount of salt in the water determines how readily it will freeze, and the oceans of the world contain varying amounts of salt. (See *July 3* for more on salt in ocean water.) Try a simple experiment adding common table salt to a glass of water and setting this solution outdoors next to a glass of plain water. Which freezes first?

. . . .

It is said that only about one-tenth of most icebergs is visible above water, lending credence to the cliche "just the tip of the iceberg."

February

The white pine has five needles growing in each bunch. That's W-H-I-T-E!

5

Identify some trees without leaves.

While there is something missing from many trees this time of year (namely their leaves!), you can still tell one tree from another by looking for other clues.

Trees have very distinctive silhouettes (with and without their leaves). Many guide books include tiny silhouettes to help you identify the trees. Trees come in all shapes and sizes, just like people! The bark also differs considerably from tree to tree, and from young to old. Again, like people the bark of younger trees is smooth and even; older trees have rough and wrinkly looking bark.

Buds offer many clues, too. Before trees even lose their leaves in autumn, they are preparing for the new leaves that will clothe them the following spring. Each bud is protected by a scaled covering, or fuzzy hairs. There is much variation from tree to tree.

Some trees are easy to identify any time of year. These are the evergreens that keep their leaves year-round (see *February 6*).

6

Take a look at some evergreens.

Do the evergreens really keep their foliage year-round? Well, yes and no. They *do* shed their leaves (as the needles are properly called), but it is an ongoing process, making the loss less noticeable.

Not all evergreen trees are conifers (cone-bearing trees such as pines, firs and hemlocks). Holly trees, live oaks, and palms are three exceptions, being broad-leafed examples of evergreens. On the other hand, some needle-leafed trees, such as larches, are deciduous and lose all their leaves each autumn.

You can tell the three major groups of conifers apart by their leaves. Here are some clues to look for.

 Firs
Short needles with blunt tips, leave round scar on branch

 Spruces
Four-sided needles that are very sharp

Pines
Needles grow in bunches, wrapped together at the base

Measuring up

Trees are the giants of the plant world, but just how big are they? (The tallest trees in the world are the redwoods, native to California—the tallest on record is over 360 feet high!) You can find out how tall trees are with a simple trick that involves two people. Have someone hold a stick upright on the ground, about 60 feet from the tree you are measuring. A yardstick works just fine. Position yourself about 6 feet farther, and, lying close to the ground, look where the top of the tree comes to on the stick. Ask your helper to mark that point on the stick (direct your helper to move his hand down the stick until you say "stop"). The height of the tree will be about ten times the height marked on the stick.

7

See how important trees are in nature.

You can probably think of dozens of uses for trees, but did you ever wonder what role trees play in nature? Take a walk outside and see if you can detect some of the ways trees serve the natural world.

You can't really *see,* but you might guess at one way that trees are important, and that is their ability to hold the soil together with their far-reaching roots. These "underground branches" prevent erosion, but they also provide safe havens for burrowing animals. Animals live in other parts of trees, too. Look for holes in trunks that squirrels and birds have made. On dead limbs, lift the bark and look for the squiggly tunnels and pinholes made by various insects. Leaves also provide shelter (check this during the summer).

Of course, trees furnish food for many animals. Not only are nuts and fruits eaten, but also twigs, bark, and leaves. The leaves serve other functions, as well. They give off oxygen and transpire great amounts of water. And when the leaves fall from the trees, they decompose and enrich the soil, as does the tree itself when it dies and rots, but not before still other creatures find food and shelter in the tree. Little wonder trees are so valuable in the wild!

Three-quarters of all timber and most paper come from coniferous trees.

February

8

Name some of the ways people use trees.

Besides benefiting from trees in their natural settings, people use trees in many ways. Look around your house, or in your neighborhood stores, for examples of tree products. You can even make a game of guessing what objects in your house started out as part of a tree.

You'll probably find many examples. Your house may be made from wood (at least in part) as well as some of your furniture, tools, and toys. Paper, and such products as fabric, photographic film and cellophane are made from cellulose (the major component of the cell walls). Food is harvested from trees (from apples to almonds) including spices and flavorings (from cinnamon to maple syrup). Gums and resins (special saps that ooze from certain trees) are used to manufacture paint thinner, soaps, and rubber goods. Some bark is used for floats and bulletin boards.

So thank a tree the next time you make a paper airplane or crack open some pistachios! Come summer, you'll be glad for the shade that trees offer, too.

9

Make rubbings of tree bark.

You can record variations in bark patterns by making rubbings. All you need is a sheet of lightweight paper and a wax crayon (dark colors show up best). Peel the paper-covering off the crayon and hold it horizontally. Smooth barks are easiest to rub, and steady one-directional strokes work best. If the paper keeps shifting, tie it to the tree.

You can bind your rubbings in a scrapbook, or frame them to hang on the wall. Include rubbings in the diary you are keeping of a single tree (see *A tree grows in* . . . on page 41).

Note: Never strip bark from trees, as that may damage or even kill a tree. You can collect bark off of fallen branches and stumps.

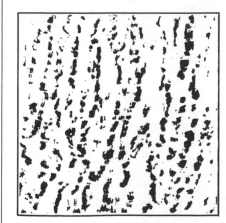

10

Count the rings on a tree stump.

Trees grow not only in height each year, but also in girth, and you can actually count the years that have passed by counting the rings on the stump of a tree. The rings also offer clues to the conditions that affected the tree during its lifetime. Wide rings show years of strong growth; narrow rings suggest that the tree was subjected to adverse conditions, such as drought, a hard winter, insect damage, fire, and even competition for sunlight and nutrients from neighboring trees.

Unfortunately, to see the rings of a tree the tree must be felled. Search your area for stumps, or take a look at a fireplace log. This activity is suggested again on *December 29,* when it is possible to determine the age of your's or a neighbor's Christmas tree.

. . . .

The oldest trees in the world are in the United States. Some of the bristlecone pines, found in the Southwest, are over 4,000 years old.

11

Guess the age of a living tree.

By measuring the girth of a tree (about five feet from the ground), you can guess the age of a living tree. Most trees will measure about one inch for every year of growth.

This method works only for mature trees and there are notable exceptions. Most poplars grow too fast, and some (such as the Scotch pine and horse chestnut) grow too slowly to make this method reliable all the time. A tree growing by itself might conform to this rule, too, whereas a tree the same size growing deep in the woods might be twice as old. Having competed for moisture and sunlight its whole life, its growth will have been stunted.

Count the number of rows of branches radiating from the central trunk of a pine (such as the white pine). Each row represents one year's growth.

Scout for trees to date, on your property or in a park or wooded area near you. Can you find any of the same types of trees growing in both open spaces and densely wooded spots? How do they compare in size, and how old do you suppose they might be? What important historical events were taking place when those trees were just seedlings?

February

12

Make a habitat diagram.

A habitat is a place where plants and animals live together. But there has to be enough of each to balance things. Here's a way of showing that balance.

Draw a large pyramid on a sheet of poster board. Cut out lots of pictures of plants and animals (or sketch your own). Take a meadow, for instance. At the base of the pyramid, paste down lots of plants. Plants are known as producers because they actually make their own food by harnessing the sun's energy (this is photosynthesis). The number of plants far outweighs all other life in a given habitat, for plants provide not only food, they also serve as shelter, and give off oxygen, and replenish the soil when they die.

The next tier of the pyramid consists of consumers, those animals that eat the plants. In a meadow that may mean insects, seed-eating birds and mice. Higher still are the secondary consumers, animals that feed on the plant-eaters, such as snakes. And at the top, the tertiary consumers, those that eat animals that themselves have eaten animals. An owl is a good example of a tertiary consumer.

There's just enough in the meadow for everyone. What do you think would happen to these animals if the meadow were turned into a shopping mall?

13

See how people figure in nature.

How do people fit into the picture? We may be animals (mammals, to be precise), but we are very different from most other animals. In bettering our lives, we have exploited many natural resources, upsetting the balance of nature in the process. Can you think of any examples of this?

Luckily, there is much we can do to put things right. You probably already know about some of the steps that are being taken to undo some of the damage. Harmful chemicals that end up in the air and water (and in our food) are being re-evaluated. Wetlands, and other valuable habitats, are being saved wherever possible. Wildlife refuges are being set aside for plants and animals. Even at home, there are little things you can do, like turning off the lights when they aren't needed, that help to conserve natural resources.

Do you think there are other ways we can make sure that there is plenty of room (and all our necessary needs are met), not only for our expanding human population, but for other animals as well?

. . . .

When you have a salad, you are a consumer. When you bite into a hamburger, you are a secondary consumer. Add chicken to the menu and you become a tertiary consumer. Chickens eat not only grain but insects.

14

Happy Valentine's Day!

In recognition of this holiday, make or do something special to show your love for nature.

Make an edible valentine for the birds by "painting" suet or peanut butter on a heart-shaped piece of cardboard, and sprinkling it with seeds. Stitch a catnip toy for your favorite cat. Sew two squares of felt together, leaving one side open. Stuff with dried catnip—you can get this at pet shops—and sew the opening shut. Bake some dog biscuits for the family dog. In a bowl, combine 2½ cups whole wheat flour, ½ cup powdered milk, 1 teaspoon brown sugar and ½ teaspoon salt. Add one beaten egg and 6 tablespoons meat drippings or margarine. Add enough water to hold the mixture together. Pat the dough ½" thick with your fingers, and cut out with cookie cutters or a knife. Bake for 25-30 minutes in a 350°F oven. This recipe makes about ten biscuits.

Give some plants that you have grown yourself to family members and friends. A gift of your time would be appreciated at a nature center or animal shelter. Volunteer to help out in some way. Oh, and Happy Valentine's Day to *you!*

. . . .

It was believed in medieval England that birds mated on St. Valentine's Day.

15

Read a story or poem about loving nature.

How do some people express their love for nature? They write stories and poems about plants, animals and the world around them. Do any of these stories and poems express the way you feel about nature and wildlife?

A Clearing in the Forest
Carol and Donald Carrick *(story)*

Feather or Fur
John Becker *(poem)*

Hurt No Living Thing
Christina Rossetti *(poem)*

Mice
Rose Fyleman *(poem)*

Nature Is
Jack Prelutsky *(poem)*

Valentine's Day
Aileen Fisher *(poem)*

Valentine's Greetings
Kathryn Sexton *(poem)*

The study of the interrelationships of plants and animals within their habitats is known as ecology.

16

Show respect for all wildlife.

Are there any animals that you really don't like? Say, worms or snakes, or the moles that make tunnels in the lawn where you play ball? If you stop to think about these creatures, they all play an important part in nature, sometimes even directly benefiting us without our realizing it.

Earthworms are terrific soil builders and truly a gardener's best friend (see *April 19* for a way to get to know these creatures). Snakes aren't really slimy (you know this if you've ever touched one); rather they are shy animals that keep to themselves and actually help rid your property of unwanted rodents. And moles? Well, they can be a nuisance, but they do aerate the soil with their tunneling.

Even unwelcome plants like poison ivy and nettles provide food and shelter for many animals. Learn what these plants look like, and remove them from play areas, but take a moment to imagine how other animals would be affected if they didn't exist. Do you think animals get a rash when they touch poison ivy?

17

Learn about endangered species.

Endangered species are those that are at great risk of extinction. While many wildlife species have become extinct throughout our earth's history—usually for failing to adapt to environmental changes—the rate at which plants and animals are dying out in recent times is alarming.

You may have heard of such animals as the humpback whale, the giant panda and Grevy's zebra. There are hundreds more, and the list includes all sorts of animals from insects to amphibians, and many plants.

What do you think can be done to help endangered species (and those that are considered threatened)? *You* can help by learning what some of the endangered species in your area are, and encouraging their survival. Learn what plants need protection, and don't pick them. Build houses to encourage birds to nest and raise families.

And look beyond your backyard to discover what plants and animals are at risk in other parts of the world. There is a lot you can do from your own home to help endangered species on other continents and in the oceans. Request information from one of the conservation groups (see *Nature conservancy groups* in the Appendix).

18

Return bottles and cans here

Do your part to care for the environment.

We can do a lot to care for our earth, starting right at home! Everyday you can strive to do those little things that add up. Conserve water and electricity; walk or bike those short distances instead of having your parents drive you in the car; save bottles and cans and newspapers to be recycled.

You can also recycle vegetable scraps by composting them (see *October 20*). You can reuse plastic food containers (save some for your nature studies). You can use the blank sides of "junk" mail for at-home notes and grocery lists. Recycling gives new life to all sorts of things!

And you can learn about conservation and recycling efforts on a larger scale. Ask your parents if they might consider mass transportation or carpooling for getting to work. How are homes and businesses heated in your area? Could some use renewable energy sources (such as wood heat or solar or wind power) rather than oil or coal or electricity?

You may not think that the changes you make at home and in your community would amount to much, but just think what would happen if *everyone* did what they could to care for our environment!

Joining hands

While there is a lot you can do on your own to care for the environment, you can make an even bigger impact by joining forces with others. You have probably heard of some of the conservation groups that act to change environmental laws, purchase land to be set aside as refuges, and fund programs to educate the public. But have you ever considered joining one of these organizations?

You'll find the names and addresses of some of the better-known groups in the Appendix, under *Nature conservancy groups*. Write them for information. Many organizations publish magazines and newsletters that are free to members (some are just for kids!). Look, too, for local groups that serve your area. Check the Yellow Pages under "Environmental, Conservation and Ecological Organizations"; ask at a nature center or humane society for the names of those groups that are active in your area.

February

A star festival called Tanabata is celebrated each year in July in Japan.

19

Do some stargazing.

While stargazing is a year-round activity, this is an ideal time of year to be looking skyward. It still gets dark early, and the stars appear very bright during the winter months. (It can be very cold, however, so dress warmly!)

Some stars are only visible at certain times of the year, but one remains constant, and that is Polaris, or the North Star. (It is also known as the "lodestar," as it's useful in navigation; the Navajo Indians call it The Star That Does Not Move.) Most star charts have you face north, which you will be doing if you face Polaris. Look for the Little Dipper—Polaris is the last star in its handle.

From there look for the Big Dipper, or Drinking Gourd. With the help of a chart look for such wintertime favorites as Orion, the Hunter, and both Canis Major and Minor. It's a good idea to know what you're looking for before you go outdoors. If you do refer to a chart outdoors, cover your flashlight with some red cellophane, so your eyes will stay adjusted to the low light. Stargazing is best done lying down, so pull up a chair you can recline in. Try to choose a spot away from distracting lights, and remember the moon (especially when full) obscures many stars with its light.

20

Make connect-the-dot constellations.

Grouping stars in constellations is a human invention, one that dates back thousands of years. In fact, many of the 88 officially recognized constellations are named for characters and objects from Greek and Roman mythology. (Orion, for example, was a Greek god who was turned into a constellation at his death, along with his faithful dog, Sirius—the brightest star of Canis Major, or Large Dog.) The Greeks used these fanciful stories to help them remember the arrangement of the stars in the sky, and so can you.

Make some connect-the-dot diagrams to help you remember the way stars are grouped. The Big Dipper looks just like a big ladle, doesn't it? (Actually the seven stars of the dipper are part of a larger constellation called Ursa Major, or the Big Bear.) Corona Borealis, the Northern Crown (not visible this time of year, so check again during the summer) resembles a crown, although not all cultures have seen it this way. The Shawnee Indians saw it as a circle of dancing sisters, the gap representing one of the sisters who was carried off by a hunter.

Make up your own stories about the stars, to help you remember the constellations. What do the stars remind you of?

21

See if you can detect star colors.

To the naked eye, stars don't look like they have much color, but they actually range in hue from red to blueish white. You can detect these differences with a telescope. Some appear red or orange, others are definintely yellow, and some are yellowish white and blueish white.

These colors correspond to the temperatures of the stars. The red stars are the coolest, the blue-white ones the hottest. You have probably noticed these same color variations if you've ever stared at a fire. Have a fire in a fireplace tonight (or ask your parents if you can burn some logs outdoors, with their supervision) and check out the range of color and heat.

Did you know that our sun is a star? It is the closest star to earth, which is why it seems so large. In fact, it is considered to be a medium-sized star, and yellow in color. (For a full week of sun activities, see *July 29* through *August 4.*) Stars generate their own light, and shine not only at night but all day long. We can't see them, however, because the sun's light is too bright.

Snip a star

Stars have been depicted throughout history with three, four, five, six, seven, even eight points! We usually think of them having five points. Here's a nifty way to cut stars from paper. They can be pasted on or hung from ceilings, or used in other decorative ways. Extra little snips taken from the stars while they are still folded create lovely, intricate patterns (similar to the snowflakes you cut from paper on *January 10*).

Fold an 8½" × 11" piece of paper in half the short way. Follow the diagrams in order, to make five-pointed stars.

1. Bring right corner to the halfway point and crease.
2. Fold right edge over to left and crease.
3. Now fold left edge over to right and crease.
4. Cut on heavy line and unfold.

22

Make a flip book of the moon's phases.

Even easier to track than the changing constellations are the changing phases of the moon, which complete a cycle every 29½ days. The moon does not generate its own light (only stars do this) so we see only the portion that is lit by the sun. When there is a full moon, the sun is shining directly on the moon; at other times our earth gets in the way, shadowing the moon so that only part of it is visible.

Make a flip-book of the moon's phases by copying the sixteen pictures shown below on plain index cards (you may want to make your drawings slightly larger). Arrange the cards in order, starting with 1 on top, and staple the left-hand side of the cards together. Flip the pages for a fast-forward look at the moon's changing face.

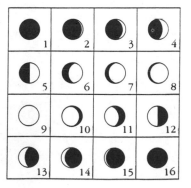

23

Watch a moonrise.

Have you ever noticed the moon during the day? At various times of the month it's visible at all hours. (Sometimes you can barely see it, at least not until the sun goes down and the darkened sky brings out the moon's outline.) And then there is the full moon, seeming to rise out of nowhere! A full moon rising is an unforgettable sight. Have you ever taken a walk when the moon was full? Did you need a flashlight?

Watch a full moonrise from indoors sometime, and mark on the window where the moon first becomes visible. Track it as it continues its arched ascent by taping small circles on the window every ten minutes or so, right over the circle of the moon itself. Some full moons are even more spectacular than others. The full moon in September (see *September 20*) moves across the sky at a lower angle than usual. It's really something to see!

. . . .

When there are two full moons in one month, the second is called the blue moon. As this happens infrequently, the saying *once in a blue moon* means "very rarely." (Some people think the term refers to the actual blue tint that the moon takes on due to atmospheric conditions, again a rare occurrence.)

24

Read a story or poem about the moon and stars.

The full moon is so bright you can almost read by its light!

February Twilight
Sara Teasdale *(poem)*

The Girl and the Moon Man
Jeanette Winter *(story)*

Many Moons
James Thurber *(story)*

The Moon's the North Wind's Cooky
Vachel Lindsay *(poem)*

The Star
Jane Taylor *(poem)*

Star Light, Star Bright
Anonymous *(poem)*

Walk When the Moon is Full
Frances Hamerstrom *(story)*

Winter Moon
Langston Hughes *(poem)*

25

Visit a planetarium.

Where can you go to see the night sky in the middle of the day? A planetarium, that's where! Many museums (and some universities and other educational institutions) have specially designed rooms where an exciting show about the stars and planets is staged. When the theater grows dark, and the music begins, you almost feel like you're travelling to worlds beyond our own. Check to see if there is a planetarium near you, and make plans to visit it soon.

Early attempts to make models of the night sky date back to ancient Greece, but modern planetariums were only developed in the 1920s. You can even put on a planetarium show of your own. There are all sorts of ways to do this, from glow-in-the-dark stars to a battery-powered rotating model that projects "stars" on the ceiling. Or make your own projector, with an empty oatmeal box (cut off the bottom, too) and a length of paper punched with holes in the shapes of constellations. Feed the paper through two slits made at one end of the box, and place a flashlight inside the box. The "stars" will show up wherever you point the box.

. . . .

Cluster glow-in-the-dark stars around a ceiling fixture where the concentrated dose of light will set them glowing for up to 30 minutes.

February

Try a delicious treat called "sugar-on-snow". Heat some maple syrup until it's boiling. Carefully pour it on some fresh, clean snow that has been packed firm. The syrup will cool to a taffy-like candy. Mmmm!

26

Build a birdhouse.

If you have ever moved (or know someone who has) you know that finding a new home is the first thing you do. Birds returning to their summer habitats are faced with the same task, and many are finding it harder each year to find nesting sites in the wild. You can help out by providing safe housing that meets the needs of these summer residents.

From a five-foot length of board (use 1″ × 6″ pine), you can cut the pieces for a basic box that will suit many hole-nesting birds. Saw the board as shown in the diagram. (Note how the cut separating the top and front pieces is angled.) Drill holes in the back (for hanging), the bottom (for drainage), and in the front (this is the entrance the birds will use). Match the entrance hole size to the birds you would like to attract (see the chart in the box below for recommendations). Look at the second diagram to see how the box is actually put together.

Use either screws or galvanized nails; buy the hinge for the top or make your own from leather or rubber.

Look for a good spot to hang your birdhouse, away from direct sun and out of reach of cats. Many hole-nesting birds make their nests in dead trees, so place the box away from shade. Put the box up well before the birds return, and watch for your new neighbors to move in!

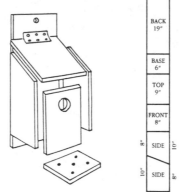
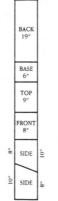

Birds welcome!

Your basic birdhouse will appeal to a number of different bird species. Just alter the size of the entrance hole, and place the house in a spot the birds will feel comfortable in. See the chart for some hints.

Bird	Entrance hole	From ground
Bluebirds	1½″	5′ to 10′
Chickadees	1⅛″	6′ to 15′
Titmice	1¼″	6′ to 15′
Woodpecker, Downy	1¼″	6′ to 20′
Wren, House	1″ to 1¼″	6′ to 10′

27

Make some maple syrup.

For a few weeks each year, some time between mid-February and early April (when warm days are followed by cold nights), sugar maple trees are tapped and the sap turned into maple syrup. It's sugaring time!

Did you know you can make your own maple syrup? All you need is a maple tree (any kind will do as long as it's at least 35″ in diameter), a hand-drill with a ½″ bit, a hollow tube (make your own by pushing the pith out of a 5″ piece of sumac with a coat hanger wire) and a bucket.

Drill a hole into the south-facing side of the tree, about 2″ deep and slanting up slightly. Insert the tube, tapping it in firmly. From a nail, hang the bucket so that it catches the drips. Cover the bucket with foil to keep out any animals. Check the bucket regularly (every few hours if the sap is dripping steadily) and when it is full, pour the sap into a large, shallow pan. If you have only a gallon or so of sap, you can boil it down indoors, otherwise do this outdoors because a lot of steam is created. With your parents' help, bring the sap to a boil and cook it until it reaches exactly 219°F (or 7° above the temperature that boils water). Drop a pat of butter into the syrup to keep it from boiling over.

When it is done, strain the golden brown syrup through a fine-mesh sieve. Cook up some pancakes and have a feast!

28

Look for the first spring bulbs.

You may have planted these yourself the previous fall (see *October 14*), or you may have inherited some planted bulbs if you moved into a new house, as previous tenants often leave them behind. Snowdrops are among the first to emerge, even from under a light blanket of snow. Others soon follow, including glory-of-the-snow, early crocuses, and scillas. These are all cultivated species, of course, although you'll find they prefer woodsy settings, lightly shaded and moist.

Bulbs outdoors continue to bloom year after year, with very little care. Each bulb actually contains a completely formed flower, surrounded by "food" to sustain it. You can cut a bulb in half to see this. Once the bulb has blossomed, the leaves make new "food" from sunlight (this is photosynthesis). That is why you always let the leaves of bulbs wither and dry up, rather than cut them away. Nature has certainly designed some clever packaging!

March brings breezes, loud and shrill,
To stir the dancing daffodil.

March

29

Choose seeds or plants for spring planting.

Gardeners start to get itchy around this time of year. Spring planting isn't far off! Even the simplest gardens benefit from planning, so take some time to choose what you'd like to grow this year.

If you are new to gardening, start small. Grow your favorite vegetable, or sow some flowers that you like. You will find most of what you need at your local garden center. The racks of seed packets offer delights of every type, from acorn squash to zinnias. (It's a bit early for plants, so check again in a couple of months.) But don't forget the many seed and plant catalogues, some of which you may have sent for (see *November 30*). There are all sorts of fantastic seeds from around the world, and healthy plants ready for the garden (these won't be sent until the weather settles). Do you want to grow mammoth pumpkins that tip the scales at 100 pounds? Would you like to grow your own ingredients for a Mexican meal? Maybe you only have the room for containers. Or you might be interested in having an herb garden (see *Let's hear it for herbs!* on page 60).

No matter where your garden is, nor how small it might be, there is something you can grow. Happy gardening!

1

Listen for the early birds.

Even in the colder northern reaches, it's not too early for some of the hardier birds to return to their summer breeding grounds. Among the first to fly north are the ducks and geese (do you hear them honking?), and the red-winged blackbirds. If you live within earshot of a marshy area, you'll hear them staking their territorial claims. That's them calling "conk-kar-ree"!

Some of the year-round residents are starting to sing again, too. The mourning dove has a melancholy song that sounds almost owl-like. Do you like the sound? As certain birds prepare to choose mates and raise families, their behavior changes, as does their tune, in some cases. The chickadee, well known for its "chicka-dee-dee-dee", adds a whistled "fee-bee" (not to be confused with the phoebe's "fee-bee" which is more abrupt and repeated over and over). Did you know that it's the male that does all the singing? They have the most to say. Their songs, after all, are meant first to keep other males away from their territory, and later to attract females to it. (For more on bird song, see *March 25* and *26*.)

2

Listen for spring peepers.

The first warming spring rains stir a number of animals to life, and in your area you may be aware of a bell-like "pee-eep, pee-eep, pee-eep" coming from the direction of a pond or marshy spot, even when there is snow on the ground. Who is making this noise? Spring peepers, tiny (postage-stamp size) frogs that awaken from their underground sleep well before most other frogs and toads.

The peeper's call is a welcome one. Not only does it mean that spring is inevitable (it's too early to say that it's on its way in colder regions!), but it means you've also found a pond where you'll be able to find other amphibians later in the spring and summer. Would you like to see what the spring peeper looks like? Good luck! The frog is so small, and so well camouflaged that it's very hard to actually glimpse the noisemaker. Spring peepers are tree frogs, but they prefer the low branches of bushes and other plants, so concentrate low down when you are hunting. Spring peepers usually wait until twilight to call, although on overcast days you may hear them earlier.

3

Hunt for woodland flowers.

Take a walk through a wooded area and search for those first flowers that poke up through the leaf-strewn forest floor. (You'll find that there is more plant life—from mosses to wildflowers—on the ground of a deciduous forest than in a stand of pines. The fallen needles from conifers make the soil rather acid, which many plants can't tolerate.) These flowers are usually delicate, and short-lived, as they require sun for their growth and blooming. Once the trees are in leaf, little light penetrates to the woodland floor.

Look for those plants that bear such descriptive names as spring beauty and harbinger of spring. Trailing arbutus, hepatica, and bloodroot are some others you may find. In clearings look for wood anemones, slender-stalked flowers that are sometimes known as wind flowers, because they dance and sway in the breeze.

March

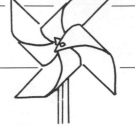

4

Make a wind vane.

Did you know that the sun is responsible for creating winds? As the air is warmed by the sun, it rises, and colder, denser air moves in to replace it. This is wind! Geographical features, such as mountains, bodies of water and deserts, help determine the nature of wind—its speed and direction.

The direction of wind (where it is blowing *from*) often affects the weather. For roughly two-thirds of the continental United States good weather is brought by northwest, west and southwest winds; bad weather is generally blown in by winds from the northeast, east and southeast. You can make your own wind vane to check wind direction.

Make an indicator with a straw and two triangles cut from thin cardboard (see the diagram). Cut slits in the straw ends and glue the triangles in place. Stick a pin right through the middle of the straw into a pencil eraser. Make sure it swings freely. Support the pencil in a yogurt container that is anchored to a board with some modeling clay. Place the vane on a flat surface outdoors and mark N, E, S, and W on the container. The arrow will point to the direction the wind is blowing from. Can you predict what weather the winds will bring?

5

Guess the wind speed.

Have you ever noticed how a gentle breeze can make an otherwise unbearably hot day almost pleasant? Or how a brisk wind in winter will send you scurrying for cover?

Wind velocity is measured on a scale of 0 to 12, known as the Beaufort scale. It is named for Sir Francis Beaufort, an English rear admiral who devised this method of determining wind speed in the early 1800s. (We have since added the figures in miles per hour.) The box on this page offers the visual clues to look for to determine the wind's speed. Can you guess how fast the wind is blowing today?

Blow ye winds, blow!

Calm
Smoke rises
0 mph

Light air
Smoke drifts
1-3 mph

Slight breeze
Leaves rustle; vanes move
4-7 mph

Gentle breeze
Leaves and twigs move
8-12 mph

Moderate breeze
Branches move; flags flap
13-18 mph

Fresh breeze
Small trees sway; white caps on water
19-24 mph

Strong breeze
Large branches move; flags beat
25-31 mph

Moderate gale
Whole trees move; flags extend
32-38 mph

Fresh gale
Twigs break; walking is difficult
39-46 mph

Strong gale
Signs, antennas blow down
47-54 mph

Whole gale
Trees uproot
55-63 mph

Storm
Much general damage
64-72 mph

Hurricane
Wide-spread destruction
72+ mph

6

Make a pinwheel.

Over the centuries people have come up with all sorts of ways to harness the wind to use it to push boats and power machinery. Wind power is currently of interest to those who would like to see us using cleaner and less expensive energy. Windmills can be used to generate electricity, and while you need plenty of wind to make this work, it's clean, and it's free!

Did you know that a pinwheel is just a miniature version of a windmill? Make a pinwheel to see how the sails catch the wind and make the wheel turn. You can make a pinwheel from a square of stiff paper (6″ is a good size), a pencil that has an eraser, and a straight pin. Fold the paper diagonally both ways and cut along the crease lines to within 1″ of the center point. Take each corner in turn and bring it to the center point (let it overlap slightly, as shown in the diagram). Push the pin through all four layers. To reduce the friction between the spinning sails and the pencil eraser, make a "bead" by rolling a strip of paper into a tube. Glue its end so that it won't unroll. Place the "bead" on the pin and stick the pin into the side of the eraser. The pinwheel should turn freely.

Experiment holding the pinwheel at different angles to the oncoming breeze. Which works best?

Kites are thought to have originated in China about 3,000 years ago.

March

7

Read a story or poem about wind.

Wind has a magical quality, don't you think? We can't see it, but it's all around us, sending spiders on their way and changing the face of the earth with its brute strength. These stories and poems have captured some of that magic.

The March Wind
Anonymous *(poem)*

The Spring Wind
Charlotte Zolotow *(poem)*

The Surprise from **Frog and Toad All Year**
Arnold Lobel *(story)*

Who Has Seen the Wind?
Christina Rossetti *(poem)*

The Wind
James Reeves *(poem)*

The Wind Blew
Pat Hutchins *(story)*

. . . .

When the wind is out of the east,
'Tis good for neither man nor beast
But when the wind is out of the west,
It sends every man the very best.

8

See how plants and animals use wind.

Have you ever watched dandelion seeds floating on air? Or seen a tiny spider attached to a single thread blow from one branch to another? Then you've seen two fabulous ways that plants and animals actually use the wind.

Take a walk outdoors and see if you can find any other evidence of plants and animals putting the wind to use. Dandelions aren't the only plants that disperse their seeds with the wind's help. Maple seeds are those funny helicopters that go twirling with the breeze. And lots of plant pollen is spread with the wind. Mushrooms rely on the wind to send their spores to new locations. (You'll have to look again in the autumn when the ripe seeds from other plants, such as thistle and milkweed, are launched with the wind.)

What about animals? Stop and watch a spider if you see one hanging by its silken thread. It's waiting for a slight breeze to blow it to a new spot. This is called ballooning. It looks like fun, doesn't it? Other animals use the wind to help them hunt (and avoid being hunted, as the case may be). Odors travel with the wind, and both predators and prey use this to their advantage. It also explains why people try to stay downwind from animals they are tracking. Our scent can give us away long before animals hear or see us.

9

Make some wind chimes.

How about using the wind to make music? You can if you hang up some wind chimes! Chimes can be made from a variety of materials, including wood, metal and shells.

Wood makes a soft sound, but you can improve upon it by hollowing out the wood you use. (Bamboo chimes, which you may be familiar with, are hollow.) Choose a wood like elderberry or sumac that you can push the pith out of (do this with a straightened wire coat hanger). Or string up some empty wooden spools (these are getting hard to find, unfortunately).

Metal chimes ring, and you can make some from washers or nails of various sizes hung with strong thread. Experiment with different combinations to make different sounds.

Shells work very well, tinkling pleasantly with the slightest breeze. Tap holes into thin shells (such as jingle shells—how do you think these shells got their name?) or wrap string around shells that have a "handle." Group several strands together for a full orchestra.

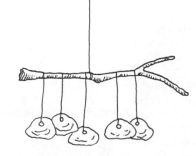

10

Construct a kite.

Go fly a kite! Here's a quick one you can make. Fly it in a gentle breeze.

You need a 24″ square piece of paper (newspaper or wrapping paper will do), a 14″ × 1½″ strip of thin cardboard, a ⅛″ dowel 18″ long, and tape. Use buttonhole thread for the flying line, wrapped around a stick.

Fold the paper in half and mark the lines shown in diagram #1. Cut away the areas marked. Fold the top sheet down and rule a line from wing tip to wing tip. Join the wings with tape along the fold. Tape along the wing edges (on one side) to keep them from tearing.

Turn the kite over and rule the lines on the fin as shown in #2. Cut as shown. Tape these edges with folded tape. Snip the corners from the cardboard and tape it to the fin, ½″ down from the wing fold, and 3″ over the wing line.

Mark the center of the dowel and tape it to the back of the kite 1¼″ above the wing line. Bow the dowel and tape the ends to the wing tips. Attach the flying line 1¼″ behind the wing line on the fin. Note: If the kite won't climb, move the line forward. Move it back if the kite spins.

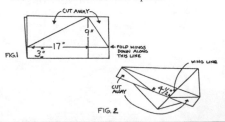

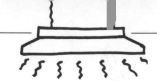

March

11

Put branches in water for early blooms.

Are you getting impatient waiting for spring to arrive? Why not help things along a little? You can coax the buds of spring-flowering trees and shrubs to open in the warmth of your home.

Forsythia branches are a good choice, and lots of people have a bush in their yard. The bright yellow blossoms are just the thing to put you in a sunny mood. How about apple blossoms? These are beautiful, delicate flowers that smell just as good as they look. Just cut the branches from the plants and either peel or mash the thick ends to help them absorb water. Change the water frequently, and depending on how close the plants were to blooming, you should have a lovely display of spring blossoms within a few weeks.

And then there are pussy willows. Pick these branches when the fuzzy catkins have developed. Don't put pussy willows in water, however, because that encourages them to leaf out. If handled with care, the dried branches of pussy willows can be kept for many years.

12

Mix up some potting soil.

Who needs potting soil when you have a yard full of dirt? Well, if you want to start your own plants from seed, or if you plan to grow plants in containers, you should use potting soil. Potting soils are simply sterilized mixes that hold moisture well without becoming waterlogged. You can buy bags of soil at garden centers (even your supermarket may sell it), but you can easily make your own.

Some potting soils have soil in them; others are soilless. If you would like to add some real dirt to your mix, you will have to sterilize it, and the easiest way to do this is in the oven. Coffee cans full of soil need to bake for 1½ hours at 350°F to kill weed seeds, insects and soilborne diseases. Soilless mixes need no special treatment. Perlite and vermiculite (both mined rocks that are heat-treated to turn them into lightweight particles) can be used interchangeably.

Soil mix
2 parts sterilized garden soil
1 part peat moss
1 part sand or perlite

Soilless mix
1 part peat moss
1 part perlite or vermiculite

Note: Neither of these mixes contains fertilizer. You will have to add this nourishment. Choose an organic blend and follow the instructions on the package.

13

Start some seeds indoors.

Some plants benefit from a head start indoors. Sow the seeds of those plants that need a long growing season, and those that you would like to have bloom as early as possible. Your seed packets will help you determine what to plant when.

You can start seeds in practically any container that is deep enough for the plants' roots, and that has drainage holes. (Punch holes in milk cartons and yogurt containers with a nail.) Dampen the potting soil before putting it into the containers. Bury large seeds about ¼" to ½" deep; sprinkle tiny seeds right on the surface, covering them lightly with more soil. Label the containers, and put them in plastic bags. Place them in a warm, dark place. Check them every day, and when the seeds have sprouted, remove the bags and put the containers in a sunny spot, or under a plant light. Keep the soil moist, but not too wet.

You'll have to transplant the seedlings as they grow, and give them "food" (as fertilizer is known) to keep them healthy. Just tend to their needs, and watch them grow!

14

Rig a plant light.

You can start your own plants from seed even if you don't have a sunny window. How? With fluorescent lights. Maybe you've seen "grow lights" that claim to simulate sunlight. You can make your own rig with ordinary fluorescent bulbs.

You may already have a fluorescent fixture in your house. Check your basement or garage. Ask if you can "borrow" it for the month or so that your seedlings will need it (make sure the room has some heat). One "cool" and one "warm" bulb used together will give your plants the right kind of light. Twelve to sixteen hours of artificial light each day are necessary for proper growth, but fluorescent bulbs don't use much electricity. If you turn on the lights in the morning, and turn them off when you get ready for bed, your plants will prosper.

Plants do best when the lights are placed only 3-4" above the foliage. That means you either will need to put the fixture on a chain (to raise it as the plants grow) or make the plant shelf so that it adjusts lower. Have your parents help you figure out the best way to do this.

15

Make new plants from cuttings.

You can fill your garden with new plants without having to spend a dime by taking cuttings from existing plants. Stem cuttings are the most common, although some plants (notably African violets and begonias) will root at the leaves. Not only houseplants can be started with this method—many herbs and flowers that are grown outdoors can be propagated by stem cuttings.

Choose a healthy 4″ to 6″ shoot, and cut it just below the spot where a leaf meets the stem. Strip the lower leaves from the stem and insert it into a pot containing clean damp sand (or vermiculite or perlite). Put in a cool but light location. Keep the sand moistened and within about 6 weeks the stem will have sent out roots. You can then transplant the cutting to a pot containing potting soil. If the cutting wilts, put the pot in a plastic bag (to increase humidity) until it rights itself.

Leaf cuttings are done much the same way. Cut the leaf close to the stem at an angle. Nestle this in some moist sand (this anchors it well). Once the leaf has put out roots, it can be potted in regular potting soil.

16

Make a cold frame.

Long before gardeners thought to start plants indoors under lights (see *March 14*), they used cold frames. Serious gardeners still find them invaluable. A cold frame is basically a sloping box that has a hinged lid made of clear glass or plastic. The air inside the box is much warmer than the outside air (thanks to solar energy), and cold frames can be used to start seeds and harden off plants.

Make a miniature cold frame with some easy-to-find materials. Look for two cardboard boxes the same size and put one inside the other (remove the tops and bottoms first). Sink the frame into the ground a few inches (dig a trench for it), banking up some dirt all around the box to keep it in place. Cut a piece of heavy plastic for the cover. It should be the same width as the box, but make it long enough so that it can be weighted with rocks or bricks when closed.

To see how effective a cold frame is, place a thermometer inside the box and compare this temperature to the outside air temperature. It's almost summer-like inside the frame, isn't it?

17

Grow some plants from pits.

Wait, don't throw that avocado pit out! You can grow a lush, green houseplant with it. Just peel the brown covering off and stick three toothpicks into the pit. Suspend it over a jar of water, fat end down. Add more water as it evaporates, and the pit will soon send out roots, followed by a green stem and leaves from its top. Transplant it to a pot of soil at this point, and pinch it back to keep it bushy and healthy.

You can do the same thing with a sweet potato. Sweet potatoes are vining plants. Plant the pits of oranges, lemons and other citrus fruits. The plants won't bear fruit, but they make nice houseplants. Or cut the top off of a pineapple and root it in sand.

A pineapple makes a long-lived houseplant. Let the cut top dry on its side for about 5 days. Place it in a shallow pot of moist sand, buried so only the leaves show. Place the pot in a warm, sunny location and in about 2-3 months the top will have rooted. You can then repot it into regular potting soil. The great thing about a pineapple is that after several years it will bear small pineapples of its own!

A tree grows in . . .

Is there a tree in your yard, or on the way to school, or in the park, that you think of as special? Maybe it's a tree you planted when you were little (or one that your mother or father did). Or maybe it's a tree that has a family of squirrels living in it that you have watched. You may have marveled at the color it turned in autumn, or collected its cones.

Why not keep an eye on your tree for the next 12 months, to learn as much as you can about the tree itself and its inhabitants? Record your observations in a scrapbook or on a wall chart. Measure the tree, photograph it and sketch it. Make rubbings of its bark, and press its leaves and blossoms at different times of year. Try to find out what animals live in the tree, from the tiny creatures that live beneath the bark to the opportunists that make their nests in any holes. This is a good time of year to begin, before the buds open and the leaves obscure the upper reaches (if it's a deciduous tree). A tree is a wondrous thing. Introduce yourself to one today!

March

Spring is showery, flowery, bowery.

18

Look for signs of thawing at ponds.

With the warming of the air, comes the thawing of the thick ice that covers lakes, ponds, and other watery areas. Many lakes suffer from winterkill this time of year. Winterkill is caused by lack of oxygen in the water, brought about, in part, by the ice, which keeps external air from stirring the waters. Once the ice breaks up, life within the lakes is roused.

You can see how the spring thaw varies from year to year. The ice may gradually become thinner and thinner, melting from the banks inward. Or it may thaw and re-form if the temperature drops. Rain may fall and raise the level of the water, breaking the ice into chunks, or melting it into patterns that are visible on the surface. What does it look like is happening this year? One thing is for certain. Once a proper thaw is underway, you can be sure that spring is soon to follow.

People in Poland celebrate the breaking up of the ice by throwing large dolls (dressed in clothes and festooned with ribbons) in rivers. Along the river banks, the townspeople sing and dance to welcome in spring.

19

See how rivers are rising.

Rivers are at their highest this time of year, full of water from melting snow and ice. Watch how rivers rush with abandon, even thundering with force. Do you see how water power might be harnessed? Many mills, of course, have been built along rivers throughout the world, to take advantage of water power. Some rivers are dammed to control their flow and are used to generate hydroelectricity.

Have you ever noticed how many small brooks come alive only in spring? They dry up in the heat of summer, as do many vernal pools (vernal, for spring) that exist only long enough to give amphibious life a start. The amount of water in rivers now will depend on how much snow there was during the winter months. Stop and admire a river, gushing with spring importance.

. . . .

March 19 is the day when the swallows are expected to return to San Juan Capistrano, California. Birdwatchers have been keeping an eye out for them since 1776. The birds do usually return within a week either side of this date.

20

First day of spring!

The first day of spring falls on or about March 20. This is the vernal equinox (equinox being Latin for "equal night"). What this means is that on this day, the length of day equals that of night, everywhere on earth. (This also happens at the autumnal equinox, around September 21.)

The sun also rises due east and sets due west today. And the length of the days will continue to increase until June 21, when night strives to overcome day once again.

As you have seen, many of the natural events that we think of as happening in spring have already taken place. But this is a special day, so do something special to celebrate spring. Take off your shoes and walk in some mud. Look for some fresh fruit in the market and make a huge fruit salad. Go fly a kite. Take in some deep breaths of fresh air and praise nature.

The rite of spring

As recently as the 16th century, Europeans regarded spring as the beginning of the year. That's not surprising, really. The spurt of plant growth and the birth of animals proved that renewal was taking place. Different days were actually set aside by different peoples, usually in connection with the spring equinox (see *March 20*). For some the new year coincided with religious celebrations which took place at the end of March. In fact, the original "April fools" were those people who refused to adopt the New Year and steadfastly clung to the old, which was celebrated with festivities that ended on April 1st. The custom of poking fun at everyone in general on April 1st evolved later.

21

Read a story or poem about spring.

Is spring your favorite season? It certainly is an exciting time for nature observers. Poets and other writers are pretty observant, too, as you'll see.

The Day the Sun Danced
Edith Thacher Hurd *(story)*

Good-by My Winter Suit
N.M. Bodecker *(poem)*

March
Elizabeth Coatsworth *(poem)*

Ode to Spring
Walter R. Brooks *(poem)*

Pussy Willows
Aileen Fisher *(poem)*

Really Spring
Gene Zion *(story)*

Smells
Kathryn Worth *(poem)*

Spring
Karla Kuskin *(poem)*

Spring Is
Bobbi Katz *(poem)*

22

Make a spring mural.

There are so many changes taking place in spring, it's hard to keep track of them all! You can with a mural. On a continuous length of newsprint, or computer print-out paper (or piece together sheets of paper), paint, sketch, paste, and stick all sorts of pictures that show spring growth and change.

Make a tree silhouette and paste down green paper leaves when the real leaves open. Glue pictures cut from old gardening catalogues, and other magazines. Paste down pictures of baby animals that are born in spring. Don't worry about everything being to scale. Label what you put in your mural, including any relevant dates.

When did the first robin start poking around on your lawn? Is there still snow on the ground? Can you feel spring in the air, or will it be a little late this year? Do you remember what it was like at this time last year?

23

Watch for flies in your house.

Some warm, sunny day you may notice flies inside your house. How did they get in, and why are there none outdoors? Most probably these are cluster flies that have spent the winter hibernating between your storm and inner windows. Warmed and wakened by the sun, these insects make their way through the tiniest openings, often ending up inside your home. Do them a favor and let them outside. (See *October 15* for more on their hibernation.)

24

Play in some mud.

With the thaw comes mud, stuck to the soles of boots and shoes and inevitably tracked into the house and car. Ask your parents if there's a spot you can play in, because mud pies just can't be made with anything else!

In some parts of the country, where the thaw is prolonged and the ground gets really muddy, this time of year is known as "mud season." It can be pretty messy, but also a lot of fun. Just make sure your boots are laced on nice and tight!

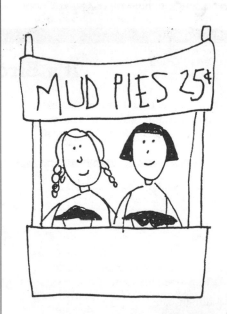

March

25

Drink your tea!

Learn some bird songs and calls.

Have you ever been wakened by the birds? The morning chorus of chirps, tweets, and squawks can be delightfully deafening! With some practice, you can learn to identify birds by sound, which is a handy skill to have. Often you will hear a bird before you see it, so if you know what bird to look for (and where to look), you'll have a good chance of spotting it.

Birdwatchers make a distinction between a bird's call and its song. A call is usually a single sound (it might be a shrill, long note or a squawk or a peep). A song is a series of sounds—a melody. Some birds have both calls and songs. Others are considered poor singers, but their calls are noteworthy.

The best way to learn a bird's "voice" is to study the bird while it is singing (or calling). Concentrate on forming a mental picture of the bird going about its business. Can you think of any funny little ways to remember the song? Many songs have been "translated" into English (and other languages). These can help you recall the string of notes that a bird is singing. (See the box on this page for some common "translations.")

Check your library for recordings of bird songs. These can be a big help.

It's Bird to me

Dr. Doolittle talked to the animals. Maybe you can too! To a lot of people many bird songs sound like human speech. Check out some of these examples.

Bird	Song (or portion of song)
Barred Owl	"Who cooks for you all?"
Chestnut-sided warbler	"I want to see Miss Beecher"
Ovenbird	"Teacher, teacher, teacher"
Robin	"Wake up, cheer up, cheerily up, wake up"
Rufous-sided towhee	"Drink your tea"
White-throated sparrow	"Ah, sweet Canada, Canada, Canada"

26

Call some birds.

Birds are naturally curious creatures, and if you imitate their calls and songs, many will come forth to investigate. Owl hoots and the mournful sounds of the mourning dove are easy to imitate; anyone can quack like a duck. But what about some of the other birds?

You can get your voice to make many of the sounds that birds make, or you can use a bird caller. The Audubon bird caller is probably the best known. It's a pocket-sized wooden cylinder with a pewter stem that is twisted to produce a variety of sounds. They don't cost much, and you can find them at nature centers and from catalogue retailers. With this simple device, you can call chickadees, catbirds and white-throated sparrows, to name a few. Try one out. What birds can you get to visit you this way?

Many birds can be drawn out into the open just by making a squeaky sound by placing your lips against the back of your hand and sucking in your breath. Birds just can't seem to resist finding out who is making this noise.

. . . .

The songs of the whip-poor-will, bobwhite, phoebe and chickadee gave these birds their names.

27

Construct a blind.

Birds may be curious, but they are cautious, too. They are easily startled and may even abandon their nesting sites if they have cause to worry. You can put birds at ease when you are watching them, by concealing yourself in a blind (or hide, as it is also called). This is a trick professional naturalists and photographers use in order to observe wildlife up close.

If you have a tent (preferably a green or tan one, or one camouflaged with paint), set it up where you can watch a nest under construction, or birds at your feeders. Lacking that, drive some stakes into the ground and drape a camouflaged blanket over and around the uprights. Branches and other foliage placed in front and around the blind will help it to blend in with its surroundings. Even just a bush that you can crouch behind works well. Enter your hiding place as quietly and calmly as possible, and the birds will soon discover that they have nothing to fear.

Use your blind to watch other animals, too. Mammals, especially, are easily spooked, so you'll want to conceal your presence. Because most mammals come out at night, make sure your blind will give you the insect protection you'll need. Dress warmly because you'll be sitting still for long periods, waiting and watching.

You'll attract seed- and insect-eating birds if you have a meadow or open area. Berry-eating species look for berry bushes, while birds that eat pine nuts will settle where there are plenty of coniferous trees.

28

Watch for birds building their nests.

The time soon comes for the birds that have staked their claims, and chosen their mates, to begin nest building. The males of some species do the work; sometimes the females take charge, and sometimes the males and females work together. Look for birds making frequent trips with twigs and grass (and even paper and bits of plastic in urban areas) held in their beaks. Follow them discreetly and watch them building their nests. Some of the birds may have chosen the house you provided for them (see *February 26*); others will be looking for concealed spots in evergreen trees and bushes, and natural cavities within dead trees. Some birds build their nests at ground level.

Nesting materials are also getting harder for birds to find. You can help by putting out short lengths of yarn and string, dried Spanish moss and dried grass. Even hair from a hair brush and stuffing from old furniture can be put to use. Hang up a mesh bag (the kind that onions come in) full of these materials, or thread the yarn pieces around a pine cone hung from a branch. Don't forget that many birds plaster their nests with mud. Keep a bare patch of ground wet for them.

29

Try building a nest.

It's pretty amazing how with only two feet and a beak, birds are capable of weaving all sorts of different sized materials into nests, daubing some with mud for added strength, and lining many with softer materials such as their own down or plant fluff. Watch birds building their nests to learn some of their techniques. Then try to build a nest yourself.

Gather up the same sorts of materials that birds find—dried grasses, twigs, scraps of paper and other trash, and even some of the materials that you have put out for the home builders. With your own two hands, weave all these bits and pieces into a nest. You can appreciate how skilled birds really are, and how patient they must be to take on the task of nest building year after year. It's not as easy as it looks, is it?

30

Record some early spring sounds.

You can make your own recordings of birds and other animals with a portable cassette recorder. While some recorders have a built-in microphone, use a microphone that has a long cord. That way you and the machine can be hidden some distance from the animals you are recording, inside your blind, for instance (see *March 27*), or behind a tree or bush.

Try attaching the microphone to the end of a broom stick, so that you can hold it close to the source of the sounds (such as a wasp's nest) without getting too close. Or clip it to a stake driven into the grass in a meadow. You'll be able to make recordings of all the insects coming and going. To help reduce the sound of wind (which our ears tune out but which a good microphone will pick up), make a simple frame to fit around the microphone's recording end. Bend some flexible wire into a balloon shape and stretch a stocking foot over it.

If you note what you are recording at the time, you can use the tapes to help you learn bird songs, or to play games with. Try stumping your family and friends. Can they guess who's making the sounds in your recordings?

Bzzzzzz

31

Learn your state bird, flower, and tree.

Can you name your state bird, flower, and tree? It's less widely known that many states have also designated other natural resources to honor. Some states have state animals (some list both a wild and a domestic animal), insects, fish, minerals, gems, grass, fruit, nuts, mushrooms, and even soil and fossils!

There's a complete listing of the state birds, flowers and trees in the Appendix under *Additional information*. Why do you suppose your state has chosen those particular plants and animals? Would you choose any of them differently?

There are about 8,600 species of birds in the world.

April

April brings the primrose sweet,
Scatters daisies at our feet.

1

See how rain is formed.

Water is always present in the air, in the form of water vapor, a gas which we can't see. It is constantly evaporating from oceans, rivers and lakes, tree leaves, and even our own bodies! The vapor rises, and when the conditions are right, clouds form. (See the week of *August 12–18* for more on clouds.)

You can catch some water vapor to prove this. Tie a plastic bag around a tree branch that is in leaf and leave it for a few hours. You'll notice that the bag is full of condensation from the water that the tree leaves have transpired. Or venture down to a river or stream on a cool morning, and you'll see the mist hanging over the water like a ghost. A mist like this even feels wet.

When there is enough water gathered in a cloud, and when the cloud cools, the tiny droplets bump together and join one another. Their sheer weight causes the drops to fall to the ground. It may be drizzly rain or a steady downpour (see *April 2* for some of the words we use for rain), but to borrow from a well-worn cliche, what goes up must come down!

2

Think of different words for rain.

Sometimes when there is a gentle rain we say it is sprinkling. Or drizzling, or spitting! Aren't these funny ways to describe rain? Can you think of any other ways to say it's raining?

What about "it's raining cats and dogs"? No one really knows where this saying came from, although many derivations have been suggested. Some people think the ancient Greeks came up with this imaginative way to say it's raining hard. Other people think the Scandinavians should get the credit. And this is but one variation on a theme. Have you ever heard "it's raining chicken coops"? Or darning needles or pitchforks? Yicks!

Dour showers

In recent years, scientists have become increasingly concerned with a problem known as acid rain. The by-products from burning fuels rise into the air and interact with weather elements, producing rain that has a high chemical content. Sulfur dioxide is one such chemical that has been raining down, killing vegetation worldwide, and threatening life on earth. Other noxious chemicals are sometimes trapped at low levels producing a dangerous smog.

Acid rain is considered by some to be a short-range problem—that is, if it is corrected quickly. Most scientists agree that there are other long-term problems that should not be ignored. They think that carbon dioxide in the air is causing the earth to warm too quickly. This would cause the glaciers to melt, and there could be widespread flooding, and many animals might not be able to adapt to the change. Others think the ozone layer in the upper atmosphere is in danger of being depleted, allowing harmful ultraviolet radiation to beam down on the earth.

While no solutions have been reached, much work is being done now to study the problems in hopes of turning the situation around in time.

3

Compare rain forests to deserts.

There are some places on earth where it rains every day. And other places that might not receive a single inch of rainfall in a whole year's time! How do you think these two places might differ?

The tropical rain forests that get so much rain, *need* that much rain. The plants and animals there expect lots of moisture. Not surprisingly, rain forests have a wider variety of wildlife than is found in any other habitat. You may only find one tree of a particular type, however, in an area as large as several acres. (Compare this to forests in the United States where hundreds of like trees grow together in a small area.)

Plants and animals in deserts, on the other hand, expect arid conditions. Some plants can sprout, flower, and bear seeds in as little as two weeks! In this way they take advantage of the rain that might fall only once a year. What would happen to these plants if there was a lot of rain?

There are also places throughout the world that have a clear-cut rainy season, lasting for many months. During the dry months, these areas may be desert-like, but then the rains change all that. Countries bordering the Indian Ocean conform to this pattern, when the monsoon winds of summer bring steady rain.

A flash of lightning is a larger version of the electrical charge you get when touching metal after walking across a carpet.

April

4

See how drought affects wildlife.

No one expects it to rain very much in a desert. But what happens when it doesn't rain for a long time in a place that normally gets plenty of moisture? A drought can be a devastating thing in such a place.

Not only is spring and summertime rain important for keeping grass green and trees watered. Lack of snowfall the preceding winter can bring about drought. Without adequate water, all plant life suffers, and as a consequence, all wildlife is affected. Those plants and animals that we raise for human consumption feel the effects, too, of course. And forest fires are a real hazard when trees and shrubs are very dry. (This rarely happens this time of year. Most droughts in the United States occur during the summer and early autumn.)

You can demonstrate the effects of drought by deliberately not watering a houseplant. See how it withers? Now notice what happens when you give it a good drink of water. It revives remarkably fast. Plants in nature are able to do the same, but of course they need that drink of water to come in time.

5

See how animals sense it will rain.

Weather forecasters don't rely on animals when it comes to predicting the weather. But amateur weatherwatchers, such as farmers and gardeners, claim that animals can provide some clues, especially for short-term predictions. They say there is some truth to such signs as general restlessness in animals, or the relative absence of others.

Lots of weather sayings comment on the behavior of animals. Maybe you've heard of some such as these.

If bees stay at home,
Rain will soon come.
If they fly away,
Fine will be the day.

Flies will swarm
Before a storm.

It is *not* true that you can expect rain when ants travel in a straight line, nor does a rooster crowing at night mean rain is in sight! These have become part of our folklore just as the groundhog seeing his shadow in early spring has (see *February 2*). What have you noticed your pets doing when a change in the weather is imminent? Are there any ways that *you* can feel rain coming?

6

Read a story or poem about rain.

Rain needn't be a reason for staying indoors! These stories and poems dispel the myth that rain and good times can't go together. What is your favorite thing about a rainy day?

All Wet! All Wet!
James Skofield *(story)*

April Rain Song
Langston Hughes *(poem)*

Rain
Peter Spier *(story)*

Raindrops
Aileen Fisher *(poem)*

Rainy Nights
Irene Thompson *(poem)*

Spring Rain
Marchette Chute *(poem)*

Umbrellas
Barbara Juster Esbensen *(poem)*

A Walk in the Rain
Ursel Scheffler *(story)*

7

Guess where lightning is striking.

A full-fledged rain storm is sometimes accompanied by thunder and lightning (especially in the summer). When the conditions are right, electrical charges build up within a thundercloud and create a flash of lightning. Most lightning jumps from one part of a cloud to another, or from cloud to cloud. Bolts of lightning only strike the earth about one-third of the time.

Then what is thunder? When the air along the stroke of lightning is heated, it expands so forcefully that it generates shock waves that we hear as thunder. Did you know that you can estimate where lightning is striking by counting the seconds that elapse between the flash and the resulting thunder? Divide that number by five, which is roughly the number of seconds it takes for sound to travel one mile. The answer will be an approximate distance in miles.

Are you frightened by thunderstorms? Maybe when you can see that the storm isn't that close you can relax a bit. Try explaining that to your dog cowering under your bed!

. . . .

During a thunderstorm, avoid tall trees, water, and anything metal. If you can't get to safety, crouch low but don't lie down. In your home, it is best not to touch metal; avoid using water, electrical appliances, and the telephone until the storm passes.

April

8

Take a walk in the rain.

A walk in the rain is a treat for the senses. Can you smell the damp earth? What does the rain feel like on your skin? Don't all the colors look rich when everything is wet?

When you venture out during a rain, you can see some of the ways that nature deals with precipitation. Leaves on trees and bushes (and you'll have to check this again when there are more leaves) are specially shaped to funnel off water, and animals shed the wet with the help of oily fur and feathers. Some animals, such as moist-skinned amphibians, make their treks to breeding grounds when it rains. Earthworms, too, surface when there is rain (for more on this, see *April 18*).

Dress for the weather, with water-proof coat and boots, and enjoy a walk that's out of the ordinary. Who wants to stay indoors when it's this beautiful out?

9

Make a rain gauge.

While you can collect rain in any container marked off in inches (or centimeters), you can make a gauge that is more precise. The best container for collecting rain is a wide-mouthed one. If you can find a wide funnel that will fit inside it, all the better, because the funnel will keep some of the rainwater from evaporating before you get a chance to record its depth. But measuring a small amount of rain in such a large container is difficult. Here's a trick for making more precise measurements.

In addition to the container you have sitting outside collecting rain, you will need a tall jar that is only 1″ to 1½″ in diameter (olives come in jars like these). Fill your collecting container with exactly one inch of water. Pour the water into the tall jar and mark the level of the water. Divide that inch (and any others you wish to mark on the jar) into fractions.

Whenever it rains, collect the rainwater in the bigger container, but transfer it to the measuring jar to see how much rain really fell.

10

Measure a patch of grass.

All plants need water to grow, but none grow as visibly as grass. Did you know that there are 10,000 species of grass, covering nearly one-third of all the earth's land surface? These include grasses that animals graze on, those that humans eat (such as wheat, rice, and corn to name only three), and even bamboo, which is both eaten (by pandas and humans!) and used as a building material.

Do you have grass growing in your yard? It has a nice cushiony feel, especially when it is kept short. Do you help mow the grass? Well, leave a tiny patch unmowed and watch what happens as the grass grows. Measure it now and keep track how much it shoots up each week, especially after a rain. Are you surprised? Did you expect the grass to look like this when it was fully grown?

. . . .

Day-light saving time begins the last Sunday in April. Remember "Spring forward, fall backward" and set your clocks ahead one hour.

11

Make rain pictures.

Have you ever been caught in the rain with your homework, or a letter to mail, written with a felt-tip pen? A few raindrops always manage to land right on the ink and smudge it! Why not use the rain to help you "paint" a picture?

Start out by painting some shapes or blocks of color with water-soluble paints (such as watercolors or poster paints) or markers. Place the picture outdoors when it's raining for a brief spell. The patterns made by the drops can be very interesting. How long can you keep the painting in the rain before it washes away? Compare the results of drizzle, gentle rain, and a full-fledged downpour. The resulting artwork might be said to have been created jointly by you and nature!

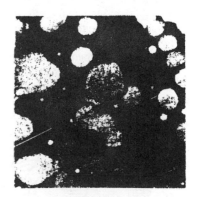

12

Look for rainbows.

Just after a rain, when the sun emerges from behind the clouds, check the sky for a rainbow (or two). Actually, it must still be raining somewhere in the sky for a rainbow to form. The sunlight is refracted (bent) and reflected (bounced back) by the raindrops, which act like tiny prisms. (For more on prisms, see *April 14.*) The seven colors we see in a rainbow are red, orange, yellow, green, blue, indigo and violet. (Just remember *Roy G. Biv* to recall the colors in their proper order.)

Rainbows figure in many folk mythologies, and they are not generally welcome signs. This is not uncommon for infrequent phenomena. In some cultures the rainbow is seen as a snake. In others, the ground where the rainbow touches is considered unhealthy. You've probably heard that there's a pot of gold at the end of the rainbow. Now that's more like it!

13

Create a rainbow with a garden hose.

You can make your own rainbows (minus the pot of gold) with a garden hose. The sun has to be shining (just like it does for the real thing), and you should position yourself with your back to the sun. Spray a fine mist in front of you, preferably against a dark background so that the colors will really stand out. Early morning, or late afternoon, is best for this experiment, because the sun's rays are slanting lower in the sky. Can you make out all the colors?

14

Make a rainbow indoors.

You can even make rainbows indoors, without getting wet! Fill a glass with water (make sure it is full to the top) and set it on a window sill in bright sunlight. It should project over the inside ledge just a bit. Put a white sheet of paper on the floor beneath the window, and a rainbow will magically appear on the paper.

A prism will do the same thing. You can hang a prism in a sunny window, or make some preparations for an even more vivid display of the spectrum colors. Just as the rainbows you made with the garden hose outdoors showed up best against a dark background, so will your prism bows work better in a darkened room. If you have pull-shades in a south-facing room, ask your parents if you can make a tiny pinhole in a corner of the shade, just big enough to let in a beam of light. Place your prism in the path of the light, and see how it projects a rainbow on the opposite wall.

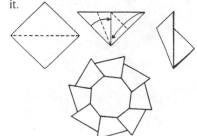

The colors of the rainbow

Which of the colors of the rainbow do you like best? They are all nice, and they work well together, too, which makes them perfect for a number of craft projects. You can use crayons and markers to make colored arcs, but don't stop there. Cut strips of colored construction paper and weave a rainbow mat. Make some play dough, divide it into seven parts and color each a different color of the rainbow. Use the dough for making three-dimensional rainbows, and coiled pots that go from red to violet. Or make your own calendar and use the seven colors to liven up the seven days of the week.

An unusual way to use all seven colors is to make a circular wreath using Japanese paper folding techniques. (Use Origami paper, too, if you can find it, because it's already cut in squares and comes in beautiful colors, including the seven you'll need.) Select the seven rainbow colors plus white. Fold each square diagonally in half, then fold the bottom corner to the top, creating a triangular pocket (see the diagram). Do this for all eight sheets of paper. Tuck the pointed end of one paper into the triangular pocket of the next, securing it with a spot of glue on the back. Start with white and work through the rainbow colors in order. Hang your wreath in a sunny window, or frame it.

April

Primitive peoples thought that mushrooms sprang from the ground where lightning had struck.

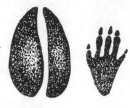

15

Look for the blossoms of early-flowering trees.

Most tree flowers blossom after the trees are in leaf, but some blossom before the leaves emerge. None of these blooms are very showy (like apple blossoms are, for instance) but they may be the only color in the tree tops this early, so they are very conspicuous.

Look for maple trees in bloom, especially the red maple which is a tree found in great numbers in the eastern half of the United States. The drooping clusters of red flowers give these trees a reddish haze. The hophornbeam is another early-flowering tree, as is the sassafras and boxelder. This last tree is in the maple family, but its common name refers to two other large shrubs that it resembles. Its leaves are like those of the elder; its white wood like that of boxwood.

These first hints of color, subtle as they are, are proof that spring has sprung!

16

Hunt for spring mushrooms.

Do you like mushrooms? On top of pizzas, and in soups and sauces? If you do, you may know that spring has its star—the morel.

The morel is considered one of the most delectable wild mushrooms. It's easy to identify and it's good both fresh or dried. (Dried mushrooms are reconstituted in water before cooking.) Morels are so highly prized that many mycologists, as mushroom hunters are called, keep their location a secret! The mushrooms fruit only briefly in the spring; but even then, areas that have yielded them for many years in the past may not in the future. Look for them in old apple orchards that have been abandoned. Or check at the base of dead elm trees. They often pop up there for a number of years before mysteriously disappearing.

Be ABSOLUTELY sure of any mushrooms you plan to eat because some look fine but are actually poisonous. (That goes for any food in the wild.) See if there are any mushroom-hunting expeditions you might join, to learn first-hand which mushrooms to pick and which to avoid.

17

Look for animal tracks.

With the spring thaw comes mud. And where there's mud, there are bound to be animal tracks! Although many animals are shy and elusive, they do leave behind many traces of their presence. You just have to know what to look for. Tracks made in soft ground are easy to find. You can even make permanent plaster of Paris casts of them (see the box on this page).

When you find tracks, you'll want to first identify them, and then see if you can piece together something about the animal's activities. By measuring the distance between tracks, and noting what part of the feet made the impressions in the mud, you can tell if an animal was walking or running. Follow continuous tracks, and you might come upon an animal's home. Do you see big and little tracks? Do you think these might be the tracks of an adult and its young? Look at the tracks you have made. What can you read into them?

Casting about

A good way to record any tracks you find in mud is to make plaster casts. Look for well-formed impressions that are clean and not full of water. You'll need plaster of Paris, a half-gallon milk carton (cut in half, with the top half cut into 1″ rings), a stick and some newspaper. You'll also need water, brought from home if you don't think you'll find any on the site. A trowel also comes in handy for digging up the casts.

Place the milk carton rings around the tracks you wish to cast. In the bottom half of the carton, mix some plaster with enough water to make it the consistency of molasses, and pour it gently into the rings. Let the plaster harden for 15 minutes before carefully digging up the casts and wrapping them in newspaper for the trip home.

When the plaster is completely hard (wait a few hours), remove the rings and clean the casts with water. Use an old toothbrush to get out all the dirt. What you've made are raised prints of the tracks. Press these into clay or play dough to make impressions like those you found. Or use the casts as molds from which to make new casts (again like the tracks you found in the mud).

Some communities have constructed tunnels under busy roads that amphibians can crawl through on their way to breeding grounds. It is hoped that this will save many species that have been endangered by cars.

18

Look for earthworms on the ground.

Or, more likely, look out! Watch your step during and after a spring or summer rain, because the ground is often liberally sprinkled with earthworms. You've heard about it "raining cats and dogs"? Well, some people wonder if it doesn't "rain earthworms"! Why else would they be lying all about?

A heavy rain will often flood the earthworms' burrows. The worms risk drowning if they don't come to the surface. There are plenty of dangers there, however. Sunlight is harmful to earthworms, and of course there are robins! These and other worm-eating birds have a field day after a rain. (And so do fishermen, who collect worms both after a rain and at night when the worms crawl out of their burrows in search of the plant material they eat. See *April 19* for more on watching worms at work.)

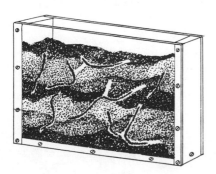

19

Construct a wormery.

With a simple set-up you can observe earthworms in your home. Make your own wormery from two panes of glass (or rigid plastic) and some 1"-wide wood strips. Glue or screw the panes to the wood, and fill the wormery with layers of various soils, such as garden soil, peat, and fine sand. Water the soils thoroughly, and add a dozen or so worms that you have dug from the garden. Take care to shield them from the light. Scatter the worms on the soil's surface, and cover them with some dead leaves or grass clippings. Cover the entire wormery with a light-proof cloth.

Check the worms now and again (sprinkling some water on the surface occasionally) to see how their tunnels are progressing. Can you see how the layers of soil have shifted? Look for the mounds of rippled soil on the surface. Earthworms burrow underground by eating the soil and eliminating it, resulting in these mounds known as casts.

When you are done watching the worms, return them and the soil to the garden. There they can continue to work the magic which gives them their nickname "gardeners' best friend."

20

Watch for salamanders.

Salamanders are some of the most reclusive amphibians. You may have seen some at night, when they are active, but you'll never find them by listening for them. Most are mute, and do not advertise for mates the way frogs and toads do.

Some people mistake salamanders for lizards, which, at a quick glance, many do resemble. Salamanders prefer cool, moist areas on land, or wetlands such as ponds and streams, unlike lizards which are reptiles and generally live in drier habitats. Salamanders can often be spotted during wet weather, especially along the routes to their breeding grounds. If you ever find a salamander in danger of crossing a road, kindly help it across to the other side.

. . . .
There are about 250 known species of salamanders. Most of these reside in the northern hemisphere.

21

See how honeybees communicate.

Honeybees stay in their hives when it rains, but you do have a good chance of seeing lots of them once the rain has stopped. The blossoms on trees and shrubs and other plants will have opened once again, and the bees will be eager to search for nectar. Be warned that these normally docile bees might be a bit touchy when finally satisfying their hunger, especially after a prolonged wet spell. You can safely watch them from a distance, but don't cross them, which is good advice to follow in any case.

Have you ever seen bees doing funny loops in the air? A bee that has found a source of food communicates its location with a dance. The other bees watch for a circular dance (which means the food is close by), or a figure eight (which indicates the food is farther afield). Watch where the bees fly off to. Can you tell how the dancing bee communicated distance, or even direction?

April

22

Plant a tree on Arbor Day.

Arbor Day is a nationally recognized celebration that serves to make people aware of the importance of trees. (Other countries honor trees in similar celebrations.) Different days are set aside in different states, to take advantage of the best time to plant trees in those areas. April 22nd is the date chosen in Nebraska, in honor of the birth of the man who started it all.

In 1872, J. Sterling Morton persuaded the Nebraskan government to start a tree-planting program to replenish the trees that had been felled by settlers. That first year, on April 10, over one million trees were planted in Nebraska! Today many millions of trees are planted throughout the United States, and millions of people learn something about trees and their role in nature.

Check to see when the holiday is observed in your state by asking at a garden center. Or write to the National Arbor Day Foundation (see *Nature conservancy groups* in the Appendix for the address). Plant a tree on your property, or join with others and plant trees in a community park or on school grounds. Long live trees!

23

Look for tree seedlings.

Before the grass is mowed for the first time in spring, look for bright green tree shoots dotting your lawn (or check in a park). Most trees drop their seeds in the autumn, but they lay dormant over the winter until the warmth of spring stirs them to life.

You can sometimes tell what kinds of trees these tiny shoots will be. Look at the leaves—they are often miniature versions of the parent tree's leaves. Maple shoots sometimes have the maple "wings" still attached. These seedlings won't have a chance once a mower is run over them. But even those the mower misses (and seedlings found in remote places) will have to fight for space and light and moisture. Many will also be eaten by animals that feast at ground level. Few will actually grow up to become trees.

Can you grow trees from seed? You sure can. Collect some seeds in the autumn. Many need a spell of cold weather, so plant your seeds in pots of soil and leave them outside in a sheltered location until spring. Some take a long time to sprout, so be patient. Tend the seedlings carefully over the summer and plant them in the ground come fall.

Just imagine—all the magnificent trees in your neighborhood were once tiny seedlings such as these!

24

Examine the roots of a plant.

The roots of plants serve to anchor them in the ground, but they also provide a way for water and nutrients to reach the plants. Take a close look at the roots of a houseplant or weed that you've pulled from the garden. Roots look like underground branches, don't they? The main roots branch off into smaller rootlets, which divide into even smaller root hairs. Water and food are actually absorbed by the tiny root hairs.

You can wash the soil off a plant's roots to see them better, or you can look closely at the roots of a bulb growing in water. (Hyacinths and other bulbs are commonly grown this way.) How can these plants grow without soil? Well, bulbs contain all the food they need for flowering within the bulb itself. But other plants can be grown in water, too, providing that the minerals they need are supplied in solution. That's how hydroponic gardening works.

Can you think of any roots that people eat? We eat carrots, beets, radishes, parsnips and turnips, to name a few. What about potatoes? Although potatoes are harvested from beneath the soil, they are not root crops. What we eat are actually swollen stems.

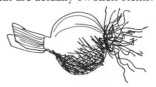

25

See how plants absorb water.

You can see how plants take up water with the celery stick trick. You need a celery stalk that still has its leaves, and a glass of colored water. (Use a few drops of a contrasting food color, such as red.) Place the stalk in the water and leave it overnight. In the morning what do you notice?

Cut a cross-wise slice from the base of the stalk. Can you see the ducts that take in the water? They show up as tiny colored dots.

Flowers can also be dyed in this way. In fact, do you remember seeing green carnations on St. Patrick's Day? The blossoms had been dyed by this very method. You can dye your own flowers. White or pale blooms work best. Just place them in colored water and wait until the dye reaches the blossoms. Or try this: Carefully split the stem of a flower along its length and place each stem half in a glass of water containing a different color. What happens to the blossoms? Pretty amazing, no?

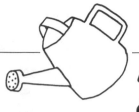

26

Grow some sprouts to eat.

Do you like to sprinkle sprouts on your salad? Or use them like lettuce in a sandwich? You can grow your own sprouts, any time of year, so that you'll always have some on hand. Here's how.

Alfalfa sprouts are the most common sprouts eaten raw, and they are very easy to grow. All you need is a wide-mouthed jar that has some fine gauze over its opening (hold it in place with a rubber band), and some seeds. Health food stores carry a wide assortment of seeds for sprouting. Soak a tablespoon of seeds in an inch of water in the jar overnight. In the morning, drain the water from the jar (without removing the cloth covering). Rinse the seeds with running water, emptying all the water from the jar when you're done. Repeat this daily rinsing as the seeds sprout and grow, harvesting the batch within 5 to 7 days.

Try sprouting different varieties of seeds, such as mung beans (used in Oriental cookery) or a combination of small seeds such as mustard or cress. Sprouting your own seeds is an inexpensive way to have them on hand when you want them. Make sure you sprout them during the long winter months, too, when a little fresh greenery is always welcome.

27

Look for the fiddleheads of ferns.

Ferns can be found growing in all sorts of places. You may even have some growing as houseplants in your home! We know that there were ferns on earth 300 million years ago (fossilized remains have been found). They've changed little since then. Today there are 12,000 species of ferns throughout the world. Most are large tree-like plants; some are even aquatic. Those native to the United States are usually found in the moist, acid soil of woodlands.

Once the ferns shoot up from the litter of the forest floor, it's not long before they unfurl. The tightly curled fronds give them their nickname—fiddleheads. Don't they look just like the scrolls carved on the peg heads of violins? Did you know that many fiddleheads are delicious to eat? The fronds of the ostrich fern are particularly good. Look for these in the woods. Or check in the produce section of your supermarket. Fiddleheads are sold by the pound for the brief time that they are available in spring. To cook them, just remove any brown scales before steaming. They are delicious as a vegetable side dish, or chilled atop a salad.

April

28

Hatch a batch of amphibian eggs.

Spring is the time for amphibians to make their annual treks to ponds and other watery places to mate. You probably have been hearing them at dusk and on cloudy days, croaking and carrying on. (See *March 2* for more on spring peepers, the earliest frogs to sing.) Go down to the water with a pail and see if you can find any eggs to bring home and hatch.

Frogs' eggs are bunched together in a clump; toads' eggs are generally arranged in long strings. You might even find salamander eggs, which are larger than frogs' eggs but found in smaller bunches. Bring only a few home in your pail, along with plenty of pond water and some algae and pond plants for the tadpoles to eat. Don't mix eggs from different species. They develop at different rates, and may feed on each other.

It's a frog's life

Even if you can't get frogs' eggs down at a pond, you can witness the metamorphosis of amphibians. Eggs and tadpoles can be ordered from the science suppliers, or you can buy a kit containing the tadpole of an aquatic frog known as the African Clawed Frog. (See *Where to purchase supplies* in the Appendix.)

Frogs' eggs will grow and change into tiny tadpoles within a week or so. Keep only one or two tadpoles, returning the others and any unhatched eggs to the pond. A tadpole soon develops hind legs and then tiny front legs where the gills were. (The gills are also replaced by lungs at this stage, although you can't see this.) Gradually the tail disappears, during which time the tadpole does not eat. Transfer your frog to an aquarium now, one with a sloping rock or a floating log, and a cover. Frogs are powerful jumpers. You should also start thinking about returning the frog to its natural habitat. Adult frogs require live food, and a lot of it, and while you could raise your own mealworms to feed your frog, you have to decide whether you can take the time to properly care for your frog friend.

April

29

Make a chart of animal characteristics.

When you think of animals, what comes to mind? Most people think of mammals, four-legged creatures with fur. But what about snails, salamanders, and sea anemones? These are all animals, too, of course.

Make a chart that outlines some of the basic animal characteristics. Divide a continuous length of paper into sections. How many sections depends on how detailed you'd like to get. Refer to the chart below to get you started. Make a heading for each section, and under it list some of the characteristics the animals possess. Illustrate the chart with pictures cut from magazines, and your own sketches.

What similarities do you notice within each group? What are some of the animals that don't conform to the norm for their group?

Some like it hot, some like it cold . . .

Here are some ideas for your chart.

Insects
- Three pairs jointed legs
- Three-part body
- Hard outer skeleton
- One or two pairs wings

Arachnids
- Four pairs legs
- Two-part body
- Hard outer skeleton

Sharks and Rays
- Skeleton made of cartilage
- Rough skin
- Unequally divided tail

Bony Fish
- Scales or bony plates
- Equally divided tail

Amphibians
- First part of life in water
- Moist skin
- Four limbs
- Webbed feet

Reptiles
- Dry skin covered with scales or bony plates
- Lay leathery-shelled eggs

Birds
- Warm-blooded
- Covered with feathers
- Front limbs are wings
- Lay hard-shelled eggs

Mammals
- Warm-blooded
- Covered with fur or hair
- Young drink mother's milk

30

See how living things are classified.

Early attempts to classify living things were made by the ancient Greeks; Aristotle's work was extensive, although he divided all living things into three groups: plants, animals, and human beings! The modern scientific classification system is based on the work done by an 18th century Swedish botanist, Carl von Linné (better known as Carolus Linnaeus, his name in Latin to match the language he chose for classification).

The classification system works somewhat like the postal system. (A letter addressed to you is first sent to the right country, then to your state, your town, and then is sorted with letters for your street. It finally arrives at your house!) First all living organisms are divided into five kingdoms. They are then sorted by phylum, class, order, family, genus, and species. (Occasionally subclass, subgenus, and subspecies are also used.)

Trace the lineage of your pet, or one of the animals you watch in the park. (An encyclopedia or other reference book will help.) Do you see how the classification system works?

. . . .

To remember the order of the classification system remember: *King Phillip Came Over For Ginger Snaps.*

1

May Day!

May Day traces its origins to Roman times, when the day was sacred to Flora, the goddess of spring. She was honored with widespread festivities. The custom spread to Europe as the Roman Empire grew, and it became especially popular in England by the Middle Ages. People gathered flowers to decorate their homes and churches, and they sang carols and gave gifts. Most villages had a maypole on the village green, around which the people danced.

Because the Puritans frowned on celebrations, the custom of celebrating May Day was not brought to the New World with the Pilgrims. In this country, few communities observe the day. But that shouldn't stop you! Plan to honor the day in some way, with a maypole (use a flagpole or a slender tree for the pole), or simple arrangements of flowers in baskets. Hang one on your best friend's doorknob. Surprise!

Many changes take place in nature come May, and it's fitting to usher them in with some fanfare.

May brings flocks of pretty lambs,
Skipping by their fleecy dams.

May

2

Compare the ways animals bear their young.

Most animals lay eggs, and most of these are left to hatch on their own. That's true of amphibian and fish eggs, laid in water. It's true of reptile eggs, and insect eggs. Birds are different, however, being warm-blooded animals. Although birds' shells are hard, they must be kept warm in order to develop properly. Did you know that there are even two mammals that lay eggs? The duck-billed platypus and the echidna of Australia both lay leathery eggs.

In nature, the young of most animals are not cared for by their parents (or any other adults). Birds and mammals are the exception. In fact, the exceptions make the study of animal young fascinating. Did you know that there is a frog in Chile called Darwin's frog that lays eggs that are then watched over by the male? Once the eggs turn into little tadpoles, the male swallows them and keeps them in his vocal sac for almost three months. Out hop a dozen or so little frogs!

Have you ever seen animals being born? What about human babies?

3

Visit a zoo.

Where can you go to see some of the many animals you have been learning about (see *April 29*)? The zoo, of course!

If you live near a zoo, be sure to visit it often. Rather than wear yourself out taking in the entire zoo in one visit, concentrate on specific areas of interest to you. If you hope to see some animal young, ask if there are any babies on display. If you are interested in what animals eat, find out when the animals are fed and see if you can watch. If reptiles are your passion, check out the snakes and lizards that the zoo houses.

Even if you don't live near one of the larger traditional zoos, there may be other places that have animals in residence. Native species can often be found at nature centers. Science museums often have animals, including insect zoos! And aquariums are zoos, too, where you can see those marine animals that make their homes in and around the sea.

Take a close look at the cages the animals live in. Can you see how you might improve your cages at home? You can also learn something about the food needs of different animals.

4

Visit a wildlife sanctuary.

What's the difference between a wildlife sanctuary and a zoo? They share some similarities (namely that they are places set aside for animals) but sanctuaries don't have the structure that zoos have. What a wildlife sanctuary (or refuge or preserve, if you like) offers is just that—sanctuary, or protection. Any parcel of land that animals can wander on and off freely, without fear of being shot by anything other than a camera, is a sanctuary. Your own property is a sanctuary, too, isn't it?

On a larger scale, there are more than 360 national wildlife preserves in this country, as well as many state-run and privately-funded ones. These are good places to go in search of animals that have little contact with human beings (which, of necessity, alters their behavior somewhat). If you are looking for migrating ducks and geese, go to a refuge that has a body of water. If you would like to explore a wetland, seek out a refuge that has one (some even have boardwalks built through the marshes so that the land will not be disturbed by visitors). There are refuges in all sorts of habitats. Visit one soon.

5

Make a study of an animal's behavior.

It's easy to fall into the habit of comparing animals to people. Some animals do possess human-like traits, but this is coincidental. The behavior of animals is tremendously varied, from their eating habits to their social behavior. Most live in relative peace among one another, with spurts of ritual fighting, which is more bluff than anything.

If you have a dog or cat, you've probably wondered why it acts the way it does. When you are mad at your dog, does it roll over on its back? Dogs are not far removed from wolves, and in a wolf pack the belly-up posture signals defeat. (Wolves play fair—they won't pick on an animal once it "gives up.") Does your dog love to lick your face? The "underdogs" in the wolf pack lick the muzzle of the dominant wolf, and to your dog, you are the dominant one.

Domestic cats practice hunting skills even though you provide their food. This is so ingrained that former pet cats do well in the wild—they become what we call feral cats. Kittens, especially, like to stalk and pounce on moving objects—your leg, if you're not careful!

What do you notice about the squirrels in the park, and the birds at your feeder? See if you can learn something about the way they maintain harmony.

May

Birds have 940 to 25,000 feathers, depending on the species.

6

Look for bird feathers.

Birds are the only animals that have feathers. They serve as insulation and aid in flight. As the feathers wear, they are periodically replaced. During a partial molt, only some of the feathers are replaced (such as when males don colorful plumage during mating season). A more complete molt takes place after breeding, and before migration (see *October 4*). Feathers are lost a few at a time from both sides of the body, so that a bird is still evenly balanced. Look on the ground for the fallen feathers.

Feathers are of two basic types, contour and down. Contour feathers are those found on the body, wings and tail. Notice how the individual strands (called barbs) lock together. Separate one of the barbs from the rest. It's like unlocking a zip-lock bag, isn't it? Birds spend a lot of time getting the barbs realigned (see *May 7* for more on preening). Tail feathers have the shaft running exactly down the middle; the shafts of wing and body feathers are slightly off-center. Down feathers are the fluffy feathers you may know from down coats, comforters, and pillows.

It's harder to tell what bird a feather has come from, unless it's an obvious one like a blue jay feather. What can you tell about the feathers you have found?

7

Make a birdbath.

To keep their feathers in peak condition, birds spend many hours each day preening them. They pass their bills over the stiff contour feathers to realign the barbs (for more on feathers, see *May 6*); some spread water-proofing oil on their feathers (the oil comes from a gland at the base of the tail). But did you know that may birds like to bathe as part of their preening ritual? Some even "bathe" in dirt! This helps keep down insect pests, and may serve to fluff the down feathers.

Watch how birds splash around in puddles! You can provide shallow water (which many birds prefer) by making a birdbath. One of the simplest to make is an up-turned garbage can lid filled with a layer of pebbles to give the birds firm footing. The pebbles also weight the lid so that it won't blow away. Birds like a place to perch after bathing, so place the lid near some brush or under a tree. Put it on the ground (in an open area so the birds feel safe) or on a pedestal. A tree stump will do, or rig the lid by tying a rock to the handle and placing it on top of a length of clay drainage pipe. Check the level of water occasionally, and watch the birds have a blast!

8

Watch birds in flight.

You have probably noticed that birds fly in different ways. Those birds that ride thermal currents (see *September 19*) hardly ever flap their wings at all. Hummingbirds, on the other hand, beat their wings an incredible 70 times per second, enabling them to fly forward, backward, and even hover in place!

Crows and robins beat their wings about two times every second; starlings beat theirs 4 to 5 times each second. Chickadees are almost up there with the hummingbirds, flapping their wings at least 27 times each second. How do they do it?

Well, birds have tremendously powerful chest muscles. And they are built for flight (at least the ones that fly are). Their bones are hollow (see *May 9*), and they are streamlined.

Try beating your arms as fast as a robin or pigeon does (pigeons clock in at 3 beats per second). How long can you keep up the flapping?

9

Saw a chicken bone in half.

The power for flight may come from the powerful chest muscles that enable birds to take off, maneuver and land (see *May 8*), but this muscle is sufficient only because birds are light enough to become airborne. Birds are light, in part, because their bones are hollow, strengthened by an inner network of tiny cross pieces.

Saw a chicken bone from the dinner table in half to see what this looks like. Compare bird bones to those from other animals. (Examine the bones from a cut of beef or pork.) Remember that chickens have lost much of their flying ability over the years through selective breeding. The bones of flying birds have an even more exaggerated inner structure.

. . . .

There are laws that prohibit collecting bird feathers. But it's okay to keep those that have naturally molted, or that you have plucked from road-side kills.

10

Make a bird beak-and-feet poster.

You can tell a lot about a bird by looking at its beak and feet. The two often complement each other. Make a poster that shows how these distinctive beaks and feet are often paired. Illustrate the poster with pictures cut from magazines, and your own sketches.

To get you going, think of the seed-eaters. They have short, thick beaks that are good for cracking open shells. Their feet are designed for perching (with three toes in front and one behind), which they do when they eat. What about pond-dwelling birds? Their beaks are flat and broad, just right for scooping (some have built-in strainers!); these birds are swimmers and their feet are shaped like paddles. Birds of prey have powerful beaks, with the upper beak hooked over the lower. Their feet, large curved claws, firmly grasp their prey.

Think of other adaptations, from the long hollow tube of the hummingbird used for sipping nectar to the gaping mouths of insect-eaters—all the better to trap them with! Birds that scratch in the dirt for their food like chickens have rake-like toes.

11

Read a story or poem about birds.

What is it about birds that so many people find enchanting? Is it their singing, or their perky presence at the birdfeeder in winter? Maybe we envy their way of getting around!

The Blackbird
Humbert Wolfe *(poem)*

The Dead Bird
Margaret Wise Brown *(story)*

Ducks Ditty
Kenneth Grahame *(poem)*

Humming Birds
Betty Sage *(poem)*

The Mountain That Loved a Bird
Alice McLerran *(story)*

The Ptarmigan
Anonymous *(poem)*

The Swallow
Ogden Nash *(poem)*

12

Watch for the first broods of chicks.

It takes birds' eggs as few as 11, or as many as 90, days to hatch once they have been laid. The number of eggs varies considerably from species to species, as well. Some birds lay only one, others as many as twenty. And some birds have several broods each year. If any eggs are lost or stolen, very often replacements are laid. (This is how some chickens are encouraged to continually produce eggs. A domestic hen might lay more than 200 eggs if they are promptly removed. If left in the nest, she would lay only 15-20.) When do you think the eggs in the nests you are watching will hatch? How many do you suppose there will be?

The frequent trips for food and the incessant peeping from the nest are unmistakable clues that the young have hatched. Keep watching the nest for the next few weeks. You'll be able to watch the chicks grow, crowding each other in the nest. You may even be able to watch them take their first trial flights. Just imagine what that moment feels like for those young birds!

Eggcentricities

Most eggshells are camouflaged to blend into their surroundings. Birds that nest on the ground lay eggs that are brownish in color, and often speckled, to visually break up the shape of the eggs. Then why are robins' eggs blue, and others white? Brightly colored eggs are often laid by birds that nest in shaded places; white eggs are most often laid in holes where they won't even been seen.

The shapes of eggs are also cleverly determined. Most eggs are oval, larger on one end than the other. This prevents them from rolling way. Place an egg from your refrigerator on a flat surface and give it a push. What happens?

May

13

Make a plant press.

A good way to preserve plant specimens is to press them. You can always stick them between the pages of a fat book (make sure you protect the book by slipping the plants between sheets of clean paper), but an even better press is a portable one you can take with you on hikes. You can make your own at home with some simple materials.

Take two pieces of ¼″ plywood or masonite cut to the size you want. A 6″ × 8″ rectangle is a good size to tote; make the press larger if you plan to leave it at home. Drill holes in the four corners of each board and attach them to one another with long bolts that have wing nuts. Cut several pieces of heavy cardboard from an old box to fit.

As you find leaves and flowers to press, place them between sheets of clean paper. Sandwich these between the layers of cardboard. Tighten the nuts evenly at all four corners to put enough pressure on the plants to press them flat. Your specimens should be dry within a few weeks. (For ways to use pressed plants, see *December 3*.)

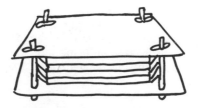

14

Start a scrapbook of tree leaves.

You may have already pressed the leaves of your "special tree" (see *A tree grows in* on page 41). A good way to get to know the different trees is to make a scrapbook of pressed leaves.

Now that the trees are in full leaf, you'll be able to find flawless specimens to press. (See *May 13* to make your own press.) Mount the pressed leaves in a scrapbook of some sort. A store-bought one will do, but you can make your own with a three-ring binder. Use poster board for pages—it holds up well and provides a firm surface for the leaves. You can glue the leaves in place (use white glue), or attach them the way scientists do, with thin strips of paper that straddle the stems and lobes. You can also keep leaves in place with a clear sheet of Contact® paper, which protects them from dust and damage.

Make sure you label the leaves. And leave some room for the trees' flowers and fruits, if you like. You might also leave space for samples of the leaves in their autumn guises (see *October 8*).

15

Learn which plants not to touch.

Have you ever broken out in a rash after rubbing against some poison ivy? You're in good company, because a lot of people have an allergic reaction when they come in contact with this plant. The best way to avoid getting plant rashes is to avoid the plants! Learn what poison ivy—and poison oak and poison sumac and stinging nettles—looks like and you'll be all set. (See *Treating poison plant rashes* in the Appendix if you haven't been so lucky.)

The poison ivies and oaks are deceptive. They can grow low to the ground, as shrub-like plants, or as vines. Both can, however, usually be spotted by remembering the rhyme, "Leaves of three, let it be." There are some other plants whose leaves grow in a similar pattern, notably strawberries and some of the Virginia creepers, but the poison plants generally have shinier leaves.

Stinging nettles are another plant altogether. Luckily their sting, painful as it is, is short-lived.

Learn what plants to watch out for and dress properly if you plan to explore an area where they can't be avoided, and you can save yourself an uncomfortable reminder of a walk in the wilds.

16

Look for mosses.

You're probably familiar with some of the mosses. The cushiony green mats can be found wherever there's moist shade. Maybe you've heard that you can tell direction by looking for moss? Supposedly it grows on the north side of trees. Well, there's some truth to that (the north side of a tree is moister and in shade) but moss is often found growing all around tree trunks. So much for that theory!

Mosses are primitive plants that have no true roots, stems, or leaves. They absorb moisture and nutrients through the entire plant. You may have heard of club mosses. These are not mosses at all—nor are Irish moss, a seaweed, and Spanish moss, a member of the pineapple family. In the woods, look for ground pine and running cedar, two club mosses that look like miniature versions of the trees they are named after.

Mosses do very well in woodland gardens (see *May 18*). Give them a log to hug, and they'll be quite content.

Many plants that made their first appearance hundreds of millions of years ago look the same but have shrunk in size. Club mosses, ferns, and horsetails once towered as tall as trees.

17

Collect some lichen.

Lichens are actually two plants living in close association—a fungus and an alga (the singular form of algae). Here's a silly way to remember what a lichen is: "A fungus met an alga and they took a *likin'* to each other!" Lichens are partly responsible for breaking down rocks. They are also food for many animals.

You've probably come across all sorts of lichens around where you live. There are three basic types. The flat, crusty lichen found growing on rocks and other surfaces is crustose lichen (just think of "crusty"). There's another type that looks like crumpled leaves. Not surprisingly, it is called foliose (like "foliage") lichen. A third group is known as fruticose lichen, from the latin for "shrub." Some of the lichens in this group do stand up and have fanciful names such as pyxie cups and British soldiers, but some are hanging varieties. There is one called beard lichen that hangs from tree branches just like a straggly beard!

What kinds of lichens can you find? What types are they? Collect some to display (they keep very well), or gather up some to dye yarn with. Some of the most beautiful Scottish woolens are dyed with lichens. (See *July 28* for more on dyeing with plants.)

18

Make a woodland garden.

Setting up a woodland garden in your home is a rewarding project in a number of ways. It's a great way to get to know the native plants in your neck of the woods. And it can serve as a temporary home for any moisture-loving animals you bring home. Just replace any plants that are eaten, and watch for insect infestation. Once set up, a woodland garden will almost take care of itself.

An old aquarium makes a good container for your garden. Place some charcoal and gravel on the bottom for drainage (and to keep the water "sweet"). Either transplant soil along with the plants you dig up, or use a soilless potting mix. Put in some large rocks, and some logs. Try to make the garden as natural looking as possible.

To keep the moisture level high, cover the aquarium with a sheet of glass or plastic. Make an alternative cover with holes to use when there are animals in residence.

The plant kingdom

Within the plant kingdom, there are all sorts of different types of plants. (Mushrooms are not considered plants. They rule a kingdom all their own!) True plants range from green, red, and brown algae (all considered separately) to mosses, ferns, conifers and flowering plants. Can you think of examples of each?

Some of these plants are rather primitive. Club mosses were growing 250 million years ago, and have not changed much since. Conifers, cone-bearing shrubs or trees, dominated the earth about 150 to 200 million years ago. They are losing ground to the flowering plants, currently represented by at least 250,000 species. Plants that bear flowers include grasses, many trees, cacti, as well as the plants we call "flowers."

19

Create a desert garden.

Everything a woodland garden is (see *May 18*), a desert garden isn't! Desert gardens are truly easy to care for; the hardest thing is remembering not to water them too much. But even desert plants can suffer from lack of humidity inside a home during the winter months. Set the pot on a layer of rocks that can be kept wet, and you'll have just enough moisture in the air.

Desert plants have shallow root systems (and require little water) which means you can create a desert garden in any low dish, even one without drainage holes. Just put down a layer of gravel and mix your own potting soil in a two-to-one mix of potting soil and sand. Plant a number of cactus varieties together. Remember to wear thick gloves or wrap a strip of folded newspaper around the plants to protect your hands from the spines.

Cacti are some of the most creatively named plants. Look for powder-puff, rat's tail, rabbit's ears, and fish-hook cactus. What do you think bishop's cap, moonstones, and old man cactus look like? Very aptly named species, wouldn't you say?

May

Use organic fertilizers. They provide benefits for the soil—not just a quick boost for this year's crop.

20

Plant some seeds outdoors.

Many seeds can be sown right in the garden. (See *March 13* for starting seeds indoors.) Check the backs of your seed packets for hints on when to sow the seeds, how deep to plant them, and how far apart.

Most instructions assume that you will plant long rows (one plant after another), but there are other ways to set up a garden. Experiment with wide-row gardening. Make your rows 3-4 feet wide, and plant several seeds (or seedlings) across the width, sowing those along the length of the row closer than usual, too. Individual plants don't grow quite as large as in conventional rows, but you can grow up to four times as much in the same area planted single file. You also don't have to weed your garden as much, because the closely grown plants shade the row. And you may even have to water less often, because every drop of water is used by growing plants (rather than ending up between the rows, as in a conventional garden).

Water the garden with a gentle spray after planting. Make sure that the soil doesn't dry out, or the seeds won't be able to break through the ground. Likewise, don't overdo it—too much moisture can cause seeds to rot. Replant any seeds that haven't germinated after a week or so.

Let's hear it for herbs!

If you had to choose one group of plants to grow, you couldn't go wrong if you chose herbs. Herbs are lovely plants; many smell wonderful and they can be used in all sorts of ways. Not only that, they are among the easiest plants to grow. Few are bothered by insect pests and many can even stand a little neglect, which is a plus if you are new to gardening.

Do you like to cook (or eat)? Grow some herbs you can use on pizza (oregano), in salads (chives) or sandwiches (dill is great with tuna). Do you like sweet smells? Grow some herbs you can use in potpourri—like mints, lemon balm, and rosemary. There are many craft ideas that call for herbs, from scented pillows to dried flower arrangements.

Discover why so many people grow herbs. Plant some today!

21

Transplant seedlings.

The plants you started from seed indoors (see *March 13*) can go in the garden when the weather warms. It's important that you gradually toughen up these plants before transplanting them. Place them outdoors for an hour or two, increasing the time they stay out over the course of a week. By the end of the week, they can stay out all day and all night, too, if there is no danger of frost. Make sure you give the plants plenty of water. They need a lot more of it than when they were indoors. Can you see how the plants are looking healthier? Are they a darker green?

When your plants are properly hardened off, as the saying goes, transplant them to the garden on an overcast day, if possible. Otherwise, provide some shade for the seedlings with newspaper tents. Plants resent having their roots disturbed (wouldn't you?), so give them a little extra TLC.

22

Make a scarecrow.

Some of the seeds you plant in the garden may never sprout even if the conditions are right. Why not? Because birds and other animals might have eaten them! As any experienced gardener can tell you, you have to expect to share some of your bounty with other animals. But can they take a hint? Put up a scarecrow and find out!

Crows aren't the only pesky creatures that help themselves to garden produce. But the name scarecrow has stuck. Make a figure from some of your old clothes stuffed with straw. Tie it to a fence post, or to a pole stuck into the ground. What do the birds think of your creation?

Or take a curved branch and paint it with weather-resistant paints to look like a snake. This sometimes does the trick. Move it around the garden so that the birds don't catch on. Or try warding off animals with a little noise. Hang some aluminum pie pans so that they bang together. (You may not be able to stand the sound either!) The sunlight reflecting off the pans scares the birds, too.

Maybe next year you should plant twice as much. Some for you, and the rest for the animals!

23

Create a hanging garden.

What can you do if you don't have any room for plants? Make a hanging garden. You can plant a hanging salad, or herb patch, or even a vining version of a cherry tomato plant or compact cucumber. Indoors and out, hanging plants are the way to go if you want to make the best use of your space.

Just make sure that you hang your plants from strong hooks. Screw these into a solid support. Check with your parents before you start making holes in the ceiling. The plants you hang indoors need to have saucers under the pots to catch the drips.

Treat your hanging plants like other container-grown plants. Water them regularly and make sure they get enough "food" to compensate for the small amount of soil they grow in. Hang your plants high in sunny windows, so that they get the light, but so does the room. Outdoors, plants look nice hanging from porches, or even from tree branches.

24

Plant some night-blooming flowers.

A lot of plants open their blossoms during certain parts of the day. (For using flowers to tell time, see *Closing time* on page 81.) Morning glories are a familiar flower that opens in—you guessed it—the morning. Did you know that there are plants that bloom at night? These are some of the loveliest, most fragrant of flowers.

You can start your own plants from seed, or purchase seedlings from a garden center. Look for nicotiania, or flowering tobacco (smoking tobacco is a relative of this plant). Ask for evening-scented stock, datura, evening primrose, moonflowers and the cactus called cereus, to name a few. One of the nice things about these plants is that they bloom during the summer months. When you are out in the garden at night, the scent of these flowers adds an unforgettable touch. (See *August 7* for watching these blooms open.) Plant some under your bedroom window for a fragrant slumber.

25

Sow some sunflower seeds.

One of the sunniest flowers going (no pun intended!), sunflowers are great fun to grow. They grow very quickly, and very tall! Make sure you choose a spot for them where they won't shade other plants. Sunflowers need to be staked as they grow (to keep them from toppling over), and you'll need to be able to get water to them, because they drink a lot.

You can grow sunflowers for the birds, or for you. You'll have to rig some netting for the huge flowers once the seeds begin to ripen, otherwise the birds will help themselves. (If that's what you want, leave them be.) Rub the seed heads with a fork to loosen the seeds and lay them out to dry. Put them away to dole out to the birds this winter, or crack some open for a nutritious snack.

. . . .

The texture of garden soil (affecting how well it holds water, and drains) can be improved by adding aged animal manure, peat, and straw.

26

Read a story or poem about gardening.

Gardening is one of the most popular hobbies for people of all ages. What do you like about growing plants?

The Buried Treasure
Djemma Bider *(story)*

The Garden from **Frog and Toad Together**
Arnold Lobel *(story)*

Little Seeds
Else Holmelund Minarek *(poem)*

Maytime Magic
Mabel Watts *(poem)*

A Spike of Green
Barbara Baker *(poem)*

This Year's Garden
Cynthia Rylant *(story)*

May

27

Name some of the ways people use animals.

The dog was probably the first domesticated animal. Who can say when this took place? It is thought that the first animals to be kept for food were cattle (at least 12,000 years ago). We have a long history of raising animals.

Can you name some of the other ways we use animals? They provide us with food, from milk to eggs to flesh. We turn their hair and hides into clothing. Other products from animal parts include fertilizers from bones and blood; glue from hides; paint brushes from bristles; violin bows from tail hair; and even medicine, such as insulin (this comes from the pancreas of cattle and hogs). Animals also play a vital role as "guinea pigs" in scientific and medical research. While still used as beasts of burden in many parts of the world, animals are ridden, shown, and bred for fun, too.

Most animals that people use are specially bred for the purpose. However, many wild species are extinct (or endangered) because too many have been killed in the name of sport or commerce. Today more and more people are aware of some of the needless slaughter and inhumane practices that animals are subjected to. How do you think we should treat animals?

28

Visit a working animal farm.

Once upon a time, every family kept chickens for eggs, and milked a family cow. Small family farms are rare these days, but some people still tend animals that "pay for their keep." Some people raise a small flock of sheep, which they shear for the wool; others have a few chickens that lay eggs. Many are happy to show you around if they have the time. (Offer to help feed the animals!) You can get a firsthand glimpse at the relationships people have with animals other than pets.

You might also live near a full-fledged commercial farm. These impressive businesses have to be large-scale these days to be profitable. Many people don't like living near working farms. They complain about the smell, and get impatient when they have to drive behind tractors and other farm machinery. Farming has become so far removed from everyday experience that most people do not appreciate what farmers do to put food on everyone's table. What do you think farming must be like? Would you like to have your own sheep, or pigs or chickens someday?

29

See how wild animals help people.

Some wild animals do a lot to help out people, too. They aren't even aware of it! What would we do if there weren't any bees and butterflies to pollinate plants? How would we find enough fertile soil to grow crops on if there were no earthworms? We gather guano (bird dung) to fertilize crops; we also fish the seas and freshwater lakes for food. What other ways do wild animals help us out?

Some insects help farmers out by eating other destructive insects. This is called biological control, and it's a much better way of keeping pests under control than dusting or spraying with harmful chemicals. You can use insects (and other animals) to protect your own plants. Encourage ladybugs, ground beetles and lacewings to live on your property. You can do this by growing a variety of plants and providing insects with hiding places (such as a leafy mulch). Although birds can cause some trouble, they do more good than harm. Insect-eating birds, especially, are a great boon. And don't forget frogs and toads. They eat a lot of harmful insects. A source of water for them to breed in, and spend some of their time near, will make them feel right at home.

30

Help take care of some animals.

People who enjoy working with animals have many job opportunities. Would you like to be a zookeeper when you grow up? Or maybe a veterinarian, or dog breeder or race horse trainer? For most of these occupations you have to go to school, but in the meantime you can learn a lot by getting some hands-on experience.

Ask the vet in your town if you can help out after school, or during the summer. There might be some simple jobs you can do that will benefit the vet's practice. Many animal breeders are people who have other jobs but raise dogs or cats on the side. You might make friends with someone who could use a hand feeding or exercising the animals, especially when they are away at shows. You can also offer your services at a nature center or science museum that has caged animals. Many places like these have small staffs, and depend on volunteer helpers to keep things running smoothly. You will be doing a good deed, while getting a chance to spend time with animals.

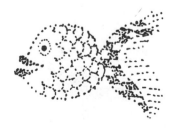

June brings tulips, lilies, roses,
Fills the children's hands with posies.

June

31

Go to an animal show.

Animal shows are held year-round, both indoors and out, so check to see what's going on near you. Which is your favorite animal? Do you like dogs? Dog shows are bustling events that draw large crowds eager to see dogs of every imaginable breed, or watch the dogs going through their paces. Have you ever seen the utility training competitions? Dogs are asked to jump over obstacles, fetch objects and distinguish items by smell, all while getting instructions from their trainers at a distance. Watch how subtle some of the signals the trainers give are.

There are cat shows and horse shows and shows where farm animals of every description are given a chance to win ribbons for their looks and abilities. These are also good places to meet people who raise animals for show, some of whom are your age!

1

Read a story or poem about pets.

If you could have any pet in the world, what would you choose? Would it be one of these?

Annie and the Wild Animals
Jan Brett *(story)*

Cats and Dogs
N.M. Bodecker *(poem)*

Chums
Arthur Guiterman *(poem)*

The Hairy Dog
Herbert Asquith *(poem)*

Hamsters
Marci Ridlon *(poem)*

Raccoons Are for Loving
Miriam Anne Bourne *(story)*

Unfortunately
Bobbi Katz *(poem)*

2

Get a pet.

Did you know that pets are good for your health? That's what some researchers have concluded after seeing how sick people often recover faster when they spend some time with animals. Pets have a way of making people happy! Do you have a pet?

Lots of animals make good pets, even some rather unusual ones. Dogs

are great, but many smaller mammals can be just as affectionate, and a lot easier to care for. Hamsters and guinea pigs are popular choices, but have you ever thought of keeping a mouse or a rat? These two animals are very smart and enjoy being handled. Some pets are not as demonstrative, but are still fun to watch. Fish are a natural, but many reptiles make good pets, too. Want to snuggle with a snake, or lounge around with a lizard?

Before you choose a pet, do some homework. Read up on the animal of your choice and talk to people who have one as a pet. Your parents are going to expect you to feed and exercise your pet (and clean its cage, too, don't forget!), but will they help you pay for it? Work out the details with your parents, and welcome the newest addition to your family!

Please pass the peas!

Some people love animals so much that they can't bear the thought of eating meat. For this reason (and a variety of others) they choose to become vegetarians. Some vegetarians will eat no animal products and prefer not to wear any clothing made from animal skins; others permit themselves eggs and dairy products. Are you and your parents vegetarians? What are your reasons?

If you aren't a vegetarian, you might want to experiment going without meat for a couple of days or a week. Ask your mother to help you plan you meals. A vegetarian diet can be very healthy, but you must take care to get enough protein. You never knew vegetables could be so delicious, did you?

June

The largest freshwater lake in the world is Lake Superior.

3

Explore a wetland.

What exactly is a wetland? It's a name given to any area that is covered much of the time with shallow water, that has visible plants growing in it, and an abundance of animal life. You may know wetlands as marshes, bogs, and swamps. You should be able to find either a freshwater or saltwater wetland near you.

Conservationists are trying hard to convince communities to leave wetlands untouched whenever possible. They support a tremendous amount of life as they are both nurseries for animals that move on to other habitats, as well as home to many permanent residents; they are also natural buffers that contain flood waters and trap silt.

Remember to dress for wet conditions when you go exploring. Wear boots or old sneakers, and dress in old clothes. Don't forget insect repellent. Wetlands are breeding grounds for mosquitos and other biting insects. Take an underwater viewer with you (see *June 5*), a net, and something to bring home water samples, frogs' eggs and animals in. In the heat of day, many creatures are still, so stake out the area in daylight, and return at dusk or early the next morning. Be careful wading through the water—the depth can be deceiving.

What do you find in wetlands near you? Did you know there was so much going on there?

4

Explore a pond or lake.

Ponds and lakes contain deeper water than do wetlands. But did you know that all ponds and lakes eventually fill in? Over the years, plants and animals that die in the water settle to the bottom. The layers build up (especially along the banks where tall plants quickly take hold) until there is no pond! But this can take a very long time. You've got plenty of time to explore.

A body of water can be divided into four habitats—shoreline, water's surface, open water, and bottom. Collect water and wildlife from these distinct areas. Use your net, and your collection jars. Don't forget to look through your underwater viewer.

At the shoreline you might catch a glimpse of animals that come to the water to drink. Many leave their tracks in muddy banks. Ducks and other birds nest along the banks. On the water's surface are many insects. Some actually walk on the water! There are floating plants, such as duckweed (a duck's favorite!) and algae. In the water, look for frogs' eggs, fish, and aquatic insects. At pond bottom, you'll come across the buried larvae of a number of insects, as well as aquatic worms and freshwater clams. Use a net shaped like a "D" to dredge along the bottom. There's more to a pond than meets the eye!

5

Make an underwater viewer.

How can you see what's going on in the water without diving in? Use an underwater viewer! You can make a very simple viewer with materials you already have at home. All you need is a half-gallon milk carton, some clear plastic wrap and a rubber band or some tape.

Cut both the bottom and the top off the milk carton. Stretch the plastic wrap over the bottom, securing it in place with a snug-fitting rubber band or some tape. Lower the viewer into the water, and place your face into the open end of the milk carton. The underwater area you are viewing will be slightly magnified. It's very much like a diving mask, only you don't have to get your face wet to use it.

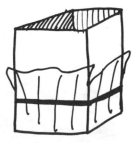

Lakes that have almost no plant or animal life are known as crystalline lakes. There are not many of these. Lake Tahoe in the western part of the United States is a crystalline lake.

6

Walk along a river bank.

Wildlife found in rivers differs from that found living in ponds and lakes. Plants and animals in rivers must be able to withstand the constant movement of the water. Many have evolved to be dependent on the abundance of oxygen in moving water, and would die if transferred to still waters. You'll notice, however, that there are little pools of water along the banks. These calm places serve as nurseries for many animals that then go on to live in the rougher waters as adults.

Rivers, too, are constantly evolving. Over time, a river's course can change dramatically. Walk along the banks of a river. Can you see any evidence of a changing course?

What kinds of plants and animals do you find living in the water, and along the banks? What do you find in the pools alongside the stream? Rivers can be full of surprises. They meander in and out of rocky outcrops; they run wide and lazy in spots. And waterfalls? This is water at its most spectacular.

7

Make a pond.

Even if you only have a small yard, you can put a pond on your property. No, you won't need to hire a bulldozer! Your pond can be as small and simple as a wooden tub sunk into the ground. Or make a slightly larger pond by hand-digging a shallow hole and lining it with thick black plastic. Ask your parents first, of course. Make sure the pond is located where it won't be in the way, but preferably not under a tree where it can quickly get clogged with leaves.

A pond about 6 feet in diameter will hold a variety of plants and animals. Dig a gently sloping hole that is at least 16″ deep in the middle. Make a narrow ledge for shallow-water plants to root on. Before laying down the plastic, make sure that no sharp rocks are sticking up. Pad those rough places with some folded newspaper.

Lay the plastic in the hole extending it well beyond the hole. Anchor the edge with stones or bricks and fill the pond with water from the hose. Cover the exposed plastic with turf or flat stones, or both.

First you need to add plants to your pond. Different species root in different depths (see the box on this page). You can collect these plants from other ponds. Next you'll want to add insects. Dredge for insect larvae at the bottom of ponds, or purchase some at a pet shop. Once your plants are established, and insects are making their homes in and around the pond, you can add other animals. They will feed, of course, on the plants and insects. Once the right balance is reached, your little pond will almost take care of itself.

Stocking up

Your pond and aquarium will need the right kinds of plants to be healthy. Make sure you have plenty of plants that give off oxygen, such as Canadian pondweed (waterweed) and arrowheads. Arrowheads and rushes and cattails do best in shallow water, so plant them on your pond's ledge. Plants that need deeper water include the pondweeds, and water lilies and hornworts. Let the plants grow for several weeks before adding any insects.

Add insect larvae dredged from ponds as well as water fleas, leeches, snails, hydras, and diving beetles collected from the water and from plants growing in the water. Once the insects are established, you can add other creatures, such as fish and frogs. Many animals will be attracted to your pond and make themselves at home.

8

Keep an amphibian or reptile overnight.

You'll probably come across lots of amphibians and reptiles when you are exploring wetlands and ponds. If you haven't found any frogs' eggs to hatch (see *April 28*) be on the lookout for some, but watch for adult frogs and toads, too. They are easily captured with a net. They will feel right at home in your indoor woodland garden (see *May 18*), or rig a make-shift cage from a cardboard box. Make sure it has a cover, and a shallow pan of water in it, because frogs, especially, need to keep their skin moist. If you are raising mealworms (see *June 27*), offer a few to your guest.

A number of turtles and snakes also spend time in and around water. Handle snapping turtles with care, because they do have a powerful bite. Snakes will attempt to defend themselves by biting, too. Most are harmless (the wound should be thoroughly washed, however), but learn what poisonous snakes live in your part of the country and avoid them.

Unless you have made plans to keep your captive for a longer stay (in which case you must know what to feed the animal and how to care for it), return it to the pond or marsh the next day.

9

Set up an aquarium.

Some of the plants and animals you find in ponds do very nicely in an aquarium. Start out with a clean tank and sterilized gravel. (Have your parents help you boil the rocks in water.) Spread the cooled gravel in the tank, sloping it gently up to the back (it should be about 1″ deep in front). Collect (or purchase) many of the same plants you stocked your pond with. (Avoid duckweed which grows too quickly.) Anchor their roots in the gravel. Lay a sheet of newspaper in the tank and pour in the water. The paper will keep everything from shifting.

After a couple of weeks, add some insects. Snails will help keep the tank glass free of algae, but add only a few. A freshwater mussel will also clear up the water. Diving beetles are fun to watch, but they may eat everybody up! You should eventually be able to add some small fish.

Once you achieve the right balance in the tank, it should take care of itself. Just siphon off the debris that collects in the front of the tank, and add more water as it evaporates.

June

The study of insects is called entomology.

10

Take a look at an insect's body.

Did you know that there are more insect species than there are bird, fish, reptile, amphibian, and mammal species combined? Almost one million species have already been identified, and some scientists think there may be three times that number! We truly live in an insect's world!

Insects are small animals that have six jointed legs attached to a three-part body. Many have one or two pairs of wings. (Spiders—with eight legs and two body parts—are not insects. Neither are a lot of other creeping, crawling invertebrates—animals without a backbone—often lumped together with insects.) Nor are all insects bugs. This distinction belongs to a certain group of insects.

Many insects can be annoying, but all play a part in the scheme of things, and many are very helpful.

Mosquitos can be a nuisance, as can those insects that pester other animals and destroy crops in fields and warehouses. But how would many of these plants reproduce without the help of pollinating insects? Some insects transmit diseases, but many others provide honey, wax, silk, and shellac—all important products. Do you like insects? Can you imagine what the world would be like without them?

Strictly speaking

Now that you know that spiders aren't really insects, do you want to know what they really are? They are arachnids, members of a large group of animals that includes scorpions, mites, ticks, and even horseshoe crabs!

Some other tiny creatures mistaken for insects are the centipedes and millipedes. Neither have the number of legs that their names suggest (count them sometime). They are both in classes of their own. What about slugs and snails? Both are members of the mollusk family which includes oysters and clams and other shelled sea creatures. Woodlice, so common in leaf litter, are crustaceans. Other crustaceans you may be familiar with are crabs, lobsters and shrimp. Yum!

What characteristics do these animals have? How do they differ from insects?

11

Hunt for insect homes.

With so many insects around, you'll have no trouble finding where they live! Insects generally don't live very long (adult mayflies live for less than a day; common houseflies last about 20-30 days) but they do find shelter for themselves in a number of places.

Look for insects under rocks and fallen logs, within the bark of trees, and in water. Spiders stretch their webs in corners, both indoors and out. Ants make anthills; certain wasps, such as paper wasps, construct fabulous homes (see *November 8*). Fallen leaves are home to many creatures that come out only at night (see *June 15*). Many insects seek shelter under leaves still on trees and other plants. They also lay their eggs on these plants. Have you ever seen a cluster of tiny eggs on the undersides of leaves?

You may be familiar with galls—swellings on leaves, stems, and other parts of some plants. Various insects are gall makers, including gall wasps, aphids, and some flies. When these insects lay their eggs on the plant, the plant responds by forming tissue around the eggs or newly-hatched grubs. The mature insects eventually leave the galls by making tiny holes to exit by. Count the holes in a gall. How many insects lived inside of it (each makes its own exit hole)? Tie some fine netting around any whole galls you find. Check the galls daily. What kind of insects lived inside them?

12

Preserve a spider web.

Spider webs aren't really homes for spiders—they are actually traps for catching small insects that spiders eat. Not all spiders spin webs, and those that do spin a variety of webs. You are probably most familiar with orb-webs, those made by garden spiders. Look for them on fences, window frames, and spanning garden plants. Have you ever come across one glistening with dew on a summer's morning?

You can preserve webs by mounting them on black paper that has been sprayed with hairspray. Place the paper in a cardboard box before spraying it to protect the area around you from the spray. Work quickly because the hairspray needs to be slightly tacky. If you want the strands of the web to stand out, sprinkle them first with talcum powder. Spray the paper with a protective coating once you get home.

Many of the webs you come across will no longer have a spider in residence. A gentle tap on the strands will sometimes alert the web's owner, thinking an insect has been caught in the sticky strands. If the web is occupied, leave it alone and find another.

Q: Why did the fly fly?
A: Because the spider spied her!

In South Africa, people roast termites and eat them like popcorn. In Mexico, a cake is made from the eggs of water boatmen.

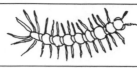

June

13

Use a cricket as a thermometer.

Have you ever noticed how crickets chirp more when it's warm? They are very sensitive to temperature. A scientist named A.E. Dolbear also noticed this and came up with a way to guess the temperature by counting the number of times a cricket chirps in one minute. He based his figures on snowy tree cricket chirps, but you can count the chirps any crickets make. Other crickets are not as reliable, but it's still fun to do.

Listen carefully, because it's sometimes hard to tell when one chirp ends and another begins. Use a watch with a second hand, and count how many chirps there are in one minute. Subtract 40 from this number, and divide the answer by four. Add 50 to this figure. This is what the temperature is in degrees Fahrenheit. Check with a thermometer. Does the formula work?

Only male crickets chirp. They rub their wings together, drawing one across the other almost like a bow across a fiddle. Crickets have two songs—one to attract females, the other to warn off other males. Can you tell them apart? Probably not, but the crickets can!

14

Read a story or poem about insects.

Insects are all around us! Creeping, crawling, flitting, and stalking. If you could choose, which insect would you like to be?

But I Wonder . . .
Aileen Fisher *(poem)*

Charlotte's Web
E.B. White *(story)*

Dragonfly
Florence Page Jacques *(poem)*

Fireflies!
Julie Brinkloe *(story)*

I Wish I Were a Butterfly
James Howe *(story)*

Ladybug
Joan Walsh Anglund *(poem)*

The Way of an Ant
Kazue Mizumura *(story)*

15

Look for insects in leaf litter.

A surprising number of tiny animals (not just insects) live under the leaves that litter the forest floor. Most spend their days under the protective layer of leaves, coming out only at night.

Gather up a handful of leaf litter to take home making sure you get plenty of the damp leaves near the ground. You can get the tiny animals to come out of hiding with a Berlese funnel (also known as a Tulgren funnel). This simple set-up is made with a funnel (make your own from thin cardboard if you don't have one), wire mesh, a glass jar and a lamp. (See the illustration.) Cut the wire mesh into a circle to fit into the funnel. Place the funnel in the jar. Put some leaf litter into the funnel and place it under the lamp. Leave the lamp on for several hours. The heat will drive any animals down through the leaves, where they'll fall through the mesh into the jar.

What have you caught? Do you find mites and woodlice? What about millipedes (they don't really have 1,000 legs!), and springtails (see *January 19*)? How many of the creatures are actually insects?

16

Make an insect growth chart.

All animals go through some pretty amazing changes as they grow. Take a look at some of your baby pictures. You've changed quite a bit over the years, haven't you? Insects go through several stages of life, too. Some undergo three changes, others four. Make a chart that shows what these changes are, illustrating it with examples.

Insects that go through three changes—egg to nymph to adult—undergo incomplete, or simple, metamorphosis. The nymphs that hatch from the eggs look just like miniature adults. As they grow they shed their outer skin. These insects may molt many times before they are adults. Some examples of these insects include dragonflies, crickets, grasshoppers, cockroaches, and true bugs.

Those insects that go through four changes—egg to larva to pupa to adult—go through complete metamorphosis. The larvae that hatch from the eggs don't look anything like the adult insects. (Think of caterpillars that turn into butterflies!) Then they become pupae, where some truly amazing changes take place. The emerging adults are fully grown. Along with butterflies, moths, bees, wasps, ants, and beetles grow in four stages.

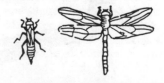

June

17

Tend your gardens.

This goes without saying, of course! But make the daily chore of weeding and watering more enjoyable by having some fun while you're at it.

Examine the weeds you pull from the garden. Did they sprout from seed or did they spread by underground runners? Leave a small patch in your garden unweeded. What happens? What happens when you don't water your plants? Are the weeds hardy enough to take over when the cultivated species wilt?

Look for insects in your garden. Capture some to observe. Which ones don't you want to have in your garden? The "bad guys" include aphids, earwigs, Japanese beetles, and whiteflies. Slugs, which are not insects, can also be a problem. Try biological controls to get rid of some of these pests (see *May 29*).

Experiment with individual plants. Let a head of lettuce go to seed (which many of them will do during a prolonged hot spell). Leave some carrots in the ground to grow and grow. How big do they get?

These are all fun things to do, but there's an added plus. Everything you learn goes toward making you a better gardener!

18

Visit a pick-your-own farm.

Fresh picked fruits and vegetables can't be beat! And you can pick your fill even if you don't have the garden space for everything you'd like to grow. Where? At a pick-your-own farm!

Strawberries and other berries are among the most popular small farm crops, and many pick-your-own farms cultivate them. You pick the berries and pay either by the pound, or by the pint or quart. (Don't eat *too* many on the spot!) Would you like to make your own jam? Pick a lot, and make up enough jars to give to all your friends. Do you like strawberry shortcake? Who doesn't! Choose plenty of strawberries to slice in half for this scrumptious dessert. Blueberries are delicious in pies, muffins, and jam, too.

Where can you find pick-your-own farms? Check with your state's department of agriculture. There's probably a listing of farms that are set up to let people harvest their own fruits and vegetables. Later in the year, you'll want to know where to go to pick your own apples, or select your own pumpkins. Always call ahead, because harvest times can vary from year to year.

19

Pick a wildflower bouquet.

One of the nicest souvenirs of a walk along a country lane or through a meadow, is a bouquet of wildflowers. Wildflowers are not as showy as their cultivated cousins, but they have a simple beauty. They are also free! But remember, don't pick too many, and don't pull them up by the roots. (See *How to use this book* for more on picking wild plants.)

Wildflowers tend to be very hardy plants. Many of them thrive in barren places. But they tend to wilt quickly when picked, so take a pail of water with you, if you can. Use scissors or a sharp knife to cut the stems—a clean cut heals faster. The flowers may droop a bit but the water will revive them. When you get home, strip the lower leaves off the stems so they won't foul the water.

Look for clovers in all sorts of colors, woodsorrels, and buttercups (do *you* like butter?) Later in the summer, you'll find Queen Anne's lace blooming, as well as jewelweed, and purple and yellow coneflowers (one of the yellow ones is the black-eyed Susan). What are your favorite wildflowers? Grow some in your garden next year!

20

Enroll in some nature programs.

Are you always looking for something fun to do once school gets out? Look no further! Enroll in some of the nature programs put on by science museums and nature centers.

There are one-day workshops where you can learn to identify wildflowers, explore a bog, or hunt for edible mushrooms; there are even day-camps that last much of the summer. What would you like to learn about?

If you and your family are museum or nature society members, you'll get word of the programs by mail. Or just pick up the telephone and call for information. You don't have to be members to participate in these programs. Don't forget that many libraries and town recreation departments also sponsor summertime programs, and many may be nature-oriented. Have a wonderful summer!

Summer is hoppy, choppy, poppy.

June

21

First day of summer!

The arrival of summer, on or about June 21, is also known as the summer solstice. It marks the day when the number of daylight hours in the United States is the greatest. The sun is also highest in the sky during this month. Have you noticed how bright the days are? And how shallow the shadows are?

Warm weather doesn't wait for this date, and you may already be enjoying your summer vacation from school, but the first day of summer is reason to celebrate! Honor the day by lighting a bonfire at dusk, which is what ancient peoples did in hopes of encouraging the sun to shine all summer. Sunny days (mixed with some rainy ones, of course) are necessary for good crops. Or take a picnic lunch into an area you have never explored. Bring home a bouquet of wildflowers to remember the day by.

. . . .

In Tokyo, hundreds of specially raised fireflies are released in celebration of the first day of summer.

Midsummer is a special time for those in love. Bake heart-shaped cookies in honor of the day.

Standing still

The word solstice comes to us from Latin. It means "sun come to a stop." For the first few days of summer (and the first few of winter) the sun doesn't appear to move once it has climbed in the sky. Have you noticed this?

22

Read a story or poem about summer.

Summer means no school, no shoes, and lots of time to spend outdoors! What is your favorite thing about summer?

How Summer Came to Canada
retold by William Toye *(story)*

A Moment in Summer
Charlotte Zolotow *(poem)*

Open Hydrant
Marci Ridlon *(poem)*

Summer
Frank Asch *(poem)*

Summer from **The Four Seasons**
Jack Prelutsky *(poem)*

23

Look for milkweeds.

Milkweeds are among the easiest plants to identify. Break a leaf or stalk in two and out oozes a milky white sap. This sticky stuff gives the plant its name. It's not a particularly handsome plant although its flowers are quite lovely, but the monarch butterfly might disagree. Monarchs have a very special relationship with milkweeds.

Monarchs lay their eggs on milkweed plants. The emerging larvae eat the plants, and none others. When they go into their pupal stage, monarchs hang their chrysalises from milkweed leaves. When the adults fly off, what are they in search of? More milkweeds!

All the milkweed the monarchs eat makes them taste bitter. This is their defense, and a mighty good one it is. Birds steer clear of the foul-tasting butterflies. A cleverly patterned look-alike, the viceroy butterfly, also benefits. They are mistaken for monarchs and are left alone, too!

June

Wise spiders with will weave webs wonderfully well.

24

Make an insect net.

The best way to capture flying insects is with a net. You can make your own from a wire coat hanger, broomstick (or thick dowel), some nylon netting, a 3"-wide strip of cotton fabric, and some strong tape.

Straighten the coat hanger hook; then bend the rest of the hanger into a circle. Tape the hanger's hook to the broomstick, wrapping it tightly with the tape. Measure around the wire circle (use a cloth tape measure to do this). Cut the netting into the shape shown—make the straight edge the same measurement as the wire circle's circumference. Sew the strip of cotton fabric to the straight edge of the net. Then sew the side seams. Finally sew the completed bag to the frame by folding the cotton strip over the wire frame and sewing it to itself.

Practice using the net to get the hang of "closing" it. Twist the handle quickly once you've caught something to keep it from escaping.

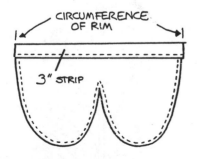

CIRCUMFERENCE OF RIM

3" STRIP

25

Visit an insect zoo.

Insect zoos are a popular feature at many nature centers and science museums. Insects that do well in captivity are kept in cages indoors (only the honeybees need access to the outdoors, and their cage has a small tube that the bees can leave by, exiting through a window or wall). You can study live insects from around the world, and you can get some ideas for an insect zoo of your own at home.

Notice how the cages are outfitted. What are the insects given to eat and drink? Ask the staff if you have any questions. And check to see if there are any special programs on insects at the facility. There's a lot you can learn about these little creatures.

· ·

American Indians believe that spiders are magical creatures. They associate them with the sun, because many webs with radiating strands look like the sun.

26

Construct an insect cage.

The insects that do well in captivity aren't too fussy about where they stay. A large glass jar (punch lots of tiny holes in the lid) works well. But a more spacious cage can be made from some materials you probably already have at home. You'll need two round cake pans of equal diameter, some screen and some modeling clay (the kind that doesn't harden).

Cut the screen a foot wide and a couple of inches longer than the circumference of the pans. Make a tube from the screen the same size as the pans (sew or tape the seam). Press some modeling clay into the two pans, and place one on each end of the screen. The clay will secure the screen and make the cage escape-proof.

If you hope to keep insects any length of time, you'll need to provide food and water. Many insects favor one food. Try offering leaves from the plants you found the insects on or near. Keep the leaves fresh by sticking the stems in a glass of water (cover the glass with foil so that the insects don't drown). Give them water by sprinkling a few drops on a cotton ball.

27

Raise some mealworms.

If you would like to keep an amphibian for longer than overnight, you will have to feed it. This isn't too hard to do if you have some mealworms on hand. Mealworms (and other live food) can be bought from pet shops, but it's easy to raise them at home.

Mealworms are the grubs (larvae) of a black beetle. Purchase some from a pet shop (a mix of adults and larvae is best) to start your own culture. Place them in a large cookie tin along with a mixture of bran, flour and pieces of dried bread. Put the tin in a warm spot, at least 77°F. The eggs the adult female lays hatch in about a week's time. The larvae take about six months to mature (this is what you are raising for food) before turning into pupae. This stage lasts about three weeks, when the adult beetles finally emerge.

Add more bread or cracker crumbs to the tin as needed. To keep the level of humidity just right, put a carrot slice or apple core into the tin, replacing it every few days.

A butterfly makes a chrysalis, a moth a cocoon.

28

Start an ant farm.

Have you ever seen an ant struggling with an impossibly heavy load? Ants are among the most industrious insects, and they are great fun to watch. You can make an ant farm (or formicarium as it is properly called) from a narrow container. Use the wormery you made (see *April 19*).

Gather up some ants in a self-locking plastic bag, including any eggs and larvae you find. Look for the queen (she is a much larger ant). A colony without a queen will dig tunnels, but will die in a couple of weeks. Life revolves around the queen because only she lays eggs. Place the ants in the refrigerator for an hour; this slows them down so that it's easier to transfer them to the formicarium. Meanwhile, fill the container with dirt. Put the ants in the container (do this outside, in case some get away!); stretch an old nylon stocking over the top and place the container in a tray of water. Any stray ants won't get far.

You'll need to cover the formicarium with a light-proof cloth, and provide food and water in small quantities. Place little bits of ripe fruit, meat, and an occasional spoonful of jam or honey on the soil's surface. Lift the cloth now and again to see what's going on. What do you see?

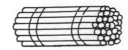

29

Make a nest box for bees.

Many types of bees are social insects that live in colonies just like ants. These include various wasps and honeybees. Some of these can be annoying pests if they make their hives too close to people's homes. But there are some others known as solitary wasps and bees, and these you can encourage to nest. Your garden will thank you!

Make a number of different nesting sites. Tape a bundle of drinking straws together, and attach them to the underside of a window sill. Plug one end of the straws with some modeling clay (face some each way). Or drill some very narrow holes ($^5/_{32}''$ to $^3/_8''$ in diameter) in a log that can stand upright. Put it in a sunny spot. Who moves in?

Bumblebees can also be accomodated by making a nest from an upturned flower pot (make sure it has a hole in the bottom, which will be the entrance). Sink the pot into the ground and put an old mouse nest in it. (The female bumblebees seek out discarded mice nests in the wild.) You might be able to get some mouse bedding from a pet store. Lay a flat rock or piece of wood over the pot (raise it up slightly) to protect it from the weather. Female bumblebees are usually in search of nesting sites in April.

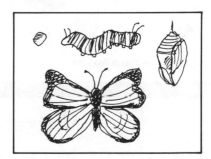

30

Watch a caterpillar as it changes.

You can witness the marvel of insect metamorphosis (see *June 16*) by caging a caterpillar and watching the changes that take place. It's not always easy to tell whether your caterpillar will turn into a butterfly or a moth. Prepare your cage for both, just in case.

Put an inch of potting soil in the bottom of your cage (this is for the moths which pupate underground). Lean some sticks in the cage for butterflies—they hang their chrysalises. Note the type of plant the caterpillar is eating when you find it. Supply fresh leaves daily. Put them in a covered glass of water.

As the caterpillar grows, it sheds its skin. How many times does this happen? Then comes the pupal stage. How long it remains a pupa, depends on the species. Generally, caterpillars found in spring and early summer turn into adults the same year. Those found later in the year remain pupae until the following spring. (Keep these in a cold—but not freezing—place, such as an unheated garage.) The insects don't eat at this time, so take away the leaves. Put a moistened paper towel in the bottom of the cage to keep the humidity the right level. Sprinkle it with water now and again.

Watch what happens when the pupa opens up. What have you got? A butterfly or a moth? Once it has dried its wings, take it outdoors to release it.

Which is it?

Adult butterflies and moths are easier to tell apart. There are three things to look for (although there are exceptions to the rules). Butterflies fly by day; most moths are nocturnal. The wings of butterflies fold up vertically when they are at rest; moths spread their wings flat horizontally. Lastly, butterflies have antennae that are long with a little knob at the end; moths have feathery feelers.

July

Hot July brings cooling showers,
Apricots and gillyflowers.

1

Find the oceans on a map.

Can you name the four major oceans of the world? In descending order of size, they are the Pacific, Atlantic, Indian and Arctic. (Some people even add a fifth, the Antarctic.) Now look on a map or globe and trace with your finger where they lie. Do you see how these oceans are really one continuous body of water?

The oceans (along with smaller

connected bodies of salt water that we call seas) cover approximately 71% of the earth's surface, which is substantial, to say the least. We've come to know quite a bit about the oceans and life beneath the waves, especially in recent years. We take advantage of the seas in many ways, and it is expected that we will come to depend on the oceans even more in the future. We can no longer regard the vast waters as dumping grounds, however, nor can we continue to carelessly pollute and over-fish the seas. Do you think it might help us to protect the oceans by remembering that the first forms of life on earth actually had their start in the oceans?

Weighing anchor

You might be happy just playing in the sand, eating fried clams, and taking an occasional dip in the water. But, if you get the chance, go out on a boat to get another perspective of the ocean. Book passage on a ferry boat that island hops, or go for a sail. You might even be able to get a few seats on one of the boats that head out in search of whales. (Whale watches are generally organized from May until October.)

Even if you don't spot any whales, these trips are a lot of fun. You can get information about whale

watches when you are down at the shore, or call a local nature center or science museum. Many sponsor trips throughout the summer, and you can book seats ahead of time. Getting that close to these big marine mammals is a thrill that can't be beat!

2

Make a marine mural.

We've come a long way since life began in the seas thousands of millions of years ago! But the seas continue to be home to all sorts of interesting plants and animals. You can get a clear idea of how life functions and adapts below the ocean surface by making a mural. A long piece of newsprint cut from a roll-end works well (or piece together smaller sheets of paper). Divide the mural horizontally into several sections, using cut or torn strips of paper, or paint, to show the shore (tan), shallow water at land's edge (pale blue), and deeper water (dark blue). Paste down pictures that you have cut from magazines, or sketched yourself.

You might want to make a comparative mural, showing the forms of life found on a sandy beach versus those found on a rocky shore. Or if you are interested in the creatures of the deep, mark the paper off in 4,000 foot increments and make a mural that shows the great ocean depths, and what can be found where. You could also use the mural to record what you have actually found on the beach. A mural like this makes a dandy souvenir of a visit to the shore.

3

Taste some water from the ocean.

You don't need to actually drink some ocean water to taste it. Just roll a spoonful or so around in your mouth and spit it out. How is that for salty? The saltiness of the oceans differs from place to place, but on the average about 3½% of seawater is dissolved mineral salts. Our own table salt, sodium chloride, is the most common ocean mineral.

The salt in ocean water is something that you can even smell and feel. When you drive down to the beach, can you notice a salty odor even before you spot the shore? After a swim in the ocean, see how your skin feels. Does it feel dry and tight, like you are covered with a fine layer of salt? Lick your skin and you can have another taste of the sea.

A simple experiment demonstrates that there is salt in the water. Pour a cupful of sea water in a clear bowl and leave it where it will not be disturbed. After several days, the water in the bowl will have evaporated, leaving only the minerals. A taste test will confirm that there are salts among them. Do you think people will ever drink ocean water?

. . . .

The four largest seas are the South China, Caribbean, Mediterranean and Bering seas.

Most streams and rivers west of the Continental Divide join other rivers that empty into the Pacific Ocean. Those rivers on the other side of the Divide drain into the Atlantic and the Gulf of Mexico.

4

Name the ways that people use the oceans.

If you've ever spent a day at the beach, you might put fun and recreation at the top of the list of ways that people use the oceans. Nothing draws people to an area like a beach does. Some people say they love the water, so cooling during the hot summer months; others just like to lie on the beach or play in the sand. What is your favorite thing to do at the beach?

We certainly do make good use of the oceans' offerings. If you were to make a list of the gifts from the seas, it might include recreation (from sailing to scuba diving), food (you might like tuna fish sandwiches, but the Japanese are partial to seaweed), medicines (cod liver oil is rich in vitamins A and D), and such varied items as jewelry (pearls come from oysters) and sponges (skeletons of another sea creature). Some minerals are extracted from sea water, and as more efficient methods are developed, there may be even more of this in the future. Currently petroleum is brought up from the ocean floor, and while it is just a coincidence that this valuable commodity is located there, you might say petroleum is one of the oceans' offerings, as well. Can you think of any other ways we use the oceans?

5

Read a story or poem about the ocean.

When you think of the ocean, what comes to mind? Is it the smell of the salt air, or the feel of sand between your toes?

Beach Party
Joanne Ryder *(story)*

Down to the Beach
Mary Garelick *(story)*

Driving to the Beach
Joanna Cole *(poem)*

maggie and milly and molly and may
e.e. cummings *(poem)*

The Paint-Box Sea
Doris Herold Lund *(story)*

The Sandpiper
Frances Frost *(poem)*

The Sea
Anonymous *(poem)*

Sea Shell
Amy Lowell *(poem)*

Until I Saw the Sea
Lilian Moore *(poem)*

6

Mark the high and low tides.

Ancient peoples thought the rhythmic movement of the tides, causing high water and low water, was created by a monster at the bottom of the seas breathing in and out. You can see how they might have thought that! We know now that the tides are created by gravitational pull from the moon, and to a lesser extent, the sun.

The high and low tides at beaches vary considerably throughout the world. The Bay of Fundy, in eastern Canada, holds the record for the greatest difference between high and low tide—an unbelievable 53 feet! By comparison, the Mediterranean Sea barely has a tide at all. Find out how your beach figures by looking for the signs of both high and low tides and measuring the difference.

A tide table of your region will tell you when the two low and two high tides will take place each day. Look for a wharf jutting out into the water, and measure where the water comes to at both low and high tides. Are you surprised at the difference?

Look, too, for signs of the shore life that must adapt to the twice daily changes in water level. Certain seaweeds need constant contact with water; other life forms make due at the "splash zone," the dry end of the shore. Look for the strand lines along flat, sandy beaches which mark the high tides and are an abundant source of treasures, especially after a storm.

7

Make a wave bottle.

The waves in your wave bottle won't knock you off your feet like real waves can, but you can get an idea how waves crest and break with this simple set-up. Fill a bottle, such as a clear screw-top soda bottle, one-third full with salad oil. Fill the rest of the bottle (and it must be full to the top) with water. Add several drops of food coloring, if you want the "water" to be blue. Screw the top on tight, and gently rock the bottle back and forth on its side. Do you see how the small waves form and break?

Real waves are caused mostly by wind. The average ocean wave is 10 to 12 feet high (measured from the trough, or low point, to the crest, or high point). Twenty foot waves are considered big. Some waves, however, are caused by movement under the water, such as earthquakes and landslides. These waves, and occasionally those that accompany storms at sea, can be huge. You may have heard of tsunamis, giant waves that tower as high as 200 feet! These waves, set off by earthquakes, are capable of travelling up to 500 miles per hour, and often batter shores thousands of miles from their origin.

July

8

Look for plants growing by the shore.

The plants you will find growing along coastal areas may look similar to plants growing farther inland. There's a major difference, however. Whether they are rooted in dry sand or in a coastal wetland, these plants must be able to tolerate salt, for both the soil and the air are heavy with it. These plants must also be able to withstand the winds coming off the water, which are sometimes harsh, especially when the occasional storm buffets the shores.

Can you find any plants that remind you of garden varieties? The beach pea is closely related to the sweet pea, a fragrant flowering plant. Did you know there is even goldenrod that grows down by the ocean (it's called seaside goldenrod)? There are beach heathers, sea oats, and seaside gerardias, all related to plants with similar names that grow elsewhere. And there are plenty of grasses, too, adapted to life at water's edge.

Because conditions along coasts impose such hardships, and because people crowding onto beaches make it still more difficult for plants to survive, do not pick any seaside plants (even if they seem plentiful). Sketch them, or photograph them, but leave them be. These flowers and grasses may save your favorite beach from eroding and eventually disappearing forever.

9

Watch for birds that live near the ocean.

You'll notice that birds along seashores have special adaptations, too, for life near the water. Can you see how many have bills that are designed for scooping food from the water, or for spearing it? Many of the birds have webbed feet, which are useful for paddling when the birds are afloat. While many seaside birds eat fish, others wait for the tide to go out and hunt for creatures that are buried just below the surface in the sand. You can search for the same clues that these birds rely on. Look for casts on the sand's surface made by marine worms. Do you see the tiny air holes dotting the beach? These are made by shelled creatures that burrow beneath the sand. Try digging in the sand to catch one of these animals. You will almost certainly not be able to keep up with these crafty creatures, as they continue to bury themselves deeper still at lightning speed.

A note: Many shore birds seen in northern areas this time of year can be found in the southern regions of the United States during the colder months.

10

Make a seaweed collection.

On rocky shores there is usually an abundance of plants growing in the water. Seaweeds, as they are loosely known, grow right on the rocks. How do they do that? Seaweeds are algae, and instead of roots they have suction-like anchors that hold them fast to rocks and other solid objects. Not surprisingly, these are called holdfasts! Pry one off carefully with a knife or sharp shell to examine it.

Closest to shore are the green seaweeds, followed by those that are brown, and lastly, those that are red. All seaweeds need sunlight to grow, so they are found in relatively shallow waters (less than 100 feet deep generally). Some, such as sea lettuce, are found on both coasts of the United States; others such as chenille weed (this seaweed looks just like strands of chenille) grow only along the Atlantic seaboard. Rockweed, found in the northeast, has bubble-like bladders along its stems, which are fun to pop when the seaweed is dry.

Seaweeds can either be hung to dry or pressed. Because they are so bulky and wet, you'll need to use plenty of folded newspapers, changed frequently, to dry them. Weight the newspapers with something heavy. Often seaweed will stick to paper as it dries. Why not take advantage of this tendency and compose some pictures with wet seaweed? Your arrangements will be naturally "glued" in place.

11

Sample some seaweed.

Are you kidding? You *can* eat seaweed; in fact you already do eat a lot of seaweed if you like ice cream, chocolate milk, pudding and toothpaste (well, you don't eat toothpaste). That's because Irish moss (which is not a moss at all but a plentiful seaweed also known as carragheen) has a substance extracted from it that is used in all of these foods. Other seaweeds that are eaten worldwide include dulse, laver, and various kelps.

Sample some seaweeds yourself. Look for the bright green sea lettuce to add to a garden salad. It's a bit tough and chewy, but it does add a festive touch to a land-based salad. Or make some Irish moss pudding. Carefully wash one cup of fresh Irish moss; add it to three cups of milk in the top of a double boiler and cook over simmering water for about 25 minutes. Discard the seaweed. Stir in a third of a cup of sugar and one teaspoon vanilla. Pour the pudding into individual dishes and chill until firm (a couple of hours). Serve either plain or with a topping of berries, perhaps some you may have gathered yourself.

· ·

Be careful when you are climbing in and out of tide pools. Seaweed is slippery! Wear sneakers on rough beaches to protect your feet from sharp rocks and shells. Watch out for jellyfish (some will give you a rash) and crabs. Crabs have a powerful pinch!

July

12

13

14

Search for seashells.

The best searching time is when the tide is going out. You'll have to be quick, however, and beat the birds to any of the whole shells. Have you ever watched gulls dropping shells onto rocks, or even roads? That is how the birds break open the shells to get to the creatures that live inside. With a swoop, the birds gobble up the tasty morsels.

Seashells come in all shapes and sizes, and many have descriptive names. Have you ever seen a slipper shell (the underside of this shell looks just like an open-backed slipper) or coffee-bean trivias (these look like whole coffee beans)? Some have musical names like periwinkle, wentletrap, and wavy turban. Some are satiny-smooth, others are rough and rugged looking.

Any whole shells you find should be dropped in boiling water (have your parents help you with this) and then picked clean once the shells have cooled. If you can't get all the little pieces of animal debris out of the shells, put them outside on the soil where scavenger insects will finish the job for you.

Display your shells in shoe box tops (glueing them in place) or in a clear vase filled with water (this brings out their colors nicely). A little mineral oil rubbed into the shells also improves their luster.

Create some seashell art.

There are all sorts of things you can do with shells besides display them. (There are even ways to use broken shells, so don't despair if you haven't found any whole specimens yet.) What have you ever seen made from shells that you would like to make yourself?

If you would like to wear your shells, you can string them on thread and make a necklace. Some, such as the thin-shelled jingle shells, can be tapped gently with a hammer and a small nail to make the holes for stringing. Or glue a safety pin to the back of a large shell to make a brooch. If you would rather hear your shells, string lots of them on strong thread and hang several strands together to make a wind chime. Large shells (plain or decorated with smaller shells) make dandy candy dishes, spoon rests, paper clip holders, and trinket boxes.

If you have found some lovely fragments of shells that you would like to use, make a hanging ornament. Glue the shell pieces (and even small bits of beach glass) onto a clear coffee-can cover with epoxy (have your parents show you how to use this strong glue). This makes a pretty sun-catcher to hang in a sunny window.

Make a mobile from beach treasures.

On your walks along sandy beaches, and in and out of tide pools, you'll find all sorts of things besides shells. Look for pieces of driftwood and beach glass; search for empty crab shells, and horseshoe crab shells (which aren't really crabs, but more closely related to spiders!). See if you can find skate egg-cases and barnacle-encrusted bits of shell and stones. If you comb the beaches in warmer areas you might find coral (some types can be found as far north as Massachusetts), or sea urchins and sand dollars.

What can you do with all these treasures? Make a mobile and hang some of your finds together as a memento of your seaside ventures. Use the driftwood as the supports and hang the smaller items with white thread. It takes some practice to balance all the elements, both artistically as well as physically, but this is a good rainy day project, when spending time on the beach is not possible.

A is for aquarium

Where can you go to see the wonders of the deep without ever setting foot off dry land? An aquarium, that's where!

Many cities (especially coastal ones) have aquariums, although many towns with science museums (and sometimes children's museums) have tanks with marine creatures, even hands-on areas where you can actually stroke a starfish or shake hands with a crab. Visit an aquarium as a prelude to a visit to the shore, or stop by one to get some ideas for setting up your own aquarium at home. You can create a salt-water habitat and populate it with sea creatures and plants, or set up a freshwater aquarium. This could be as simple as a couple of goldfish in a bowl to a complex filtered system that houses dozens of tropical species. You'll have to do some homework to see what would work best for you. Fish and other water creatures don't require daily exercise like a dog does, but you still need to provide food and clean living conditions for your aquarium animals.

July

15

Examine rocks from a pebbly beach.

The constant tumbling of the waves smooths the edges of rocks found along coastlines. Depending on the predominant type of rock in the region, you may find round rocks, or you may find flat slices of rock that are good for skipping over the water. How many times can you make a flat stone skip?

Collect some rocks and smaller pebbles and display them with your shells or on their own. A little mineral oil will bring out their color. Or arrange them in a water-filled container which will do the same.

Small round rocks can be used in flower arranging. Place a handful of pebbles in a clear vase to separate and anchor the stems of flowers. Besides being useful, they add visual interest to arrangements. Larger rocks can be simply displayed, or put to good use, too. They make good paperweights and doorstops.

. . . .

The largest salt lake in the world is the Caspian Sea in Eurasia. The saltiest (ten times saltier than average ocean water) is Lake Assal in East Africa.

16

Collect sand from different beaches.

Did you know that most of the sand found on beaches actually came from inland areas, and was washed down to the shores, often by rivers and streams? Some coastal sand is full of tiny bits of broken shells and other marine debris, but most is made up of minute particles of rock that have settled along coastlines. Ocean waves and currents spread and shift the sands where water and land meet.

The color of sand differs from beach to beach, depending, of course, on the kind of rock that predominates in a particular area. Much of the sand in the United States is greyish in color, but you can find white coral sands in Florida, and Hawaii boasts blackish-green sands (these are mostly volcanic rock particles).

Collect small amounts of sand at different beaches. Self-locking plastic bags work well. Be sure to label the sands you collect (you may want to remember where and when you found them). Look at some sand closely with a magnifying glass. Are the different grains of sand all the same color? (See the chart on *July 17* for the origins of common sands.) Can you guess what types of rocks the particles are from?

Far from the ocean breezes

Seashores aren't the only places you'll find sand, of course. Remember where most coastal sand comes from? From places inland! So look for sand along rivers, and along lake shores. If you still can't find any, bring the sand to you. Check at a local sand and gravel pit, where natural sand is screened for size and cleaned. Although this sand is primarily for the building trade, you can usually purchase a small truckload of sand for your sandbox.

You can also find salt water far from the ocean breezes. There are many salt lakes throughout the world. The best known in this country is the Great Salt Lake in Utah. Its water is eight times saltier than average ocean water, and getting saltier by the year. Today the lake is only one-twentieth its original size. As the water evaporates, the lake shrinks, and the mineral salts become even more concentrated, resulting in a very salty bath.

17

Test black sand for magnetism.

On Hawaiian beaches, black sand is mostly finely particled lava. In other places, however, the dark color may indicate minute bits of iron in the sand. You can test this by passing a magnet over the sand and seeing what it attracts. The tiny iron particles will be picked right up and cling to the magnet.

What other colors does sand come in? Check the chart below.

Color	Composition
Black	lava, iron particles
Grey	granite, feldspar
Light brown	granite, quartz
Yellow	quartz
Gold	mica
Red	garnet
Pink	feldspar
White	coral, seashells, quartz

. . . .

Glass is made from sand, which when combined with soda and lime (and other ingredients for special kinds of glass) and heated to melting point can be blown or molded into many shapes for varied uses.

18

Make a sand bottle.

Fill a bottle with layers of different sands (they can be from different areas of the same beach) for a lasting memento of seaside ventures. Even if you only have two types of sand (or sand and small pebbles), you can alternate layers in a pattern of stripes. Choose a clear, straight-sided container, and carefully funnel the sand into it, tipping the container slightly to create undulating (wavy) layers, if you like. Be sure to fill your container to the very top, and seal it with a cork or screw-top, so that the sands won't move around and mix together.

Do you want to remember where you found each type of sand? Make simple labels noting where and when the sands were collected.

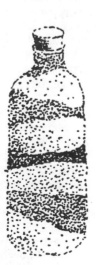

19

Make some sand castings.

Sand has long been used as a way of molding shapes that are then filled with "liquids" such as molten metals or melted wax. You'll be using plaster of Paris mixed with salt water to fill your sand molds.

Here's a craft project you can do right on the beach! Make a shallow hole in the sand and line it with treasures you have picked up along the beach. Arrange shells and pebbles in interesting designs, or just group them randomly. Pour in the plaster and let it harden (see *Casting about* on page 50 for more on working with plaster of Paris). Dig it up when it has set, letting it dry several more hours before you clean away all the traces of the sand. Or pour some plaster into a small hole, allowing the plaster to harden only slightly before lifting it out of the sand. With a skewer or other thin stick, poke lots of holes into the rounded dome of your casting. You can use this as a container for dried flower arrangements.

Don't forget that your own footprints in sand make ideal subjects to cast. Just remember that when you are done, you must clean up after yourself, leaving no trace of the activity on the beach.

20

Paint a sand painting.

In the United States, the most famous sand painters are the Navajo Indians (although they learned the art from the Pueblo Indians, who are thought to have learned it from the Spanish). The Navajos use colored sands as well as crushed charcoal, cornmeal, mineral ores and pollen for their elaborate paintings. They (and other cultures throughout the world) use sand paintings for healing and ceremonial purposes. The paintings are always nonpermanent, and are left to blow away with the breezes, or are intentionally destroyed.

You can make your own permanent sand paintings using different colored sands. On heavy cardboard, paint shapes with slightly watered-down white glue. While the glue is still wet, sprinkle sand over the painted area, tipping away the excess after the glue has had time to set. Repeat with different sands, making abstract designs, or elements of nature, as the Navajos do.

21

Make some castles in the sand.

Actually sand castles are only a beginning. If you've ever seen some of the truly fantastic sand sculptures that have been made during sand sculpting competitions, you know what an amazing material sand is to work with. And all that work and time goes into making something that will disappear forever with the tide! Maybe sculpting in sand is a healing pastime not unlike painting with sand.

See if your community will be sponsoring any sand-sculpting competitions. Then spend some enjoyable hours "practicing"! Search the beach for shells, rocks, and other treasures to adorn your sculptures. Take a spray bottle to the beach with you to mist the sand. An assortment of tools will come in handy, too. Good luck!

Protect yourself from the elements when you are down at the beach. The sun, reflecting off light-colored sand and water, produces a quick burn, so take along a brimmed hat to shade your eyes, sunscreen, and a sweatshirt or jacket if you are there early in the morning or once the sun goes down.

July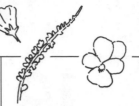

22

Harvest some herbs for cooking and crafts.

Can you believe how much your herbs have grown? (See *Let's hear it for herbs* on page 60 for more on growing herbs.) This is a good time to harvest leaves and flowers for crafting and cooking. Pick the herbs in the morning, after the dew has dried, but before the hot sun brings out the aromatic oils.

You probably have been pinching back plants all along (this encourages them to branch out). Now you can cut back many plants almost to the ground. (The plants will grow almost as high again by autumn.) The long stems can be hung to dry, or the leaves can be stripped off and placed on a screen. Herbs that don't dry well can be preserved in other ways. Chives (always cut right down to the ground) can be cut into ¼″ lengths with scissors and frozen. Basil leaves can be packed in oil, or made into pesto (check a cookbook for the recipe).

You might want to press some herbs; you might want to dry others for potpourri. The herbs that you are growing for their seeds (such as dill, coriander, and fennel) may not be ready to harvest yet. When the seeds start to turn brown, cut the stems from the plants and place them upside-down in a paper bag. Let them dry for a week or so. The bag will catch the seeds as they fall from the stems.

23

Press some leaves and flowers.

Many annual flowers are in bloom now and the best blossoms can be pressed flat for pressed flower pictures (see *December 3* for instructions and hints). You can press foliage and flowers in fat books (use protective paper so that you won't soil the pages) or in the plant press you made (see *May 13*).

Don't worry about getting all the petals of flowers to fan out perfectly, and don't fret if leaves don't lie flat. Instead, let the blossoms and leaves curl naturally and even overlap. These casually curved stems are easier to work with because they are very natural looking (you can, of course, press some individual leaves and blossoms to add to your pictures). You'll find that some flower compositions just "make themselves"!

Most plant material will be ready to use in 2 to 4 weeks, depending on the thickness of the leaves and blooms, and somewhat on the weather, too. You may want to store your pressed plants in a shoe box or other sturdy container, to free up your press (or that book you were reading!).

24

Dry some flowers in sand.

What do you do with those flowers that are so fat they can't be pressed flat? You can dry them in sand. Drying flowers in sand is a centuries-old technique. Only the sturdiest blossoms work well, so check your zinnias for perfect blooms and ransack the roses for some beautiful buds.

First you need to clean your sand. Put it in a pail, fill the pail with water and stir. When the sand has settled, skim the water for floating debris. Do this several times. Dry the sand in a warm oven for several hours. Then, put a layer of sand in a container that can be made airtight (a cookie tin or a shoe box will do). Place your blossoms on the sand, petals up, and sift sand over them, tipping the box and using a toothpick to push sand into any crevices. Cover the flowers with another inch of sand; seal the box with tape, mark the contents and the date and put the box in a warm, dry place. After two weeks, check a blossom. It's ready if the petals feel dry and crisp like paper. If the blossoms need more time, re-cover them for another week or so.

When they are "done," take the blossoms out and dust them clean with a small paintbrush. Brush the petals with a little oil to add sheen. Wire them with florist's wire and they are ready to be used in all sorts of arrangements.

25

Preserve some leaves in glycerine.

You may have heard of glycerine. It's an old-fashioned ingredient in hand lotions (rosewater and glycerine). You can still buy small bottles of it at drug stores. You can preserve all sorts of foliage with it (from oak leaves to ferns) and even a few flowers, notably hydrangeas. The plants turn color somewhat, but these are usually pleasing shades.

Prepare your foliage by stripping the bark from the thick lower stems (or mashing them slightly). Dilute the glycerine with water—one part glycerine to two parts water. Bring the solution almost to a boil (have your parents help you here) and pour 4-6 inches of it into a container tall enough to support the foliage. Place your greenery in the solution and leave it in a cool, dark place until the leaves begin to turn color.

Check the plants regularly to see that there is enough solution in the container and to monitor how the conversion is going. If plants are left too long in glycerine, mildew might set in. The leaves should feel slightly greasy, but there shouldn't be oily beads on the surface of the leaves. If the tops of your branches droop, hang the plants upside down to let the glycerine soak down to the very tips of the leaves.

Wipe the leaves with a tissue, and arrange them in a vase. Lovely!

26

Search for edible wild plants.

What do you think people ate before there were supermarkets? Go even farther back in time: What do you think they ate before they learned how to farm? Early peoples did very nicely foraging for their food (and hunting game, too, of course). And we can do very nicely today doing the same thing.

There are wonderful edibles out in the wilds free for the taking. All you have to know is how to positively identify any food you would like to taste. Do you like strawberries? Then you'll love wild strawberries, tiny morsels that are even better than the kind you find in markets. Do you like a little bite in your salad? Then hunt for some watercress and toss a few leaves in with the lettuce. Have you heard that almost all of a cattail is edible? It's true. You wouldn't go hungry if you could find only cattails to eat.

You might want to start out with some plants you already know, like dandelions (the young leaves are good in salad and the roots make a nice tea), or wild mint (the minty smell is unmistakable). Use a clear field guide (and your parents' help) so you'll know what is what (and what look-alikes to avoid). Enjoy your gourmet gathering!

27

Make a daisy chain.

There are all sorts of things you can do with daisies (remember, "He loves me, he loves me not") but none prettier than a daisy chain. Start your chain by crossing two stems at right angles. See how the vertical stem lies over the horizontal one and loops behind it, making it lie alongside the horizontal stem. This method prevents tying any knots in the stems which would fray them. Now add another verticle stem over the two horizontal ones and loop it as shown. Continue in this way until your chain is as long as you would like it. Finish it off by weaving any loose strands in among the others for a neat look.

Dandelions also make good chains. First snap the flowers off the stems, and then make links by inserting the smaller end of the stem into the larger. Stems with flowers can later be woven into the chain to add some color.

28

Dye some yarn with plants.

Dyeing with natural dyes is fun and easy to do. Wool takes dyes more readily than cotton or other fibers, so why not dye some yarn that you (or your mother) can make into something? Knit up a handsome scarf, or some mittens. Stitch a needlepoint pillow or a wallhanging for your room.

You need to boil up some leaves, bark, or nutshells to extract your dye. (In general, you need two pounds of fresh materials, and one pound of nutshells, bark, or berries in order to dye a pound of yarn.) Strain the dye and put it into a large kettle filled with enough water to cover the wool. (Your wool should be sitting in a mordant bath, made the previous day from 4 ounces of alum mixed with one ounce of cream of tartar in a kettle of water. Add your wool and bring it to a boil. Cook for one hour, then let sit overnight.) Add the mordanted wool and place this kettle on the stove (have your parents help whenever you use the stove). Poke the wool gently with a spoon as the water gets hot, and the wool takes on the color you want (remember it will be lighter when it's dry). Let the wool cool in the kettle. Rinse it with cool water until the rinse water runs clear. Gently squeeze the water from the wool and hang the yarn to dry in a shaded spot. Now get out your knitting needles!

Goldenrod flowers will turn your wool yellow-brown. Bark from a maple tree will yield a rosy-tan dye. Onion skins will dye wool a burnt orange color.

 ## A rose is a rose

Colors are commonly given descriptive names, and many are the names of plants. Just think of grass green, lemon yellow or tomato red. Some colors are the names of the fruits themselves, such as orange or peach. In and out of fashion come such shades as avocado, aubergine (or eggplant), and apricot, to name a few.

Think of the many shades of green, yellow, orange, red, and purple with plants as part of their names. What about blue? Well, there's robin's egg blue, and sky blue, for instance, but you won't come up with too many plant names that are blue. Unless you think of blueberry blue, but then, aren't blueberries really more purple than blue . . .

July

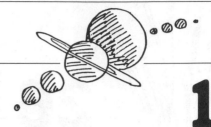

29

Show how the sun makes day and night.

Despite the fact that we say the sun rises and sets, the sun does not move at all! It's our earth, turning on its axis, that provides the movement, giving the illusion that the sun makes its way across the sky each day.

Do you remember how you used a globe (on *January 3*) to show how the earth was tilted in relation to the sun, to explain the seasons? You can use that same globe to show how the earth makes one complete revolution every twenty-four hours, to explain night and day. Or you can demonstrate night and day with just you and a light source. When you are facing the light, it is day (pretend the United States is situated on the tip of your nose). Turn around slowly. When your back is facing the light, it is night. And so on.

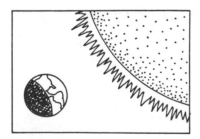

. . . .

Q: What is dark but made from light?
A: A shadow.

30

Name some of the ways the sun affects nature.

Ancient peoples worshipped the sun, and no wonder! Without the sun there would be no life on earth. The sun provides our planet with the necessary ingredients—heat and sunlight—for plants to grow, and the plants, in turn, feed all the animals on earth, ourselves included. But did you know that the sun does even more?

The sun is responsible for wind, created when warm air rises and cooler air moves in to take its place (see *March 4* for more on wind); the warmth from the sun also causes evaporation, which sends moisture into the air to later return to earth as precipitation (a fancy word for rain and snow). The sun also plays a part in certain rhythms, such as movement of tides (it shares this job with the moon) and the changing of the seasons. Which is your favorite season? The sun is even responsible for all the colors we see (see evidence of this on *April 12* when looking for a rainbow). Did you ever wonder why everything looks black at night?

Our sun may just be a medium-sized star (one of more than 200 million in our galaxy alone!) but seeing how it's in the right place at the right time, we owe a lot to this life-giving sphere.

. . . .

Scientists think the sun is 5 billion years old.

31

Read a story or poem about the sun.

We may no longer worship the sun, but we continue to be spellbound by this fiery ball in the sky. Does a sunny day put you in a sunny mood? Let some of these stories and poems light up your day!

Crayons
Marchette Chute *(poem)*

Spider in the Sky
adapted by Anne Rose *(story)*

Sun After Rain
Norma Farber *(poem)*

Sun Grumble
Claudia Fregosi *(story)*

The Sun's Asleep Behind the Hill
Mirra Ginsburg *(story)*

1

Make a display of the planets.

Our earth isn't the only planet that has a special relationship with the sun. There are eight other planets that revolve around the sun, some too close to it to support any life (it's much too hot), some too far from the sun's warming rays (brrrrr). Can you name the other planets in our solar system? Did you know that six of the other eight planets also have moons?

You can make a table-top display of the planets with foods and things found right in your kitchen (well, you may not keep a beach ball there). Use the chart below to round up the foods, or roll small bits of colored clay or play dough into balls that match the relative sizes shown.

Sun - beach ball (27″)

Mercury - tiny pea (³⁄₃₂″)

Venus - pea (¼″)

Earth - pea (¼″)

Mars - small pea (⅛″)

Jupiter - orange (2¾″)

Saturn - tangerine (2¼″)

Uranus - walnut (1″)

Neptune - walnut (1″)

Pluto - small pea (⅛″)

Here's a good way to remember the planets in their proper order: *Men Very Early Made Jars Serve Useful Needs, Period.*

August brings the sheaves of corn,
Then the harvest home is borne.

2

Use the sun to dry some foods.

Have you ever heard the expression, "It's so hot you could fry an egg on the sidewalk"? Do you think you could really do this? Why not let the sun "bake" some foods for you instead. How about some raisins or dried apple slices?

The sun is still used to dry foods throughout the world. (The drier continents, especially, rely on this method of preserving food.) All you need is a screen on which to lay the food—preferably a cloth screen or a piece of loosely woven cotton fabric stapled to a frame (metal screens, no matter how clean, give food a metallic taste). Peel and slice apples; pluck the grapes off the stems. To speed up the drying, you can blanch your food—by boiling it in water for 2 to 3 minutes and cooling it immediately with cold running water—but this isn't necessary for fruits. Lay the food on the screen and cover it with more screening (try to keep the covering from touching the food). Find a sunny spot to lay your screen and keep an eye on the weather. Turn the foods now and again to insure even drying. It's hard to say how long it will take the foods to dry—much depends on the weather. A temperature between 70° and 80° accompanied by a breeze is ideal. You can always finish up the job in a warm oven if the sky clouds over.

3

Make some solar prints.

Did you know that you can use the sun to make art? With special light-sensitive paper, you can make solar prints of leaves and flowers, and just about anything that will hold still for a few minutes! Many nature center gift shops, and toy and hobby shops, carry this special paper. Ask for sun-printing paper.

Carefully arrange your items on the paper (some paper comes in a kit that includes a sheet of clear plexiglass that can be used to hold the objects steady and flat on your paper). Expose the paper to sunlight for about five minutes. Then, remove the objects and put the paper in water to "fix" the image (your print is now permanent). The objects you placed on the paper will show up white; the background will be a rich, dark blue.

Frame your prints and hang them, or use them to create more art. Trace around the outlines to make pictures that you can color, or make a collage with lots of different solar prints. Cut the sheets of paper into smaller sizes and use them to make greeting cards. Just glue the prints onto folded note cards for some original art-by-mail.

Closing time

If you didn't have a sundial in your garden to tell you when it was time to eat lunch, you could just plant the right types of flowers that would let you know! That's what the 18th century naturalist, Carl von Linné did (also known as Linnaeus—see *April 30* for more on this man). By watching for the opening and closing of the blossoms, he claimed the "clock" was accurate to within half an hour on a sunny day. Do you think this really works? Plant some of these flowers to find out!

6 am - Spotted cat's ear *(opens)*
7 am - African marigold *(opens)*
8 am - Mouse-ear hawkweed *(opens)*
9 am - Prickly sow thistle *(closes)*
10 am - Common nipplewort *(closes)*
11 am - Star-of-Bethlehem *(opens)*
Noon - Passion flower *(opens)*
1 pm - Childing pink *(closes)*
2 pm - Scarlet pimpernel *(closes)*
3 pm - Hawkbit *(closes)*
4 pm - Small bindweed *(closes)*
5 pm - White water lily *(closes)*
6 pm - Evening primrose *(opens)*

4

Make a sundial.

One of the ways that people told time long ago was with a sundial (or shadow clock as it was sometimes known). A sundial will only work on a sunny day, of course, so other early timekeepers included a water clock that measured time as the water dripped, and sand clocks, much like the egg-timers still in use today.

You can turn back the clock and tell time with a sundial yourself! All you need is some thin cardboard, a protractor, and a 12″ square block of wood or heavy cardboard. Cut a right-angle triangle from the thin board, matching the dimensions shown in diagram #1 (use the protractor to measure the angles). This is the gnomon. Fold it along the dotted line (scoring with a knife first) and tape upright on the wood block. See diagram #2 for positioning (you may need to brace the gnomon with a second smaller triangle).

Place the sundial on a flat surface outdoors with the triangle's highest point facing south. Starting early in the day, every hour on the hour, mark the line where the gnomon's shadow falls. Write down the hour next to each line. The next sunny day you'll be able to tell time by reading the shadows. Is it time for lunch yet?

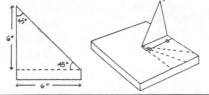

August

5

Catch a firefly.

Fireflies, sometimes known as lightning bugs, are actually neither flies nor bugs but a type of beetle that uses flashing lights as a means of attracting mates. Both sexes flash signals, although the females of most species are wingless and signal from the ground. Can you notice the variations of color, ranging from yellows to greens? You can even detect differences in the timing of the signals. Different species hope, no doubt, to attract only their own kind with their particular flashing.

Who can resist trying to catch fireflies? You can use a net, gently sweeping the air, or position yourself with an open jar, ready to clamp down the lid when you've captured one of these elusive insects. Fireflies prefer tall grass to mowed lawns, so keep this in mind. The beetles usually start signaling at dusk and continue until midnight, and can be witnessed from mid-summer until early autumn.

You may be astonished by how very ordinary these insects look in the light. They are smaller than their bright lights suggest and are a dull brown color.

. . . .

As you might have guessed, glowworms are the larvae of fireflies.

6

Listen for nocturnal animals.

The night comes alive with the sounds of nocturnal animals starting their "day." You don't need to live near a wild area to hear a number of different animals that have adapted to foraging and hunting for food once the sun has gone down. Raccoons, skunks, and mice are among the mammals that live near people. They benefit, in fact, from our habit of storing trash outdoors and from planting food gardens in our backyards.

Why do these animals come out at night? Many are sensitive to the sun's drying effects (these are mostly insects and amphibians); others hope to avoid competing for the same foods with daytime feeding animals. Many welcome the protection that the dark provides.

Notice how many of these nocturnal animals have large eyes (to be able to see in low light); their hearing and sense of smell are particularly acute. Some animals, such as bats, have a specially developed way of getting around in the dark called echolocation. Nearly 700 of the 1,000 bat species worldwide use this method of emitting high-pitched sounds which bounce off nearby objects, returning to the bats' ears as echoes. Bats dart out of the way of stationary objects (and hone in on the flying insects that they eat) by judging the distance between themselves and whatever blocks the sound waves.

7

Watch for the opening of night-blooming flowers.

The plants of night-blooming species that you started from seed (see *May 24*) or purchased as plants, should be blossoming soon. Make it a point to watch these lovely oddities open some evening. You might even witness the arrival of nocturnal moths that pollinate these plants, much as bees and butterflies do with plants that bloom during the daylight hours.

How do these moths find these plants in the dark of night? The heavy fragrances of these blooms suggest that the moths are attracted to the scent of these flowers. They are probably aided by sight, as well, because you'll notice that many of these flowers are white and stand out in the darkness, reflecting what light they can from the heavens.

. . . .

The moonflower is the night-blooming relative of the morning glory.

8

Read a story or poem about night.

The night is a time for quiet, and for sleep, but not for everyone! Read one of these stories or poems to see who's out and about at night. (For related works about stars and the moon, see *February 24*.)

At Night
Aileen Fisher *(poem)*

Grandfather Twilight
Barbara Berger *(story)*

Night in the Country
Cynthia Rylant *(story)*

The Night Is a Big Black Cat
G. Orr Clark *(poem)*

The Silent Concert
Mary Leister *(story)*

Night is a shadow, the earth itself blocking the sun.

9

Notice how your senses are affected by the dark.

When you are outdoors, concentrate on how your own senses respond to the darkness of night. We rely so much on our eyes, that our other senses are sometimes forgotten. It takes the human eye as long as 45 minutes to become fully receptive to the dark, but even then our eyes are not nearly as useful in low light as an owl's eyes are, for instance. What about smell and touch and hearing?

You might come to the conclusion that human beings are not particularly well equipped to be out and about at night! It's true that we tend not to trust our other senses as much as sight. But take a moment to really listen in the dark, and to smell and feel your surroundings, even if you have to close your eyes or blindfold yourself. Do the little sounds of night come alive? Do you think you might be able to identify a tree by touch?

Close your eyes during the day sometimes, too. You will discover the fabulous variety of textures and sounds and smells that are a part of nature.

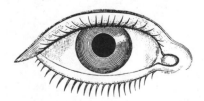

10

View the summer constellations.

You'll find some of your old friends (the Big and Little Dippers, for instance) in the summer sky, and some new ones. Easy to spot in late summer are three very bright stars that form a triangle, although each belongs to charted constellations of its own. Look for this trio, composed of the stars Deneb, Vega, and Altair.

You'll also be able to find the Northern Crown, Corona Borealis (see *February 20* for more on this cluster of stars), and some other fascinating constellations. Cygnus, the Swan, is commonly known as the Northern Cross, and it does resemble a cross (although it's not hard to see a swan, either). The swan's feet are formed by Deneb, one of the three bright stars mentioned earlier.

Enjoy the balmy summer nights, but don't forget your insect repellent, something with long sleeves to put on if it gets cold, and a comfortable place to watch from. (See *February 19* for more hints on stargazing.)

11

Watch for meteor showers.

Wow! Fireworks in August! Well, not quite, but meteor showers are just as exciting. Around August 10-13, stargazers stay up late to watch the Perseid shower, an eagerly awaited summertime event. An average of 65 meteors light up the sky each hour as they move towards the earth. The best time for viewing is after midnight, but you'll see plenty earlier.

One hundred million meteors are thought to enter the earth's atmosphere each day (!), most vaporizing high in the air. Occasionally fragments fall to earth, but this is a rare occurrence. When actual pieces of rock are found, they are known as meteorites.

While shooting stars (as they are popularly known) can be seen on almost any clear night, there are certain times during the year, such as in August, when large numbers of them can be seen. The Perseid shower is actually the second largest of the annual meteor showers. The most spectacular takes place around January 1-3 and is known as the Quadrantids. An average of 100 meteors can be seen making their descent each hour at that time.

The sky is falling!

The following table lists those annual meteor showers that are eagerly anticipated by stargazers.

Pull up a comfortable chair, grab a warm blanket, and watch the show!

Date	Shower	Location in the Sky	
January 1-3	Quadrantids	E	between Boötes and head of Draco
April 20-22	Lyrids	NE	between Vega and Hercules
May 4-6	Eta-Aquarids	E	SW of the Square of Pegasus
August 10-13	Perseids	NE	from Perseus
October 20-23	Orionids	E	between Orion and Gemini
November 3-10	Taurids	NE	between Taurus, Auriga and Perseus
December 10-12	Geminids	E	near Castor in Gemini

August

If you have "your head in the clouds," you are said to be confused!

12

Learn some of the cloud formations.

Why are there no clouds on some days and a whole sky full of them on other days? There is always moisture in the air (see *April 1*), but it bunches together into clouds only when the conditions are right. The tiny droplets of water need something to cling to, such as dust or pollen; the air temperature and wind play a part, too. Some clouds are light and wispy, others heavy and dark. Do you know what some of these clouds are called?

Clouds were first categorized and named in 1803 by a British pharmacist named Luke Howard. He came up with the three basic groups: *cirrus* (from the Latin for "lock of hair"), *cumulus* ("heap") and *stratus* ("spread out"). The modern classification of clouds uses Howard's three terms plus *alto* (meaning "high") and *nimbus* ("dark rain cloud"). These terms are combined into various combinations to cover ten basic cloud formations. The box on this page shows these clouds and where in the sky to look for them.

13

Make cloud pictures.

Have you ever looked up into the sky and thought the clouds looked like huge cotton balls floating on air? These were probably cumulus clouds, puffy shapes that form close to the earth. Why not use some cotton balls to make some cloud pictures?

You can even make a three dimensional cloud chart with cotton! (Let the box below guide you.) Bunch up the cotton balls for those dense clouds; stretch the cotton out to show the wispy ones. White glue will hold the cotton in place. Add a little grey paint (mix black and white for different shades of grey) to add realism to the gloomy rain clouds.

14

Create a cloud in your kitchen.

For even more realism, create a cloud in your own home! You can even make it rain. You've probably noticed the steam that comes out of the kettle spout when you boil water for cocoa, coffee, or tea. This steam is formed as the water vapor escaping from the kettle meets the colder air beyond (water vapor is normally invisible). The steam is a cloud, not too different from the clouds we see in the sky.

To make it rain, you need to hold a cold object (such as a metal spoon or a cold cookie sheet) in the way of the water vapor. (Have your parents help you here; steam is very hot and can burn you.) The vapor will con- dense quickly and little drops of water will form and fall. This is "rain"!

This experiment demonstrates what happens when clouds form and it rains, although the process in nature is a more gradual one. It is the sun, heating water in rivers, lakes, and the oceans that causes the rising vapor, rather than a stove.

Clearing the clouds

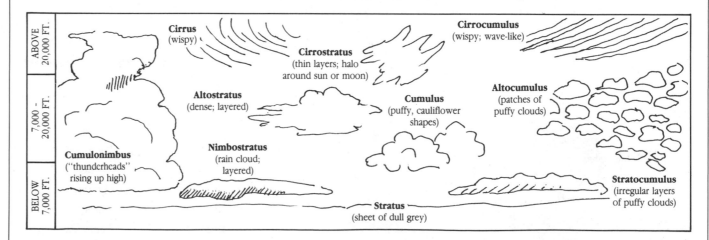

ABOVE 20,000 FT.

7,000 - 20,000 FT.

BELOW 7,000 FT.

Cirrus (wispy)

Cirrocumulus (wispy; wave-like)

Cirrostratus (thin layers; halo around sun or moon)

Altostratus (dense; layered)

Cumulus (puffy, cauliflower shapes)

Altocumulus (patches of puffy clouds)

Cumulonimbus ("thunderheads" rising up high)

Nimbostratus (rain cloud; layered)

Stratocumulus (irregular layers of puffy clouds)

Stratus (sheet of dull grey)

15

Predict the weather by watching clouds.

Weather prediction is certainly a science, and even the scientists don't always have it right! Meteorologists (those who study the atmosphere) take into account many factors when making weather predictions. They know that air temperature and pressure and humidity play a part in determining the changes that will take place. They use lots of fancy tools and instruments to help them, but they also can tell a lot just by looking at the sky.

You can make some weather predictions yourself by looking at the clouds. Do you see those wispy clouds high in the sky? Those are cirrus clouds, and they are the first sign of an approaching warm front. A warm front brings moisture (when the water vapor in the warm front collides with a mass of cold air, it condenses), so rain or snow may be on the way. Stratus clouds (layered clouds that lie low) often bring precipitation. Nimbostratus clouds are so thick that they completely block the sun. The puffy cumulus clouds usually indicate fair weather, especially when there is plenty of space between them. So don't worry about rain when you are lying on the grass watching *these* clouds go by.

. . . .

Fog is actually a low lying cloud, often forming at night.

16

Read a story or poem about clouds.

Have you ever watched a story unfolding in the clouds? Some of these writers have. Let your imagination soar when you stare at the clouds. What do you see?

The Cloud Mobile
May Swenson *(poem)*

Clouds from **Mouse Tails**
Arnold Lobel *(story)*

Dragon Smoke
Lilian Moore *(poem)*

The Rain Cloud
Mary Rayner *(story)*

Small Cloud
Ariane *(story)*

17

Slice a hailstone in half.

You would expect the only precipitation in summer to be rain, wouldn't you? Rain certainly is the most common thing to fall from clouds (except in the higher elevations where it continues to snow), but have you ever been in a hailstorm? Ouch!

Hailstones are formed in thunderclouds, where they start out as rain, but are something else again by the time they hit the ground. The drops are hurled and tossed about within the thunderclouds, and each is coated with many layers of ice as it goes on this wild journey. Most hailstones are the size of small grapes, but many become even larger—as big as tennis balls, in some cases! As you can imagine, hailstones can be very destructive. Fields of crops can be flattened within minutes. Even cars can get dented.

If you can get a hailstone without endangering yourself, bring it indoors and slice it in half with a sharp knife (have your parents help you). Can you see the layers?

18

Look for the trails made by jets.

Have you ever looked up into the sky and noticed a long white cloud arching across the sky? Is it really a cloud? Well, yes and no. What you are seeing is a trail left by a jet-propelled airplane (sometimes it is so high up that you can't even see the plane). Pilots prefer to fly in a part of the sky known as the stratosphere, which is from 5 to 11 miles above the earth, above the clouds and winds. The moisture from their engines condenses, forming clouds of fine ice crystals that slowly dissolve. They are man-made clouds, certainly, but clouds nonetheless!

. . . .

A good place to keep a cloud chart is in the glove compartment of your car. When you are out for a drive, you can check to see what kinds of clouds are in the sky.

August

Coal is a rock that formed when huge fern-like plants decayed millions of years ago and were pressurized. Petroleum is mainly of animal origin—in this case single-celled marine animals.

19

Get to know some rocks and minerals.

The terms "rocks and minerals" are so often lumped together, have you ever wondered what the difference is? Minerals come first, actually. They are either elements or chemical compounds that are found naturally on earth. More than 1,500 minerals have been identified, although only about 150 are considered common or widespread. Minerals are a diverse group, and include such members as common table salt, graphite (use in pencils), gold, and diamonds.

Rocks, on the other hand, are the solids that are composed of one or more minerals. Aha. To confuse things slightly, rocks are further classified by how they were formed. The three categories are *igneous* (rock that was formed when hot, molten materials cooled), *sedimentary* (rock created by settling particles), and *metamorphic* (rock that underwent change with intense heat and/or pressure). Take limestone, for instance. This is a sedimentary rock made up chiefly of the mineral calcite. However, under pressure this can become marble, a very different looking and feeling rock, but one composed of an identical mineral.

The field of mineralogy is complex, but you can have some real fun getting acquainted with the ground on which you stand!

20

Name some things made from minerals.

Did you know that an entire period in the early history of man was known as the Stone Age? This was a time when tools and weapons were made from rock. The Bronze and Iron Ages followed, when more sophisticated uses for minerals, especially those we call metals, were found. In modern times we rely heavily on minerals, from gold (the standard of world currency) to granite (a stone that is used for building).

As you go about your day, note how minerals play a part in everyday life. Your house might be constructed of stone, or brick, or concrete block, in whole or in part, not to mention the glass in windows and various other metals used both structurally and for decorative purposes. Most likely you will cook and eat your meals in either metallic or pottery containers, seasoning with salt, perhaps. During the course of the day, you may ride in a car, watch television, write with a pencil, read a book by lamp light. Minerals play an important role in all of these activities. Try to imagine how your life would be without the many minerals we make use of each day.

Birth brights

Assigning each month a birthstone dates back thousands of years. (Actually, each astrological sign had its own birthstone originally.) Which is your birthstone?

What's your stone?

Opal, what's yours?

January - Garnet
February - Amethyst
March - Bloodstone
April - Diamond
May - Emerald
June - Pearl *(the only organic choice)*
July - Ruby
August - Sardonyx
September - Sapphire
October - Opal
November - Topaz
December - Turquoise

21

Examine a gem.

Do you remember Dorothy's ruby slippers in the *Wizard of Oz?* They were endowed with fabulous magical powers. Is there anything truly magical about gemstones (or gems, for short)?

Gems are simply minerals with ornamental value. Current fashion dictates what a gem is worth, although each kind possesses certain inherent characteristics. Hardness and durability, color (and sometimes transparency), and rarity are all taken into account when evaluating gemstones. Some, like rubies, emeralds, and sapphires are considered precious; others, such as garnets and amethysts are semiprecious. The two terms don't mean anything scientifically.

Take a close look at some gems. Does your mother have a diamond engagement ring, perhaps, or an heirloom brooch set with her birthstone? Have you ever seen the jewelry made by the Indians of the southwest? They favor turquoise, which is polished into rounded cabochons (rather than cut into facets) and set in silver. Some gems, such as opals, have "fire" in them, colorful specks that glimmer. Some even have star shapes that reflect light. Ask a friendly jeweler to show you some of the beautiful gems he has for sale, too.

22

Hunt for fossils.

Dinosaurs may come to mind when you think of fossils, but they are only one example of the remains of animals and plants that have been preserved over the years (billions of years, in some cases). The frozen carcasses of woolly mammoths are also fossils, as is amber, a glassy substance that once was the resin of now extinct coniferous trees. Have you ever found any fossils?

If you live near an area that has a lot of sedimentary rock, such as shale, limestone, or sandstone, you have a good chance of coming across some fossils. Ammonites and trilobites are fairly common. These sea creatures were turned to stone, as it were, when their bodies were covered with sediment in the bottom of the sea. Over millions of years, minerals gradually took the place of organic matter, and their shapes were preserved in the stone.

Remember that much of the earth was formerly covered by water, so you don't need to hunt near the shore to find fossilized sea creatures. Look for fossils in quarries (get permission to do this), or where roads have recently been blasted through bedrock. And be on the lookout for the imprints of plants and other flat objects. Happy hunting!

23

See how the earth's face is changing.

We use the term "as hard as rock," but we tend to forget that rocks undergo change. Softer stones are subject to erosion by wind and water, and even harder rocks wear away. Quick changes take place when there are earthquakes and volcanoes.

Did you know that more than a million earthquakes occur worldwide each year? (We can only feel a few thousand of them, and only an average of 15 or so each year are significant.) The earth's crust is not a continuous layer of rock, but is broken into large areas known as plates, that are continually shifting and jostling one another. Most earthquakes occur when there is an abrupt shift in the earth's plates.

Most volcanoes occur in the same areas where there are earthquakes. The colliding plates sometimes create an opening from which magma, or molten (hot, liquid) rock, is released from deep within the earth. You may never see a volcano in action, but there are plenty of remnants of volcanic explosions. There are crater lakes (bodies of water that collect in the depressions left by volcanoes) and volcanic necks (lava plugs left standing long after the elements erased the volcano itself).

24

Read a story or poem about rocks.

Scientists, naturalists, and artisans aren't the only ones who feel strongly about rocks. Here are some solid pieces about rocks you will enjoy reading.

All Upon a Stone
Jean Craighead George *(story)*

The Mountain That Loved a Bird
Alice McLerran *(story)*

Old Stones
Elizabeth Coatsworth *(poem)*

Rolling Stones
Aileen Fisher *(poem)*

Skipper Stones
Aileen Fisher *(poem)*

. . . .

"Rocks" is slang for diamonds.

25

Look for rock formations.

Whenever you are in the car, keep an eye out for unusual rock formations. You can literally drive through bedrock—that is when you are driving on a road that has been blasted through a hillside. Although the crust of the earth is 3 to 22 miles thick, the folds and configurations you see from the road can give you an idea of what lays beneath our feet.

In some parts of the country you will see huge boulders plunked down in the middle of meadows. These we know were swept along by glaciers plowing their way through valleys. Out west there are carved "bridges" and spires of rock that have been eroded by wind and water. Even mountains offer clues to their formation. Some are jagged arrangements known as fault-block mountains; others resemble giant wavelike folds that run parallel to one another. Some mountains are actually volcanoes, extinct in many cases; active in others.

August

26

Visit a rock shop.

What can you expect to find in a rock shop? Just about anything your heart desires if you are a rock hound. If you'd like to get started collecting rocks and minerals, a rock shop is a good place to begin. Look at all the samples that are on display and for sale. You'll notice that most are very small. You should keep this in mind when you are collecting your own samples. Rocks may seem plentiful, but you should take only what you need.

You'll find tools for collecting (all of which can be substituted with tools you may already have at home), field guides, and ideas for displaying your finds. The nice thing about rock shops is that so much is out in the open for you to touch. Don't be afraid to ask the shop owners any questions you have. Rock and mineral enthusiasts are always happy to make new friends!

27

Start a rock collection.

A rock collection can be anything you want it to be. You might choose to limit your collection to rocks found in your area, or in your state, or you might want to extend your horizons and add rocks from far-off places.

When you are off on a rock expedition, don't forget to pack a hammer, a chisel, and protection for yourself (gloves and goggles—you can even use a diving mask or swimming goggles). Take along some tape, a pen, and a notebook. It is best to mark your specimens on the spot with a bit of tape, giving each an identification number that can be matched to information that you enter into the notebook—such as where and when the specimen was found. Wrap crumbly rock (or delicate samples such as fossils) in newspaper. Remember to take only the smallest bits of rock.

The tops of shoe boxes make excellent display cases. Just glue the rocks in place and label them. Or put them to use, much as you did pebbles from the beach (see *July 15*). If your specific collection lacks a sample or two, perhaps you can purchase the missing pieces from your local rock shop or one of the science suppliers.

28

Dig a hole in the ground.

While turning over some soil in the garden in the spring, you may have noticed how the soil was layered (differing in color and in texture). Dig a hole now, in a place that will present no danger to people or pets, and look closely at the layers. Uppermost is the topsoil, the darkest layer of soil, which usually contains plenty of organic matter (especially if it is rich and fertile). The depth of this layer can range from a few inches to six feet. The second layer, known as subsoil, is lighter in color and contains little organic material, but it plays an important role in drainage. (Fertile soil that is waterlogged can only sustain certain types of plants.) Beneath this is what is called the parent material or matter, consisting mostly of broken rock. The final and lowest layer is the bedrock.

How deep were each of the layers you uncovered? What kind of plants do you think will grow best on this soil?

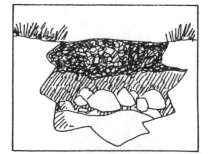

29

Visit a quarry or mine.

The region that you live in may have rock quarries where huge stones are cut from hillsides, or you may know of mineral deposits that are mined. Quarries and mines that are in current use are not always open to the public, but some are, so ask if you can visit. Modern machinery bears some of the burden of cutting, lifting, and moving the vast quantities of rock that are quarried from the earth. Do you remember how the pyramids were built, with only human muscle power?

Your area might also boast some natural attractions such as caves, or trails through unusual rock formations. There are more than 140 cave sights open to the public in the United States; in fact, the world's longest cave system is in this country. Mammoth Cave, in Kentucky, has 200 miles of passageways!

If you ever come across what you think is a cave, do not enter it on your own. Spelunking (as the hobby of exploring caves is called) is a potentially dangerous activity, and one that requires certain skills and equipment.

. . . .

Some caves have magnificent structures rising from the floor or hanging overhead. Stalagmites form on cave floors; stalactites "drip" from ceilings. To remember which is which, think of stalac*tites* holding *tight* to the ceiling.

30

Make some rock candy.

What snack might you take with you when you go rock hunting? Rock candy, of course! Did you know that you could make your own rock candy (or candy crystals, as they are sometimes known)?

Pour half a cup of water into a saucepan, and bring it to a boil. Add about a cup of sugar to the water, spoonful by spoonful, stirring so that the sugar completely dissolves. Keep adding the sugar until it is a clear syrup. Take care that the syrup doesn't boil over (have your parents help you, in any case, at the stove). Let the syrup cool for about ten minutes before carefully pouring it into a glass that has a weighted string hanging in it. (Tie a paper clip to the string for a weight.)

This part was easy. Waiting for the crystals to form might be harder. It will take about a week before there are crystals forming along the string. Check the glass every day, and carefully break the crust that forms on the top of the syrup, to allow evaporation to continue. The less the solution is disturbed the better the crystal formation will be. Yum!

31

Make rock rubbings.

Rocks have all sorts of interesting surface textures, and you can make rock rubbings the same way you rubbed tree bark (see *February 9*). This is a handy way to record something about those large rocks that you just can't bring home with you. You might want to include some rock rubbings in your rock collection. A profile of the rocks in your state, for instance, might include small specimens of various rocks, rock rubbings, photographs of local rocks used in architecture or sculptures, and relevant statistics. Or create some art for art's sake: a collage made from rock rubbings makes an interesting abstract piece of art. Something the Flintstones might hang in their living room!

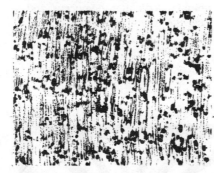

In 1975, someone with a sense of humor marketed an item known as the Pet Rock®. More than 1.2 million rocks were sold for $4.00 a piece (the rocks came with an *Owner's Manual*), and were said to be the perfect pet.

1

Make some paint from crushed rock.

Have you ever seen color photographs of the cave paintings in Lascaux, France? These powerful paintings (dating back over 15,000 years!) have also taught us what prehistoric peoples painted with. Their paints were generally made with crushed rock mixed with either water or animal blood or fat. Red clay mixed with blood gave them red; yellow was made with ocher, a clay containing iron oxide. White paints were made from white clay or lime; and black was either charcoal or ground-up manganese ore.

Modern paints are still made with many natural pigments (see *November 13* for more on nature's art supplies), and you can make your own paint right at home. Look for nicely colored material (such as clay or crumbly rock) and crush it into a fine powder. (Use a hammer or a mortar and pestle.) This is your pigment. To turn it into paint, you need to bind it with a medium. Try liquid starch or soap flakes mixed with water. Corn starch and even corn syrup can be used. Egg yolks are also a possibility (these are actually used to create a paint known as egg tempera).

Other binders can be found at an art supply store. Glues and polymers are used in commercial paints and can be bought for making your own. Read the labels on tubes of watercolors or oil paints to see what minerals are used for the various colors. You might get some ideas for your own paints.

Earth works

Did you know that pottery fragments have been found that are 9,000 years old? Prehistoric peoples discovered that clay could be shaped when wet, yet it would harden when it dried (or, better still, was baked at high temperatures). Have you ever made anything from clay?

If you have a clay deposit near your home, you can dig up some free clay. (Otherwise pick up some at a craft or hobby shop.) Roll long, thin ropes of clay to coil into jars. Or roll it out into thick slabs that can be joined together at the seams (just wet the clay at those points). Clay can be imprinted with all sorts of objects. Use your own fingers to pinch and poke the wet clay; or press shells and fleshy leaves into the clay for some designs from nature.

Note: Your clay will harden at room temperature, but it will never be waterproof. You can seal it with acrylic paints, if you'd like your pieces to hold water.

September

2

Look for autumn wildflowers.

Some plants don't flower until late summer or early autumn. In colder regions, these may be the last to bloom until the following spring.

You may know the lovely gentians, plants that grow in moist meadows and along steams. Most species are violet or blue, although there is a yellow gentian. Yellow is also the color of one of the most familiar fall flowers, the goldenrod. Goldenrods come in all sorts of shapes. Some are wand-like; others are full and feathery. People who suffer from hay fever often blame the goldenrod. Actually, ragweed and other wind-pollinated plants in bloom at the same time are the culprits. Goldenrod blossoms dye yarn a lovely golden color (see *July 28*).

Asters bloom in late summer, too. These plants, ranging in color from white to pale blue to deep purple, are sometimes confused with the flea-banes. (Fleabanes bloom earlier in the season, and have fuller looking blossoms.) The name aster comes from the Greek for "star." What color asters can you find growing near you? You may even have some in your garden. Asters, generally with showier blooms than the wild varieties, are popular garden plants.

3

Watch a September sunset.

Have you ever wondered why sunsets (and sunrises) are so colorful? When the sun is low on the horizon, its rays shine through the lower atmosphere, which is full of floating particles, from dust to industrial pollutants. The impurities scatter the light so that only the red and yellow wavelengths are visible to the human eye. In late summer, the amount of dust and pollen in the air is even greater, which is why sunsets this time of year are so spectacular.

In fact, you may have noticed how colorful sunsets are in urban areas. Air pollution plays a big part. Other air disturbances, such as dust storms and floating volcanic ash also contribute to unusual sunsets. Out west in dry, desert regions, the sunsets are especially vivid, as any cowboy who's ridden off into the sunset will tell you!

4

Look for flying ants.

Did you know that ants have wings? In late summer, the queens and males grow wings as part of the mating ritual.

Sometimes you'll see a whole swarm of flying ants. It's a pretty impressive sight, especially when you realize that all the males will die after this point in their lives. Their sole reason for living is to mate with the queen. Once they have fulfilled this bargain, they don't return to the colony. They are eaten by birds and other animals.

The queens, however, go into hibernation until the next spring. The eggs they lay will develop into the new generation of workers (the majority of ants—those that construct the colonies, look after the queens, and raise the young) and mating males.

5

Dig up some edible roots.

The roots of cultivated crops—carrots and beets, for instance—aren't the only plant roots that are delicious. This is a good time of year to dig up some of the edible roots that grow in the wild.

Cattail rhizomes (the proper name for the roots of this plant) are very good. In fact, the shoots, stalks, rhizomes and pollen are all edible! Cattails grow in marshy areas, so dress properly for wading in water. Take a spade with you to dig up the plants. Peel the rhizomes and cook them like potatoes, or dry them and pound them into a flour that can be used like wheat flour.

Other edible roots include the tubers of the day lily, which can be dug up any time after blooming; groundnut tubers; and Jerusalem artichokes, not artichokes at all, but native American sunflowers! Take only what you really need, because the plants have no way of regenerating when you take roots and all.

September

6

Make a seed chart.

On a breezy day in late summer or early autumn, you can witness one of the marvels of nature. Along roadsides and in untamed meadows, the air is often thick with the floating seeds of the thistle and milkweed plants. The downy parachutes sometimes travel several miles before settling to the ground! Why do you suppose they do this?

If the parent plant just dropped its seeds, the seeds wouldn't stand a chance. The parent plant (especially if it's a perennial that lives year after year in the same spot) is already using the available water and space and sunlight, so many seeds are designed to travel some distance to find a spot of bare earth.

Make a chart that shows some of the ways seeds get around. Divide a large sheet of paper or poster board into six sections, one for each method of dispersal. (See the box below.) Glue or tape down actual seeds as you find them. Many can be found this time of year, but check in the spring and summer, too.

Every which way

Seeds have some pretty clever ways of getting around. Check these out!

Helicopters
Maples
Elms
Ashes

Hitchhikers
Burdocks
Cockleburs
Beggar's ticks

Parachutists
Dandelions
Milkweeds
Thistles

Delectables
Apples
Cherries
Berries

Floaters
Coconuts
Cranberries
Lotuses

Missiles
Jewelweeds
Witch hazels
Wood sorrels

7

Collect wildflower seeds.

If you would like to attract a wide range of animals to your property, grow some wildflowers. Cultivated blooms are very lovely, but many birds, bees and butterflies prefer the native plants. How do you go about planting wildflowers?

You can buy seeds (and plants, too) for many native species, but why not collect your own seeds? On your walks through meadows look for plants that you would like to grow in your own garden or lawn. Mark the plants with some kind of waterproof marker (dab a bit of paint on the end of a stake), because when it's time to gather the seeds, many plants will have lost their petals. You may not recognize them. Collect the ripe seeds before they disperse. Only take what you really need.

Many wildflower seeds need several months of cold before they are ready to sprout. Either plant them in your garden now, where they will lay dormant until the spring, or put them in a plastic bag in the refrigerator until it's time to plant in the spring.

8

Make a burdock figure.

Burdocks are among the plants that send their seeds hitchhiking. Have you ever come home from a walk through an overgrown field with round burrs sticking to your clothing? Long-haired dogs have a rough time of it when they come in contact with burdocks, too. The barbed burrs get tangled in their fur in no time.

Burdock burrs not only stick to other things, they stick to one another. You can use burrs to make figures, such as people or animals. Or make them into a ball, or a pyramid. One man was so impressed by the way that burrs stick to things, that he began playing around with a man-made version. Do you know what he invented? You guessed it—Velcro®!

September

Remember to wash your hands after you handle wild mushrooms.

9

Plan a meal from your garden.

By now you've probably eaten a lot out of your garden. Why not plan an entire meal with the vegetables and fruits you've grown?

Ask your mother to help you come up with ways to creatively use the produce. Make a steaming vegetable soup, or toss some finely diced veggies into an omelette. Make a vegetarian pizza; toss a spectacular salad. And for dessert, serve up some slices of zucchini bread, or whip up a strawberry shortcake with some frozen strawberries that you picked earlier in the year.

Don't forget to include some edible flowers. Nasturtiums give salads a little punch! Other kinds of petals can be candied and used as edible decorations on cakes and cookies. Make your own candied violets, mint leaves, and rose petals. Paint the fresh, dry leaves and petals with a little beaten egg white (just whisk it for a minute or so). Dip each into some extra-fine granulated sugar, and let dry on a sheet of waxed paper.

10

Hunt for autumn mushrooms.

Autumn is one of the best times to go hunting for edible mushrooms. A walk through the woods in search of them is a treat for the senses. Everything smells so earthy. Just like mushrooms!

Some of the choice mushrooms you'll find include the boletes, oyster mushrooms, cauliflower fungus (how do you think this mushroom got its name?), and hen of the woods. Hen of the woods, growing near the ground on tree trunks and stumps looks just like the ruffled feathers of a sitting hen.

Don't eat **any** mushrooms unless you are ABSOLUTELY sure they aren't poisonous. Don't go by the pictures in a book. Have an *expert* make sure that the ones you have found are edible.

Look for artists' shelf fungus, a shelf mushroom that grows on dead trees. You can draw on the underside with a pencil (be careful not to leave any fingerprints). When the fungus dries, the drawing will be permanent.

11

Make mushroom spore prints.

Mushrooms reproduce by means of spores. (Remember mushrooms are a type of fungi, they aren't plants at all.) What do these spores look like? Make a spore print and find out.

You need to use a gilled mushroom, like the kind you buy in the supermarket. Remove the stem and place the mushroom flat side down on a sheet of dark construction paper. Cover the mushroom cap with a small bowl to keep any drafts from blowing away the tiny spores. Carefully lift the cap after several hours. Do you see the pattern the spores have made?

In nature, spores that land in moist soil or other favorable places develop into mycelium, an underground network of threads. Mycelium is often present for years, undetected until a rain makes the threads swell and pop through the soil. These swellings are mushrooms!

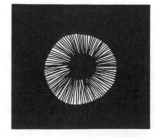

12

Make vegetable prints.

Potatoes are among the most versatile vegetables. You can bake them, boil them, mash them, and fry them. But did you know that you can also print with them?

Cut a potato in half and carve a design on the cut surface. Only the raised part will print, so cut away what you don't want to show. Let the potato dry for at least an hour (the ink will adhere better). Use real ink or slightly watered-down poster paints. Dip the potato into the ink, or brush it on carefully with a small brush. Press the potato onto paper, positioning it carefully so that it won't smudge.

Try printing with apples. They have a ready-made design right inside them! Cut an apple in half across its middle. Do you see the star-shaped cavity? Slice an orange in half for another interesting print (let citrus fruits dry for 2-5 days first). Slice green peppers, cauliflower and broccoli flowerets, and mushrooms for other unusual shapes.

Print your own greeting cards or wrapping paper (use a grocery bag split open). Experiment with different combinations of vegetables and fruits.

13

Bring houseplants indoors.

Any houseplants that have spent the summer outdoors should be brought back into the house soon. It is best to return them well before the heat is turned on, so that they can make the adjustment with no trouble. Even so, your plants will probably lose some of their leaves, so don't worry if this happens.

It's a good idea to wash your plants before you bring them indoors. If you can, isolate them from other plants for a while, too. A lot of insect pests move indoors right along with your plants. Keep an eye out for white flies, aphids, and spider mites. If you catch these insects before they get a chance to multiply, your plants will thank you.

14

Make a harvest figure.

Making harvest figures goes back a long way. In England, where *corn* refers to any grain, such as wheat, rye or oats, they are called corn dollies. Traditionally, the braided dollie represented the corn spirit that ensured a plentiful harvest. The dollie was made with the last sheaf of wheat in the fields, and saved until the following year when a new one was made.

Why not make a harvest figure from the plant Americans call corn? All you need to make a corn husk doll is some fresh or dried husks (soak the dry oncs in water to soften them), string, and a small bit of cotton.

Place the cotton in a piece of husk, twisting and tying it to make the head. Make arms by rolling a single strip of husk and tying it near the ends for hands. Slide the arms through the husk under the head. Tie the waist with string. Arrange five or six husks around the doll's waist (see the illustration) and tie them in place. Carefully fold them down to make a long skirt. Cut the skirt straight across at the hem for a woman; divide the skirt in two and tie each half at the ankles to make a man. Let the doll dry completely. May the harvest be a good one!

15

Bake a loaf of bread.

Do you and your family ever bake bread at home? There's nothing like a hot loaf fresh from the oven!

A very special loaf can be made in celebration of the harvest season. Some breads have two or three types of flour in them, but this one has seven grains! (See the recipe below.)

You may need to go to a health store to find the rye, barley, and rice flours, since most supermarkets only stock wheat flours. Gather all the ingredients together, read the recipe instructions carefully, and fill your house with the smell of freshly-baked bread!

Seven with one blow!

This bread is as delicious as it is nutritious!

Seven Grain Bread

1 envelope yeast	1 cup rye flour
2 cups lukewarm water (105-115°F)	1 cup whole wheat flour
1 teaspoon sugar	1 cup barley flour
1 cup rolled oats	½ cup rice flour
2 eggs, slightly beaten	½ cup cornmeal
1½ teaspoons salt	2-3 cups all-purpose flour
½ cup honey	

Dissolve the yeast and sugar in ½ cup of the lukewarm water. Pour the rest of the water over the oats in a large bowl. Let stand for 10 minutes. Add the yeast to the oats; then add the eggs, salt, and honey. Stir until well blended. Add the remaining ingredients, using as much all-purpose flour as you need to make a fairly stiff dough. Knead the dough on a lightly floured surface until it is smooth and elastic, about 10 minutes.

Place the dough in a large greased bowl, cover with a towel and let rise in a warm place until doubled in bulk, about 1½ hours. Punch down and knead briefly. Divide the dough into two equal pieces, shape into loaves and place in two greased loaf pans. Cover with a towel and let rise for about 1 hour.

Bake the loaves in a pre-heated oven (375°F) for about an hour, or until the tops are nicely browned and the loaves sound hollow when tapped on the bottom. Remove from the pans and cool on a rack. Makes 2 loaves.

September

16

Note the first frost.

The first frost of the season can take you by surprise, but you don't want to let that happen if you still have tomatoes on the vines, or other plants in the garden that will wither with cold. How do you know when the first frost will hit?

Well, you can't be sure without listening to a weather report every evening. But your local nursery will be able to tell you when the first expected frost will be. Based on records that are kept every year, they know when the autumn frost is likely to occur. But, of course, it does vary from year to year.

Why don't you keep a record of when the first killing frost of each year occurs? Make a note, too, of the last spring frost. This information can go into a gardening journal, and be referred to every year.

17

Watch for monarch butterflies.

Everyone has heard of birds migrating, and even whales and caribou, but did you know that a number of insects also travel long distances from summer to winter homes? The monarch butterfly is probably the best known of these, as millions of them head south, joining with others as they leave Canada and make their way to Florida and Mexico.

The butterflies that can be seen now are not the same that made their way north the preceding spring. Those that leave the warmer climate in spring lay eggs along the way, and are replaced by newly-hatched adults that continue the journey. But the adults that fly south in autumn are truly remarkable. For most, the journey is a 2,000 mile one!

Until we meet again

Birds and butterflies aren't the only animals that migrate. Some fish make long trips. You may have heard about salmon. They migrate from the streams where they are born to the Pacific Ocean, where they live two to five years before returning to the very same streams to spawn and die. Several species of turtle migrate, as do a number of mammals. Whales living off the coast of California and caribou in Canada make regular trips from breeding grounds to feeding grounds.

Other continents have their migratory species, as well. There are eels that hatch off the coast of South America that make a three year trip to Europe. There they live for several years before making the return journey to this side of the Atlantic to spawn and die.

18

Pot bulbs for indoor blooms.

The bulbs you plant in the garden now won't bloom until the spring (see *October 14*), but you can pot some that will bloom earlier indoors. Look for tulips, narcissus, and hyacinths wherever bulbs are sold.

Bulbs can be planted in pots with or without holes (use sand or small pebbles for containers that have no holes). Water them thoroughly and place them in a cold spot, such as an unheated basement, cold frame or even your refrigerator! (The temperature needs to be about 35° to 50°F.) Tulips require 12 to 14 weeks of cold; narcissus 10 to 12; and hyacinths and crocuses each need about 6 to 8 weeks. (See *December 6* for moving the bulbs indoors.)

Bulbs that are forced for indoor enjoyment can't be re-forced, nor do they do much if planted outdoors in the garden. Compost them and buy new ones the following year. There are some bulbs, though, such as amaryllis, freesia, and calla lilies, that *do* continue blooming for many years, with proper care. Their culture differs from the bulbs that bloom just the one time. Ask for them at your local nursery.

. . . .

You can root bulbs in water. There are clear vases specially shaped to cradle bulbs, with plenty of room for their roots.

September

19

Go on a hawk watch.

Most migrating birds fly at night. They spend their days resting and refueling for the long trip. But some fly by day, and among the most spectacular are the raptors, or birds of prey.

Hawks aren't the only ones that can be seen heading south during the day. (Eagles, storks, and pelicans all do the same.) They are just the most recognizable. Why do these birds fly during the sunlit hours? They need to fly during the day because they take advantage of rising warm air currents known as thermals. Watch these birds, rising in the air in a spiral. When they are high enough, they soar ahead to the next thermal mass. These enormous birds barely need to beat their wings to propel themselves!

The best thermals occur along cliffs and mountain ridges. Is there some place near you where you can go in search of the birds, which often travel hundreds at a time? Call your local nature center or science museum. They often organize hawk watches. Even if you can't get to a likely spot to watch from, look up in the sky whenever you have a chance. You may catch a glimpse of a few of the graceful gliders on their way south.

20

Watch the harvest moonrise.

The full moon in September is called the harvest moon, and it's a very special full moon. It rises in the sky at a much lower angle than usual. It looks like it's moving almost parallel with the horizon!

This full moon is huge, or at least that's the way it seems. When the full moon (any full moon) first clears the horizon, it's right behind the familiar shapes of trees and buildings. Once the moon is high in the sky it seems so much smaller, although, of course, the size never changes. Prove this by cutting a circle of paper to size when the moon is low and comparing it to the moon when it's way up high. (Do this indoors, tracing the moon on a thin piece of paper held against a window.) Because the harvest moon stays near the horizon for longer, it seems bigger than ever.

The harvest moon is often brilliantly colored when it first rises, too. Like the breathtaking red and orange sunsets of late summer and early fall (see *September 3*), the moon takes on these fiery colors because of all the dust and pollen in the air.

21

First day of autumn!

The 21st or 22nd of September signals the arrival of autumn, one of the most colorful seasons of the year. While it means the end of the growing season in most parts of the United States (at least the outdoor one), autumn is a wonderful time to be out-of-doors. Gone are the bothersome insects and the scorching heat of summer. There's lots to explore before the real cold and snows of winter set in.

Autumn is also called fall, although that term really belongs to the time when the leaves are falling from the trees. This day in September is actually the autumnal equinox. Like its counterpart in spring (see *March 20*), this means that the length of day equals that of night, everywhere on earth.

In recognition of the first day of autumn, plan a simple outing in the woods, or cook up a special harvest dish. Gather up some of the autumn-blooming wildflowers to decorate your home. Autumn's here at last!

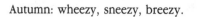

. . . .

Just after the death of the flowers,
And before they are buried in snow,
There comes a festival season
When Nature is all aglow.

22

Read a story or poem about autumn.

There's a special look, feel, and smell to autumn. What do you like best about this season?

Autumn Song
Elizabeth-Ellen Long *(poem)*

Fall from **The Four Seasons**
Jack Prelutsky *(poem)*

Harvest Home
Arthur Guiterman *(poem)*

Julian in the Autumn Woods
Milena Lukešová *(story)*

September

23

Look for woolly bear caterpillars.

Who doesn't know the woolly bear caterpillar? This hairy brown-banded black caterpillar is found everywhere this time of year. It is popularly thought that the wider the brown band, the worse the winter will be! There is no truth in this, of course.

What *is* true is that the woolly bear spends the winter curled up beneath logs and in hollows. Wrapped in its cocoon, it doesn't stir until spring, when it emerges as a rather plain and surprisingly delicate moth known as the Isabella tiger moth.

24

Watch for woodchucks.

The end of September is about the last time you'll see the woodchuck before it retreats to its winter den to hibernate. You can see woodchucks up on their haunches, or scurrying back to their burrows as they fatten up all they can before settling down for the winter.

Woodchucks spend their summers in one type of burrow, a complex network of underground chambers, often built into hillsides. Come September, they seek refuge under the roots of trees. The tangle of growth offers them some protection when they are in the defenseless state of hibernation. (For more on hibernation, see *January 17*.)

Woodchucks are among a number of animals that truly hibernate. They spend roughly half of their lives in this state! A good deal of attention is paid them, possibly because of the annual observance to which they lend their other common name—Groundhog Day (see *February 2*).

25

Watch squirrels hoarding food.

Throughout the fall, squirrels are busy gathering food that will help carry them through winter. Here's another myth you may have heard. The more food the squirrels are seen hoarding, the worse the winter will be! Once again, our furry friends can't be trusted as weather predictors.

It is also commonly supposed that squirrels remember where they've buried nuts, and later return to dig them up. Squirrels actually rely on their sense of smell. Some hidden nuts that they don't unearth sprout and grow to become trees.

What kind of squirrels do you have on your property or in a nearby park? Are there any red squirrels in residence? These are smaller than gray squirrels, and not quite as noisy! There are also nocturnal squirrels known as flying squirrels. They don't actually fly, but with the help of wide flaps of skin, they can glide for up to 30 feet from one tree to another.

. . . .

The *nuts* in "Here we go gathering nuts in May" is a corruption of the word *knots*, and refers to knots of flower garlands gathered for May Day celebrations.

26

Look for masses of ladybugs.

Ladybug, ladybug, fly away home! Home for the ladybugs this time of year may be your lawn. Ladybugs hibernate in large groups, nestled in among the roots of grass. You can sometimes spot them preparing to go under.

Ladybugs are not true bugs. They are a type of beetle; in fact, their other common name is ladybird beetle. They are among a number of animals and plants with the word "lady" in their name. Have you ever heard of lady's mantle or lady's bedstraw? The "lady" is in honor of the Virgin Mary, often referred to as *Our Lady*.

27

Pick some apples.

Fall is apple picking time! See if there's a pick-your-own orchard near you (see *June 18*), or stop at one of the roadside stands that offers a variety of apples. You'll be lucky if you find twenty different kinds of apples for sale. Did you know that at the turn of the century nearly one thousand varieties were available in this country?

Commercial growers need to concentrate on apple varieties that ship and store well. But some of those apples skimp on taste. Have you ever had a Northern Spy? Or a York Imperial? The names are almost as delicious as the apples! They are usually found near where they are grown.

What can you do if you can't find any of these interesting-sounding apples? Grow your own! There are currently about 60 varieties available to home gardeners. Don't despair if you only have a small yard. Most varieties can be grown as dwarf or semi-dwarf trees. Remind your parents that "an apple a day. . . .!"

28

Make some applesauce.

Mmmm, applesauce! Applesauce is great as a side dish with pork, as a dessert, or eaten as a snack. Have you ever made your own? It's as easy as . . . applesauce!

Most applesauce is a blend of two or more varieties of apple. Experiment with the kinds you find at your supermarket or roadside stand. Core and peel six apples and put them in a heavy saucepan that has a tight-fitting lid. Add a little water or juice to the pan to keep the apples from sticking. Cook them over low heat until they are soft. (Have your parents help you at the stove.) Let the apples cool slightly before mashing them with a fork or potato masher.

Good tasting apples need no sweetening, but a sprinkling of cinnamon or a few drops of lemon juice adds a nice touch. Chill the applesauce thoroughly in the refrigerator before serving. Yum!

. . . .

Remember Johnny Appleseed? John Chapman was a real man, but the stories that are told bend the truth just a little!

29

Gather some ripe nuts.

Are you ready to go nutting? Nuts in backyards and back woods are ripening and getting ready to fall from the trees. Try some of these tasty morsels. You'll have to be quick, though, and beat the squirrels to them!

True nuts are hard-shelled, one-seeded fruits. Acorns and hazelnuts are two examples of true nuts. (You probably know that peanuts aren't really nuts, but neither are almonds, Brazil nuts, or cashews!) Many nuts, true or otherwise, are delicious. Look for acorns, beechnuts, butternuts, hickory nuts and pine nuts, to mention just a few of the delectable varieties.

What do you do with the nuts you've found? The box below offers some preparation and cooking hints.

Acorns roasting over an open fire . . .

You may have heard that acorns are bitter. Many are, but the nuts from the bur, live, white, and gambel oaks are not as bitter as some. Even so, boil the shelled kernels in water to get rid of any traces of tannin. Cook them for 15 minutes; pour off the liquid, add fresh water, and boil them another 15 minutes. Do this until the water no longer turns brown. Roast the nuts in a 300°F oven for about an hour. Chop them up to use in recpies that call for nuts.

The black walnut and the butternut (a relative) are both delicious, but among the messiest nuts to harvest. You have to strip the husks off before the inner kernels get saturated with bitter juice. But the husks are hard to strip from the shells, and they contain a dye that leaves clothes and skin stained. (You MUST wear old clothes and rubber gloves.) Even the shells are hard to crack! Try hammering them on a rock placed in a box (to catch the flying debris).

The nuts from nut-bearing pines such as the ponderosa and piñon are very small but scrumptious! Spread a tarp under the trees and shake the nuts loose. Eat them raw or roasted (put them in a 300°F oven for about an hour or until the shells turn brittle). Spread the cooled nuts on a table and roll over them with a rolling pin to crack the shells.

September

30

Find out which birds winter in your area.

Soon the sky will be filled with birds that are flying south for the winter. How far south do they go? It depends, but many species that spend their summers in Canada, feel they have gone far enough south once they reach the United States. Some birds don't travel very far at all. Others are considered permanent residents wherever there is enough food for them year-round.

Do you know which birds will be spending the winter where you live? Do a little detective work. Check out some of the bird identification books. Many include maps that show the summer and winter ranges of the birds. Or ask at your local nature center or science museum. The Audubon Society is also helpful. Their annual Christmas count (see *December 16*) includes all the species that are spotted in December in various locales.

Learn which birds you are likely to have as visitors to your feeders during the winter months, and plan to include some of their favorite foods.

1

Make a bird feeder.

Birds eat a lot of food in winter in order to stay warm. You can help out by supplying them with some of the foods they enjoy. With a few bird feeders on your property, you can entice all sorts of birds to visit you during the winter months.

Some birds prefer to eat at ground level, so scatter some seeds for them. (When there is snow, tramp down a patch so the seeds won't sink.) But many birds can be tempted with food placed higher up. Make a simple table feeder for them.

Use a scrap piece of lumber about 20″ long by 10″ wide. (This gives the birds lots of room to perch.) Nail or glue down thin strips of wood along the sides, leaving gaps at all four corners for drainage. (See the illustration.) Nail the platform to a pole, placing it about 5 feet from the ground. Or hang it from a tree branch with chains screwed into all four corners.

Put just enough seed on the table that will be eaten in a day or so. Make sure you clean off the shells that accumulate, as well as any wet or spoiled seed. Rig a roof over the table if wetness is a problem.

See the box below for other feeders you can make with materials you may already have at home.

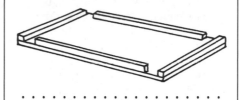

Birds feed in the morning hours, so hang a feeder where you can see it from the breakfast table.

Food for all

You can recycle all sorts of containers and found objects and turn them into bird feeders. Here are some suggestions to get you started.

For seed
- Coffee can with half a plastic cover on both ends
- Glass jar hung horizontally
- Empty coconut shell cut in half

For suet
- Mesh bag (the kind onions come in)
- Coconut shell filled with melted suet
- Drill holes in log and fill with melted suet

Other ideas
- Slather peanut butter on pine cones
- Hang coconut half upside down (some birds love coconut!)
- String peanuts on wire or heavy string

2

Collect wild food for the birds.

There's a wide assortment of food you can put out for birds that is free for the taking. Many fall-ripening berries can be harvested and dried to be put out later. Look for red-cedar berries (which are actually tiny cones!), serviceberries, devils-walkingstick berries and elderberries. (Try some elderberries yourself!) Many birds also enjoy the fruits of the hawthorn known as haws and crab apples.

You can crack open some of the hard-shelled nuts you find in the wild for the birds, too. Many relish walnuts and butternuts. Of course, sunflower seeds are a staple for many species. Leave them growing on the plants for the birds to find on their own, or harvest them to put out later. (Grow your own sunflowers—see *May 25*.)

3

Make a suet bell.

Many birds benefit from some fat in their diet during the winter. Put out a piece of suet (get this from the meat department of your supermarket), or make a suet bell.

Round up some fat such as suet, lard or the drippings from roasts and bacon, and some filler. You can use purchased seeds, bits of dried fruit, cake and cookie crumbs, and cheese—or whatever else you might have on hand. Use roughly ½ pound of fat for every pound of filler. Melt the fat in a heavy saucepan (have your parents help you at the stove) and add the dry ingredients. Mix well.

Let the mixture cool slightly before pouring it into a yogurt container that has a piece of string or wire stuck through a small hole in the carton's bottom. Make sure enough is hanging outside the carton so that you can hang the bell when it's done. When the fat has hardened, pull off the yogurt container and hang the bell from a branch outdoors. What birds come and nibble on it?

4

Watch for migrating birds.

One of nature's mysteries is the mystery of migration. Scientists have learned a lot about the kinds of animals that migrate (including people!), but there are still some unanswered questions. How do animals know where to go each year? And when to go? How do they navigate (many fly over open water for hundreds of miles)?

Have you ever seen flocks of swallows on their way south? They arrange themselves by the hundreds on telephone wires. These birds have a long flight before them. Some fly as far south as Argentina! The Arctic tern summers in the Arctic, only to fly 11,000 miles south for the winter!

You may see some of these birds assembling by day, but most birds fly by night. Have you ever seen birds flying by the light of the moon? When the moon is full (or nearly full) focus on it with a pair of binoculars or a telescope. You may be able to see whole flocks flying by, silhouetted against the moon.

. . . .

Bald eagles and ospreys start migrating as early as August; golden eagles depart as late as November.

5

Read a story or poem about migrating birds.

The time has come to bid adieu. Goodbye, farewell! See you next year!

Back Again
Aileen Fisher *(poem)*

How? Part 1
Aileen Fisher *(poem)*

Journey of the Storks
Ivan Gantschev *(story)*

The Restless Robin
Marjorie Flack *(story)*

Something Told the Wild Geese
Rachel Field *(poem)*

6

Look for owl pellets.

Owls are among the birds that are permanent residents in much of the United States. They are nocturnal, but even if you've never seen one, you've probably heard one. "Hoo, hoo-hoo, hoo," hoots the great horned owl (whose "horns" are really tufts of feathers). "Who cooks for you all?" cries the barred owl.

You can find where owls live by looking for their pellets. Because birds have no teeth, they swallow their food whole. For owls (and other birds of prey) this means bones and all! What these birds can't digest they eliminate. Instead of passing this hard matter through their intestinal tracts, it is coughed up out of their beaks as pellets.

Pellets vary in size and shape from species to species, but most are oblong, with bits of bone, fur and feathers sticking out. Fresh pellets are covered with a slimy mucus (all the better to slip out with!); weathered pellets are dry and hard. Look for pellets at the bases of trees, and in barns (where barn owls live).

Dissect a pellet to find out what the bird has been eating. Break one in half and soak it in warm water until it loosens up. Pour off the water and pick the pellet apart with a toothpick or a darning needle. Can you identify any of the tiny bones?

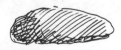

October

7

Watch for leaves turning color.

Sometime in late September or early October, the leaves on the deciduous trees in the northern parts of the United States begin to turn colors. And what a display it is! Some leaves turn brilliant red; others fiery orange. Some turn a shimmering gold. There's even a rich purply-red. Why do leaves turn color?

These colors are actually always present in the different leaves, but are masked by the chlorophyll which our eyes perceive as green. Once the chlorophyll (which is the substance trees use to make their own food) begins to break down and separate from the proteins in the leaves, the underlying colors show through.

Among the first leaves to change color are the sumacs and Virginia creepers, followed by willows and ashes and then the red and sugar maples. Other trees follow, including birches, hickories and ending, roughly, with the oaks and beeches. Keep track of the trees on your property or in a park near you. When do they start to turn? Which ones go first?

8

Press some autumn leaves.

Finding autumn leaves to use in various projects will be an on-going activity. Tree leaves turn colors in a certain order, and you'll want to collect the leaves fresh from the trees as they turn.

There are lots of things you can do with the vividly colored leaves. But don't forget to press some of the better samples you find. You may want to add some autumn leaves to your tree leaf scrapbook (see *May 14*). Include some in the profile of your special tree (see *A tree grows in . . .* on page 41). Smaller leaves can be used with other pressed plants in pressed flower pictures.

Enjoy the display of color! It won't be long before most of these leaves fall from the trees and turn brown. Fall is all too short.

9

Print with leaves.

Leaves come in all shapes and sizes. Some are squat, some are long and skinny. Each has its unique design of veins and lobes. You can really see these differences when you make leaf prints.

You can make prints from the leaves that are turning, as well as the leaves from houseplants and other garden plants. (Just make sure you ask before you trim any plants!) Use leaves to print patterns on wrapping paper and note cards. Or use them to adorn trays, gardening pots, and drinking glasses.

You can use poster paints for printing cards with, but acrylic paints work best wherever you want a waterproof design. Paint a little paint on the underside of the leaf where the veins are more pronounced and make a better print. Carefully place the "inked"

leaf where you want the image printed. Cover the leaf with a piece of folded paper toweling. Roll a brayer (a small roller used for making prints), a rolling pin, or a spoon over the paper with firm strokes. Remove the paper towel and carefully lift the leaf. Presto!

Quick change artistry

Many states (especially those in northern areas) have whole forests of the kinds of trees that turn beautiful colors in autumn. Would you like to make a special trip to view the fall foliage?

Keep in mind that the farther north, the sooner the leaves turn. Nature is also unpredictable, and some years the trees may turn and lose their leaves earlier or later than usual. You can find out when the trees are expected to "peak" by contacting the tourism department of the state you'd like to visit. Many have up-to-the-minute taped recordings that you can listen to for the price of a phone call (some are even toll-free). Foliage reports are generally available from mid-September through the middle of October.

10

Make leaf stencils.

Leaves can also be used as stencils, which makes a reverse impression. This technique works best with pressed leaves. Keep the leaves in place with small pieces of tape folded over itself, and placed on the under-side of the leaves. With a small sponge, or stubby bristle brush, dab paint around the outline of the leaves. The leaf shapes will show up white or whatever color paper you're stencil-ling on.

You can also use the splatter tech-nique. Dip an old toothbrush into watery paint and draw a popsicle stick across the bristles to make the paint splatter. This is a messy activity at best! Make sure you protect yourself and your work area from the flying paint.

11

Make leaf rubbings.

Fleshy leaves are good for making leaf rubbings. Here pressed leaves just don't work as well as fresh. Place the leaves wrong side up—that is, with the raised veins showing. Place a sheet of lightweight paper over the leaves and carefully feel where they are. Rub over them with the flat side of a crayon. You can even match the leaf colors by choosing crayons that are close in hue.

Try using shoe polish instead of crayons. Polishes come in an array of autumn colors. Remember to wear rubber gloves to protect your hands from stains.

· · · · · · · · · · · · · · · · · · ·

Most leaves are simple (this means there is one blade). Some are com-pound (each blade is divided into three or more leaflets).

12

Rake up a pile of leaves.

Autumn has its share of chores, and raking leaves is one of them! Do you help out when it's time to rake?

Make sure you rake up a nice big pile to flop in! You'll even be doing your parents a favor. All the jumping helps to break the leaves into smaller pieces. The leaves that you add to your compost pile (see *October 20*) will decompose all that much faster and not take up nearly as much room.

There are all sorts of ways you can have fun with a pile of leaves. Rake a mountain of them beneath a tree, and jump out of the tree into them. Rig a jump to ride your bike over—and make the landing safe with a big pile of soft leaves. Or play hide-and-seek in the leaves. You really can lose yourself in them. Are there any special games you like to play in the leaves?

13

Compost fallen leaves.

Not long ago, leaves were raked and piled in most communities and burned. The smoke pollution and the hazards of fire put an end to that, and not knowing what to do with all the leaves, most homeowners took to bag-ging them in plastic and putting them out with the week's trash.

Leaves are not trash! In nature they are recycled and turned into soil. You can do the same. Leave some un-der bushes and low-growing plants on your property. Add the rest to your compost pile (see *October 20*).

Leaves take a long time to decom-pose, but you can help speed things along by shredding them. The easiest (and certainly most fun!) way to do this is to play in them. They'll be bro-ken into little bits in no time.

October

14

Plant some spring bulbs.

Before the ground gets too hard, you should plant your spring-flowering bulbs outdoors. Just like the bulbs you potted for indoor blooms (see *September 18*), outdoor bulbs need to lay dormant in the ground for several months.

You can plant bulbs in the same gardens where you have other flowering plants growing (the bulbs will bloom and the foliage die back before the other plants take up the space), or you can "naturalize" them. To do this, toss them on the ground in a random pattern under trees and in open areas where the grass is not mowed. Where they land, is where you'll plant them.

Check the instructions that came with the bulbs. They will tell you how deep to plant the bulbs, how far they should be placed from one another, and how tall they can be expected to grow. Most bulbs appreciate soil that drains well, so loosen the soil to about 10″ and mix in a little bit of sand and peat moss or compost. A small handful of bonemeal mixed in each hole will give the bulbs a boost. Plant the bulbs, cover them with soil, and water them. You'll be glad you planted them, when they bring a little color to a winter-weary landscape.

15

Watch for sluggish houseflies.

With the onset of cool weather, you may suddenly find houseflies buzzing lazily inside your home. These insects respond to the drop in temperature and the decreasing daylight and start looking for protected places to spend the winter. They often make their way inside buildings. Some lie dormant between storm and regular windows. They can squeeze their way through the smallest openings!

Before you shoo them outdoors, take a good look at these insects. Some are so sluggish you can hold them in the palm of your hand. (Remember to wash your hands well after because flies get into all sorts of dirty things.) Do you see that flies have only one pair of wings? That's true for all true flies, which include fruit flies, bottle flies, robber flies, cluster flies, and mosquitos! These are only a few of the nearly 15,000 species of fly that live in North America.

16

Watch for queen bees and wasps.

In the autumn, you might come across some solitary bees and wasps flying around. Maybe a lone bald-faced hornet, or a yellowjacket. Or even a fuzzy bumblebee. These are the queen bees and wasps, the only members of their colonies to live through the winter. While you are watching, the queens are searching for a place to hibernate. Can you find where they finally settle?

What has happened to all the other bees and wasps? The details vary somewhat from species to species, but generally the female workers and the male drones all die in the fall. (The drones first mate with the queens.) The following spring, the queens will come out of hibernation and look for a place to lay the eggs that will become the next generation of workers and drones.

Honeybees are the only bees that remain active year-round. Their winter habits are somewhat different (see *October 18*).

. . . .

Bald-faced hornets and bumblebees hibernate underground. Polistes wasps frequently spend the winter within the walls of old houses.

17

Listen for migrating geese.

Most waterfowl are strong fliers, and many migrate great distances every year. You are probably familiar with Canada geese, large handsome birds that fly both by day as well as by night. You can often hear them coming—they are loud honkers! You know it's them when you see their characteristic V-formation.

The V-formation is a wondrous way of making the flight easier on the birds. The lead goose helps reduce air resistance for those birds flying behind. From time to time the geese switch places, relieving the lead bird. Other birds also fly in V-formation, including cormorants, ducks, swans, and gulls.

If you live near a pond or wetland, you may even get to watch the birds when they alight for a well-deserved rest.

A compost pile that is decaying properly actually heats up. It may be as hot as 150°F in the middle of the pile!

18

Leave out some honey for honeybees.

This time of year you can often attract honeybees to a food source, such as some honey on a plate, placed in an area that still has flowers in bloom, or that once did. If your offering is discovered, you can be sure that the news will be spread, and many bees will gather up the honey to add to their winter's supply.

Honeybees keep warm by beating their wings, and the honey they make and store fuels this activity. (They also bunch together as a way to insulate one another.) They spend much time when it's very cold within their hives (usually a hollow in a tree), venturing out only to get rid of bodily wastes. They can store fecal matter for long periods of time. They usually wait for warm spells when they emerge on their so-called cleansing flights. If there is a prolonged cold snap, and the bees can wait no longer, many leave the hive and die. Have you ever seen bees on a winter's day?

19

Prepare your garden for winter.

If you enjoyed gardening this year, and would like to do some more next year, there are a few things you can do now to make the spring chores a little lighter.

This is a good time to clean up the garden. Pull up all the annual flowers, vegetables, and herbs that have died. Compost any healthy plants. Dig some manure or compost into the soil. It will weather over the winter and your soil will be both more fertile as well as easier to work in the spring.

Take a look at your perennials. Some of them can be divided to make new plants. (Ask someone at your local nursery which plants can be divided in the fall.) Dig up the whole plants, separate them into smaller pieces at the roots, and replant each new "plant."

Once the ground has frozen solid, you might want to cover some of the perennials. That way the ground around them won't heave when there's a thaw mid-winter. Round up straw, seaweed, evergreen boughs, and even burlap bags to cover them with when the time comes.

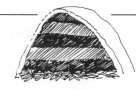

20

Make a compost heap.

Compost is the name given to decaying plant material that is added to soil to improve it. The more organic (living) matter, the better it is.

In nature, compost happens naturally. When leaves fall from the trees and annual plants die in autumn, they decay and become part of the soil. In a garden, however, things are kept neat and tidy. Compost has to be added.

If you just spread some grass clippings and old tomato vines on your garden, they would eventually rot. But it would take a long time. Compost heaps, or piles, speed things up.

There are many ways of containing the compost (see the box below).

Using a layer of twigs for circulation, place a 6″ layer of plant material. Throw in fruit and vegetable peels, coffee grounds, egg shells, grass clippings, dead plants and anything else you can think of. (Steer clear of meat or fat scraps.) On top of this, put a layer of animal manure or use blood meal or a compost activator. Continue making these layers, then wet the pile with water and cover it with an old tarp or rug.

In the spring, your pile will have shrunk, but it will have magically turned into a rich, crumbly substance that will make your garden soil better than ever!

Heap ho!

The simplest compost heap is a free-standing pile that gets narrower as it goes up. The trouble is, this kind of pile tends to dry out. You have to then stir it and turn it inside out, as it were. The whole thing usually just falls apart!

Put your compost into an enclosure made from chicken wire wrapped around four sturdy stakes sunk into the ground. Or use a 50-gallon drum that has lots of holes punched in the bottom and sides. Fancy compost bins are made of bricks or wood, divided into sections for compost in various stages of decomposition. Put your bin where it won't be an eyesore, or in the way, but make sure it's close enough to the house or garden so that you use it!

October

21

Make a maple leaf crown.

And regal you shall feel, sporting a crown made from the richly colored leaves of the maple tree!

You don't have to use maple leaves, of course. Any pretty, flat leaves will do. What kinds can you find? Make a long chain of leaves by piercing the stem of one leaf into another. Pull the stem through as far as it will go. (The knobby ends of the stems will help keep them from pulling out of the slits in the leaves.) The next leaf you add to the chain will hide the stem. Continue in this way until you have enough to go around your head. Make a circle by poking the last stem into the very first leaf you used.

How is that, your Majesty?

22

Pick dried grasses and seed heads.

Many plants look very different once the growing season is over. Have you ever seen black-eyed Susans without their petals? Before the seeds disperse, the seed heads look like fuzzy brown gumdrops stuck on the ends of sticks!

You can gather these and a number of other plants in the fall to be used in dried arrangements and other craft projects. Poppies and teasels both have interesting seed heads. Milkweed pods are very distinctive, too.

Tall grasses are especially beautiful. Many have interesting flower heads. You'll find plume-like flower heads on reedgrasses growing in marshes and along streams. You'll find arching spikelets (the proper term for the flowerheads of grasses) on some of the grama grasses found in dry regions. What do you think the grass growing on your lawn would look like if you didn't mow it? Let a patch go and find out.

Gather up an armload of grasses and wildflowers and put them in a vase. (Don't put any water in it.) As the plants dry, they'll arch gracefully, turning soft shades of yellow and brown. Other than a light dusting now and then, your dried arrangements need no care, and will last all winter long.

23

Mix up some potpourri.

Did you know that *potpourri* is French for "rotten pot"? What a funny name for such sweet-smelling stuff! Originally, potpourris were made with fresh petals and leaves, and allowed to ferment. Dry potpourris are more popular nowadays.

You can make potpourri with just about anything that grows! Fragrant herbs, spices, and flowers are used to perfume the mixture. Colorful blooms add just that—some color. Use dried herbs and flowers you've grown yourself (see *July 22*), or gathered. Don't forget the spice cupboard in your kitchen, too. To help the fragrance last longer, a fixative is usually added. Ground orris root is the most common (look for it wherever potpourri ingredients are sold). Some recipes call for essential oils (concentrated oils distilled from plants). You can buy small bottles of these.

Follow one of the recipes below, or make up your own! Mix the ingredients well, and store the potpourri in a covered container (not made of metal) in a cool, dark place. Let it age for about six weeks, stirring it now and again. Package it creatively (see *December 8*) to give to family and friends.

Sweet scentsations!

There are literally hundreds of potpourri recipes. Here are two simple blends that smell wonderful.

Rambling rose
- 3 cups dried rose petals
- 2 cups dried lavender
- 1 cup dried lemon verbena
- 1 tablespoon dried lemon peel
- 1 tablespoon ground allspice
- 1 tablespoon ground cinnamon
- 1 tablespoon ground cloves
- 1½ tablespoons ground orris root

Mix together the last five ingredients before adding the herbs and flowers. Stir well. Let cure in a covered jar for 6 weeks.

Spice delight
- 6 whole nutmegs
- 5 cinnamon sticks
- 3 vanilla beans
- ½ cup whole cloves
- 1 tablespoon anise seed, crushed
- 1 tablespoon ground allspice
- ½ cup ground orris root

Break the whole nutmegs and cinnamon sticks by placing them in a paper bag and hitting them with a hammer. Cut the vanilla beans with scissors. Mix all the ingredients together, and let cure in a covered jar for 6 weeks. This is a spice mix that men and boys like a lot!

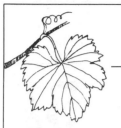

Cones range in size from the tiny cones of the hemlocks (about ¼″ long) to the enormous cones of the longleaf pine (these can be as big as 18″).

October

24

Make a vine wreath.

You can make wreaths from the vines you have on your property, or from those you find growing wild. Grape vines are perfect for wreath-making, and the spiralling tendrils add a nice touch. Honeysuckle and bittersweet also work well. (If you want the bittersweet berries on your wreath, cut the vines in early autumn when there are still leaves on the vines.)

To make the vines more pliable, soak them in water for a short time. Bend the vines into a circle (or make an oval or a heart shape!), weaving the ends in and out. Wrap smaller vines around the basic shape for a sturdier wreath.

Vine wreaths look nice just as they are, but you can adorn them with cones, dried flowers, and sprigs of herbs. Add something different for each season!

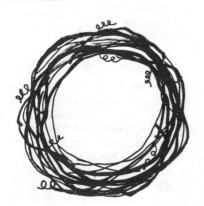

25

Collect cones.

Pines aren't the only trees that bear cones even though a lot of people call all cones pinecones! Spruces, hemlocks, firs, and cedars all are coniferous trees.

The woody cones you find on these trees are the female cones. Most conifers have both female and male cones on the same tree. The male cones are smaller, softer clusters found most often in the spring. (They are generally short-lived.) The female cones can take up to two years to mature and open.

Collect some cones for making cone wreaths (see *December 5*) and other decorations. Many of the cones you find will have already released their seeds; others may not have. When you bring the cones indoors, you'll be able to see how they detect when the conditions are right for letting go of the seeds. Do you notice how the cones open in the warmth of your house? Put them back outside and they'll close up again. Why do they do this? The cones are responding to the moisture in the air. They won't release their seeds if it's too wet—the seeds might rot. They wait until it's a little drier and warmer.

. . . .

Most cones hang down from the branches of coniferous trees. All the firs bear cones that are upright.

26

Make a corn necklace.

Did you grow any Indian corn in your garden this year? (If you didn't, grow some next year!) You can find Indian corn at garden centers and florist shops—even at some supermarkets. The kernels come in a rainbow of colors.

Most Indian corn is hung as a harvest decoration, but you can use the kernels in a number of ways. They are especially nice strung up as a necklace. Choose some colorful ears of Indian corn and break the kernels off of the cobs. Soak the kernels in water for a day or so until they are soft enough to draw a needle through. (Ask your mother for a blunt tapestry needle.)

Remove the kernels from the water and string them one by one on strong thread. (Use buttonhole thread or several strands of embroidery floss together.) When the strand is as long as you want it—about 24″ to 30″ so that it will slip over your head easily—tie the two ends of the thread into a knot.

27

Make some walnut shell boats.

Want to command your own fleet of ships? Make some boats from walnut shells!

You can make simple boats from walnut shell halves, modelling clay, toothpicks and small squares of paper. Press a little clay into each shell half, stick in the toothpick masts, and add the paper sails. Make different designs (or numbers) on each sail, and you'll be able to race the boats and know who's won. Launch the boats on a moving stream, and watch them go!

With your parents' permission and help, outfit your little boats with birthday candles instead of masts. This might be something nice to do on your birthday! Light them, and set them out on a body of still water, such as a swimming pool, or small pond. (Make sure you collect the shells when you're all done.) Lit at twilight, these make an enchanting sight.

October

28

Carve some apples into faces.

Have you ever noticed how a very old person's face is sometimes wrinkled like a wizened-up apple? You can carve an apple and make it look just like an old person!

Peel and core a good-sized apple. With a knife, carve some of the apple away, to suggest two eyes, a nose and a mouth. Place the apple in a bowl filled with salted water or lemon juice for about half an hour. Dry the apple gently, and spear it from below with a pencil. Place the pencil in a long-necked bottle. Let the apple dry there for three or four weeks. As it dries, it will shrink and take on the look of a weathered face!

Paint some simple clothes on the bottle, or glue some scraps of cloth onto the bottle to look like garments. Do you think that's what you will look like when you are very old?

29

Stick a face on a pumpkin.

Most people carve pumpkins. That's what you have to do if you want to put a light inside them. But have you ever made a three-dimensional face using a pumpkin? Try it this year!

You can create a whole cast of spooky characters with different-sized pumpkins. Gather up an assortment of goodies that you've found on your walks through fields and woods. Use pinecones for crazy curls. Make protruding noses from corn cobs. Stick individual stalks of grass in holes made with a skewer or ice pick for a head of hair that sticks straight out! Don't forget those vegetables that would make interesting features, either. Experiment with carrots, cucumbers and squash.

Pumpkins have pretty tough skin, but you can attach the features to your pumpkin with toothpicks. It's usually easiest to stick the toothpicks into the firmer surfaces first. That means poking a toothpick into the pumpkin first, then sticking on, say, a cucumber. Sometimes (such as with pinecones) you'll need to glue the toothpicks in place. Poke a hole in the pumpkin with a slender skewer where you want the cones to go.

. . . .

Want to choose your own pumpkins right on the vines? Look for a pick-your-own farm that grows pumpkins.

30

Roast some pumpkin seeds.

Is there anything you can do with the seeds that come out of the pumpkins you do carve? There sure is! Roast them for a delicious snack.

Scooping the seeds out of the pumpkins is messy business at best. Place the seeds in a colander and wash them under running water, untangling them from as much of the stringy fiber as possible. Any fiber remaining will bake hard in the oven, and can be rubbed off the cooled seeds if you don't like the way it looks.

Spread the seeds on a cookie sheet and sprinkle them with salt. Put them in a preheated oven set at 350°F. Bake the seeds for about 30 minutes shaking the pan every now and again, or until they are dry and crackly. Don't let them brown, or they will taste burned. Let them cool before you eat them. Yum!

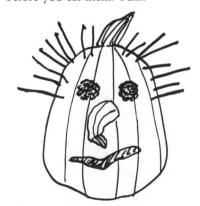

31

Happy Halloween!

You may not want to part with any of the pumpkin seeds you've roasted (they're good, aren't they?), but there are all sorts of other natural goodies you can offer your friends who come trick-or-treating.

Pop up some popcorn, or crack open some nuts. Or make a batch of pumpkin cookies. Here's a simple recipe that makes light pumpkiny morsels.

Pumpkin Pecan Bites

1 stick butter or margarine
½ cup sugar
1 egg
½ cup cooked pumpkin
½ teaspoon vanilla
1 cup all-purpose flour
½ teaspoon baking powder
¼ teaspoon baking soda
¼ teaspoon salt
½ teaspoon cinnamon
¼ teaspoon ground cloves
½ cup chopped pecans

Preheat the oven to 375°F. Cream the butter and sugar together in a medium-sized bowl. Add the egg, pumpkin, and vanilla. Sift the dry ingredients together (except for the nuts) and add to the bowl. Stir in the nuts.

Drop by heaping tablespoons onto a greased cookie sheet. Bake for about 15 minutes, or until lightly browned. Makes about 30 cookies.

Dull November brings the blast,
Then the leaves are whirling fast.

November

1

Pop some popcorn.

Have you ever wondered what makes popcorn pop? It's the moisture trapped inside each kernel that expands when it's heated. Under that kind of pressure, the kernels explode!

You've probably seen some of the crazy colored popcorn that's for sale. What do you think of the red kind? Or the black kind? No matter what the kernel color, popcorn always pops white.

How far will a heated kernel jump? Experiment with an electric skillet set on a clean sheet. (Have your parents help you.) Put a few kernels in the heated skillet with the top left off. When it's good and ready, the kernels will fly into the air. Pop a whole batch this way. It's snowing popcorn!

You can even grow your own popcorn. Next year set aside a part of your garden plot for some corn—the popping kind!

Make a wish upon a seed

Everyone knows that if you blow out all the candles on your brithday cake in one try, the wish you've made will come true. But did you know that you can wish upon dandelion seeds? If you blow all the seeds from a single stem in one breath, your wish will be granted!

Superstitions surrounding plants and animals go back thousands of years. Which superstitions do you know of? Did you known that you can tell if a person likes butter by holding a buttercup under his chin? If there's a golden glow there, he does! Have you heard that you can tell if someone loves you by plucking the petals from a daisy? Say "he loves me, he loves me not . . ." as you pick them off one by one. Does he (or she) love you?

Nature is also one big toy store. From walnut boats to launch on a winding stream to honeysuckle flowers to sip, children everywhere make playthings from plants. Have you ever made a pea shooter from a hollowed out piece of elderberry stem? (The pith pushes out quite easily with a coat hanger wire.) Or signalled to your friends with a grass whistle? Hold a blade of grass between your two thumbs (held side by side). Blow through the hole made by the curve of your thumbs. What a noise!

What are some tricks you know?

2

Make pomanders.

Long ago, pomanders were used to mask unpleasant odors. Pomanders (from the French *pomme* for "apple", and from ambergris, a waxy substance secreted by the sperm whale, long used as a fixative in perfumery) are now largely decorative items. They do smell nice, however, and add an old-fashioned touch to closets and dresser drawers.

You can make your own pomanders. All you need are some oranges (or lemons and limes for smaller pomanders), and some whole cloves. If you want to hang your pomanders, leave some room for ribbons. Mark crossing paths with narrow masking tape. Stick the cloves into the fruit, about a clove's head distance from one another; they'll end up closer as the fruit dries and shrinks.

Roll the pomanders in equal parts of ground cinnamon and orris root (a fixative found wherever potpourri supplies are sold), and wrap each in tissue paper. Let them cure for 4 to 6 weeks, before tying ribbons around them (see *December 7* for a reminder). Pomanders make lovely gifts, and not just for your grandmothers!

3

Grow a mystery crop.

If you dig up a bit of woodland soil (or take a spade to part of your garden) and put it into a pot and water it, what do you think will grow? It's a mystery!

The seeds that would normally lay dormant until the following spring can often be coaxed into life in the warmth of your home. It's fun to try to identify what is sprouting, although for best results you should put the plants under your plant lights (see *March 14*). The dwindling natural sunlight only confirms the plants' suspicions that it really is November!

November

4

Watch for white-tailed deer.

White-tailed deer are quite common in much of the United States. They generally keep hidden in wooded areas during the day, but can be seen grazing in open fields, or munching on fallen apples in old orchards, early in the morning or at dusk.

Only the underside of this deer's tail is white. Tails are raised up as a signal of alarm. Any other deer nearby (which are usually few, as deer travel in very small groups—say, a doe and her twin fawns) will see the flash of white and be on the alert. Have you ever heard the expression "to hightail it"? Do you think this saying might refer to the way deer lift their tails as they run from danger?

At this time of year, deer look for mates. During the rutting season, as it's called, the stags are very jumpy and irritable. If two stags meet, they usually end up fighting. Fawns are born in late spring. They are cleverly camouflaged with spots, and for the first few weeks they are virtually odorless. How do you think this helps the fawns?

5

Collect birds' nests.

Once the leaves have fallen from the trees, you can see where many birds have cleverly positioned their nests. Most birds construct new nests every spring, so you are free to take down any you find. Just be careful high up in trees!

It is best to wear leather gloves when handling abandoned birds' nests. They will guard against the bites of any insects which may be living in the nest. You may also discover that a larger animal, such as a mouse, has moved in! (In that case, leave the nest there.)

Place the nest in a plastic bag with a couple of mothballs, and leave it for a few days. The insects will crawl out and die.

Do you know what kinds of birds lived in the nests? Even if you didn't see the birds when they were living in the nests, you may be able to find out. Check in one of the bird identification guides that includes pictures and descriptions of typical birds' nests.

6

Listen for crows.

Crows are not considered migratory birds as such, but they do move around in response to the weather. When it grows cold and stormy, they head for low lying areas, even venturing south a ways. Small groups of them can be seen during most of the year, but in late fall you might get a chance to see large flocks assembling in stubbly fields.

Crows cry out with the familiar "caw-caw," a piercing sound if there ever was one! Some people confuse crows and ravens, which is easy to do as the two birds are closely related. Ravens are larger, for one, and they call out with a deeper "wonk-wonk." Ravens are also wary of people, so are more common in wilderness areas.

Crows (and ravens and bluejays, another relative) are considered to be rather smart birds. Seeing how scarecrows rarely work at scaring crows, there is probably some truth in this!

. . . .

Eagles and owls use the same nests year after year.

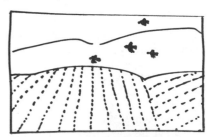

7

Search for witch-hazel flowers.

In woodland areas, now airy and open, you might find one of the tree flowers that blooms for the first time this late in the year. The witch-hazel grows to be a large shrub or small tree, and is in flower during the month of November and beyond. The bright yellow thread-like flowers are as vibrant as the leaves which recently fell from its branches.

Also maturing in autumn are the witch-hazel seed capsules. Pick some to bring home. When they dry out a bit, the seeds are ejected from the capsules with great force. They have been known to travel as far as thirty feet!

An extract from the bark, twigs, and leaves is used as an astringent in lotions and gargles. Water diviners (people who claim to be able to locate underground sources of water by holding a stick along the ground, letting it twitch and point to water) often choose the forked branches of the witch-hazel for this purpose. Do you suppose that is where the "witch" in witch-hazel comes from?

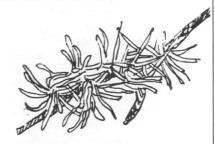

8

Examine a wasps' nest.

The nests of most wasps are abandoned each fall, so it's safe to take down any that you have found. Different wasps construct different types of nests, but some of the most beautiful are those made by the paper-making wasps.

These nests are made from tiny bits of wood—taken from trees, fence posts, and houses—which the queen, and later the workers, chew and mix with their special saliva. The pulp, very similar to the pulp used in making paper, is formed into six-sided configurations (like honeycomb). The construction of nests begins in early spring, and ends in the autumn when all the wasps, save the queens, die. Look for the nests hanging in protected spots, even under the eaves of your house.

Some wasps make their homes in trees. The bald-faced hornet builds an impressively large structure that is entwined around several branches. Now that the leaves have fallen from the trees, you can see where these are located. These nests, too, are safe to collect (just be careful climbing the tree!).

9

Scrape some resin from a pine tree.

The resin oozing from pine trees can be scraped off and boiled in some water, to release the pine scent that even city dwellers are familiar with. Pine essence is used in many household products, from disinfectants to room fresheners. (Maybe everybody has a secret desire to live deep in the woods!) Do you like the smell?

Pine resin is sap. (All plants contain sap, from the sap of the sugar maple which yields maple syrup—see *February 27*—to the "milk" of the milkweed.) It's very sticky! Nail polish remover will help get it off your hands and clothes. Do you have a cold? Sometimes taking deep breaths of the pine essence will unblock a stuffy nose. Ahhhh!

10

Dig a hole for a live Christmas tree.

If you have the room to plant a live Christmas tree outdoors once the holidays are over, ask your parents if they would consider buying a live tree rather than a cut one this year. Many nurseries sell live conifers, balled and burlapped and ready to go into the ground after they've spent just a few days inside your home.

This is a good time to dig a hole for the tree before the ground is too hard. Dig a good-sized hole, and fill it with some peat. Cover it so that no one will stumble into it by mistake. You can even pick up your tree now, provided you keep it in a sheltered place outdoors until about a week before Christmas.

A drastic change in temperature can be fatal to any plant, and these trees are no exception. From the outdoors, move the tree to an unheated garage for a day or so, before bringing it inside your home for 3 to 4 days at the very most. (Reverse the steps after Christmas.) It's always a bit of a gamble whether the tree will take and survive the winter after being subjected to such temperature extremes. With a little luck, your live tree will continue to bring enjoyment outdoors for many years to come.

Best dressed

The most popular trees grown and harvested for Christmas include the Scotch pine, Douglas fir and balsam fir. You can plant these, as well as several other conifers, if you choose to have a live Christmas tree this year.

Spruce trees aren't available everywhere as cut trees (the needles are painfully sharp!), but they are perfect for home yards. The blue spruce is an especially beautiful tree. White pines are bushy when they are young (perfect for hanging garlands on), but remember they grow to be enormous trees! You have to have plenty of room for them. Hemlocks are slow-growing trees that bear tiny cones. Your local garden center can help you make a wise choice.

November

11

Examine designs in nature.

From the way that seeds are arranged on a sunflower, to the spiraling tendrils of a grape vine, nature has come up with some ingenious and beautiful designs. Look around you, and you'll see all sorts of interesting shapes and patterns.

What can you find that is six-sided? The hexagon (as this shape is called) is the most economical shape. Do you see how many cells can fit in just a small piece of honeycomb? Snow crystals are also hexagonal.

Spirals are common in nature, from the spectacular nautilus shell to the fiddleheads of ferns. Circles (and variations such as spheres) are also wide-spread. Mushroom caps, flowers with petals that radiate from a central disk, and drops of water are circular.

Look for other shapes and patterns, too. Take tree bark and leaves, for instance. There are such variations! And don't forget color! Color in nature ranges from raven black to the iridescent shades in a peacock's feather. Can you imagine what the world would be like if everything was just black and white?

12

Look at nature's influence on art.

How do you think nature has influenced artists over the years? Look at some art to find out! An art museum is a good place to begin.

There you'll find drawings, paintings, prints, and sculptures that were created over the centuries. From landscapes to still lifes, from botanical illustrations to impressionistic pieces, nature is well-represented in art.

Nature has even influenced architecture. As you walk down the main street in your town or city, gaze up at some of the buildings and look for decorative motifs taken from nature. Some of the earliest structures we know of in Egypt were decorated with representations of flowering plants. This trend continued for centuries. Modern buildings are not very ornate, but there may be examples of flowery (no pun intended!) architecture where you live.

If you can't make it to an art museum or gallery, check your library for books on art. What are some of your favorite paintings? What do you like to draw?

13

Find art supplies derived from nature.

You saw how paints could be made from the earth (see *September 1*), but did you know that many paints that you buy are made from natural sources? Not to mention many other art supplies!

Artists depend on nature for supplying them with paper (made from cotton and wood fibers) and canvas (usually cotton or linen). Many pigments used in paints and inks are of mineral or organic origin. Pigments are bound with different mediums, from linseed oil (in the case of oil paints) to gums and glues (gums are derived from plants; glues from animal hides).

There's graphite and charcoal—two natural substances used in drawing. Sculptors work in everything from wood to clay to marble and metal. Even photographers owe a debt to the natural world. Photographic film is made of several natural ingredients, including silver, gelatin, and cellulose.

Where would artists be without nature? What natural substances do you use in any of your artistic hobbies?

14

Start a nature notebook.

Have you ever noticed how much more you really *see* when you walk rather than drive along a familiar street? You can also "see" more in nature when you take the time to draw what you find.

You may not consider yourself much of an artist. But did you know that most skills come with practice? You can practice by recording what you find in a nature notebook!

It doesn't have to be anything fancy. All you need are some blank sheets of paper and some pencils. Try drawing little things (like a single flower) and bigger things (such as a field covered with snow). You'll soon get the hang of it! Do you see yourself noticing more now that you're drawing some of what you see?

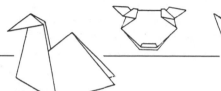

15

Make folded paper plants and animals.

The Japanese art of paper folding known as Origami, has a long and venerable history. The techniques were brought to Japan from China during the sixth century. Paper was a rare and precious commodity, so objects were folded only for ceremonial purposes. Today, children and adults all over the world enjoy paper folding.

There's no end to the plants and animals you can fold from paper. Use specially packaged Origami paper, or cut your own squares from thin paper. Follow the instructions below to make a funny frog that really jumps!

Fold a frog!

Make this frog from a square sheet of paper no larger than six inches across.

Use green or brown, or color your own sheet in a camouflage pattern!

1. Place the paper colored-side down. Fold in half, first one way and then the other.
2. Fold each corner to the center.
3. Fold the sides in, meeting in the middle.
4. Fold the bottom up.
5. Fold the sides in, with the points meeting halfway.
6. Fold the bottom up, about one third of the way up.
7. Fold the bottom down.
8. Fold the top point down.
9. Press your finger down on the frog's back. Slide your finger off and . . . watch the frog jump!

1.   2.   3.

4.   5.   6.

7.   8.   9.

16

Listen to music composed on themes from nature.

The natural world has inspired musicians, too. Even classical composers have written pieces that illustrate aspects of nature.

Here's a sampling of some well-known pieces. You may have some of these recordings at home. Or look for them at your local library. When you listen to this music, can you picture what the titles suggest?

The Carnival of the Animals
Camille Saint-Saëns

Flight of the Bumblebee
Nicolai Rimsky-Korsakov

The Four Seasons
Antonio Vivaldi

La Mer (The Sea)
Claude Debussy

On Hearing the First Cuckoo in Spring
Frederick Delius

The Planets
Gustav Holst

The Rite of Spring
Igor Stravinsky

17

Make a musical rattle.

The first musical instruments were percussion instruments—things to bang on, scrape together, and shake. They were made with materials found in nature. How would you like to make your own musical rattle?

Gourds make terrific maracas, or rattles. Use the hard-skinned kind known as calabash gourds. First you have to take the skin off the gourd. Do this by wrapping the gourd in an old towel soaked in a solution of liquid household cleanser and water. (Wear rubber gloves to protect your hands.) When the skin has softened (after several hours), scrape it off and leave the gourd to dry for 3 or 4 days.

Carefully cut a hole in one end of the gourd (start the hole with a nail; round it out with a hacksaw). Remove the pulp and seeds from inside the gourd with a spoon. Try to get as much out as possible. Let the gourd dry for a few more days. Then fill it with a handful of dried beans and plug the hole with a handle (cut a piece off an old broom handle, or find a stick the right size). Secure the handle with some glue and let dry. Give it a shake!

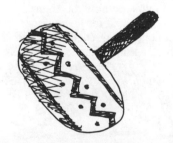

November

There are more kinds of plants and animals in tropical regions—but relatively few of each species. In cold regions, there are few species but many of each kind.

18

Make a world animal map.

The United States has a wide variety of animals (and plants, too) because it has so many different habitats. But just think of all the other animals that can be found throughout the world. There are all sort of wild and crazy creatures!

To get to know some of these animals and where they can be found, make a world wildlife map. You'll need a large map of the world (look for one wherever school and office supplies are sold, or make your own by drawing the rough outlines of the continents on a large sheet of paper), tacks, string, and 3″ × 5″ index cards (or cut-up pieces of tagboard).

Start collecting pictures of animals. Cut them from magazines, or sketch your own. Glue them onto the index cards. Put your map on a wall that has plenty of room for the map plus pictures tacked all around it. (Get your parents' okay before you start making holes in the walls!) Stretch pieces of string between tacks that hold up the pictures, and those that are stuck into the map to show where the animals can be found.

Do you see how the animals are specially adapted for living under different conditions? There are some pretty unusual creatures, aren't there?

19

See how the continents have drifted apart.

Do you notice how many animals that live thousands of miles from one another—often oceans apart—look very much alike? Many have evolved along similar lines in response to similar conditions (desert animals, for instance, are much alike everywhere), but there may be another reason.

Scientists think that all the continents were once united in one huge land mass. (Geologists actually think there were separate land masses that came together about 200 million years ago.) This supercontinent is referred to as Pangaea (that's Greek for "all lands"). Pangaea gradually broke up into many pieces, which drifted farther and farther apart. In fact, the continents are still adrift! Every year they move a couple of inches, which may not seem like much, but when you multiply it times hundreds of thousands of years, it's not hard to see how the continents got so far.

You can see how the continents all fit together by tracing their shapes and cutting out the basic outlines from construction paper. Move them close together. Do you see how they fit together like puzzle pieces? What do you think will happen in another 100 million years?

20

Find out where some food plants originated.

If you could buy only fruits and vegetables that were native to the United States, the produce section of your supermarket wouldn't be very big at all. Did you know that most all the plants we eat have their origins elsewhere?

Take apples, for instance, the most popular fruit in this country. The first apples were found growing in Southwest Asia, and from there they spread to China, Babylon, and parts of Europe before they ever made their way across the Atlantic! (We can thank the English for bringing apples with them.)

The only native foods we eat include some berries (such as strawberries and raspberries) that are descendents of native species, and the Jerusalem artichoke (not an artichoke at all, but a sunflower with edible tubers). Every other plant got its start somewhere else. Use an encyclopedia to help you find where some of your favorite foods were first found growing. Are you surprised by your discoveries?

21

Collect wildlife postage stamps.

Stamp collecting is a great hobby. All the countries of the world issue beautiful stamps (yours for the price of a stamp!) that honor various aspects of national pride. Many stamps celebrate nature in one way or another.

Start a stamp collection that concentrates on the plant and animal life of different nations. You can learn a lot about native flora and fauna (that's another way of saying plants and animals) from stamps. China is very proud of its pandas, and they are featured in some of their stamps. Australian stamps have a tiny kangaroo in the corner. Other countries, including the United States, help to focus attention on plants and animals deserving of recognition, including endangered species. Do you think these stamps help make more people aware of the natural world?

What are some of your favorite wildlife stamps? Where do they come from?

November

22

Learn which animals help people worldwide.

A wide variety of animals has been domesticated throughout the world. Many may seem unusual to us, but if you think about it, they are all logical choices.

Did you know that elephants do the work of heavy machinery in many parts of Southeast Asia? (These animals are not actually domesticated—they are caught in the wild and tamed.) And why not? They don't break down, they don't pollute, and they have a lot more character than machines! In South America, llamas are herded. They are not only invaluable as beasts of burden (they are well adapted to the thin mountain air high in the Andes), but their wool is fabulously warm!

What other animals can you think of that are domesticated throughout the world? Some animals have very specialized jobs. In China, cormorants are used to catch fish. And in France, pigs are used to find truffles, highly prized fungi that grow underground.

23

Play a nature game from another culture.

The games that children play in one part of the world often are very similar to those played elsewhere. Sometimes only the names have changed! Many games include regional customs, and a lot refer to plants and animals of national importance.

In Taiwan, children play a game called "Growing Rice." In Ghana, they play "The Boa Constrictor." The games of North American Indians typically celebrate the natural world. Both the Dakotas and Cheyenne play games about bears; the Eskimos have a game they call "Musk Oxen." The Pueblo Indians of the Southwest play "The Coyote and the Sheep."

Have you ever played any of these games? There's one from Denmark you'll like. It's called "The Fish Game." See the box below for the rules.

Swim for your lives!

"The Fish Game" is for 6 to 30 players, and can be played either indoors or out. Divide the players into couples. One couple is chosen to be It—they are the Whales. All the other couples seat themselves on chairs (or pillows or folded paper bags). Each couple secretly chooses the name of a fish.

The Whales walk about, calling out names of fish. If a couple's name is called, they must get up and march behind the Whales. The Whales continue calling out as many fish names as they like; then they say, "The ocean is calm!" All the children must rise and march behind the Whales. Without any warning, the Whales call out, "The ocean is stormy!" and all the players run as couples to get seated. The two children left without a place to sit become the Whales for the next round.

24

Invent your own animals.

How about inventing some creatures of your own? You won't find these in your backyard, or anywhere else!

On some 3″ × 5″ plain index cards, draw or paste down pictures of all sorts of animals. Center the animals as best you can on each card. Cut each one in half right down the middle. Now comes the fun part! Take the front half of one animal and pair it with the back half of another. What zany creatures can you come up with?

What about a jackalope (half jack rabbit, half antelope)? Or a kangalo? Ever seen an octocoon? Make up some stories to go with your kooky creatures. Where would the animals you invent live? What would they eat? Would any of them make good pets?

There are some real animals that are a cross between two different species. Mules are part horse and part donkey. In Asia, yaks and cows are bred together to make "yakows!" These are strong animals that give more milk than plain yaks do.

November

25

Make Thanksgiving decorations.

The first Thanksgiving in the New World is said to have taken place in 1622. The Pilgrims had a lot to be thankful for! Borrowing from centuries-old harvest celebrations, they ate, drank, and were merry.

In the United States, on the fourth Thursday of November each year, we recreate that harvest feast. Much time and preparation goes into the Thanksgiving meal, but it's fun to decorate the table and house with special touches, too. Look to nature for some good ideas, and for materials.

Bundle some corn stalk sheaves together, and tie some Indian corn in bunches for some traditional decorations that honor the harvest. Give your vine wreath (see *October 24*) a new look. Decorate it with seed heads, cones and tiny gourds. Make a display of nature's wild bounty—assemble birds' nests, feathers, shells and dried plants for an unusual centerpiece. For fun, make up some silly turkeys (see the box below) that will tickle your funny bone. Wishbone, that is!

Turkeymagigs

Here are two very silly turkeys you can make with materials you probably already have at home.

Look through your cone collection for some squat pinecones. Turn these into turkeys by twisting yellow pipe cleaners through the cones and bending them into legs and feet. Glue tiny circles of felt for eyes, and snip pieces of red felt for the wattles.

Or make a turkey from a pear, two zucchini, a carrot, two whole cloves and a handful of toothpicks. Slice the top off one zucchini for the head. Slice the rest into ¼″ pieces. Cut a 2″ piece from the narrow end of the carrot. Slice the rest into ¼″ pieces. Stick the cloves into the head for eyes; then attach the head to the neck with

half a toothpick. (It's easiest to push the toothpicks into the carrot and zucchini slices first. Then attach the slices to the pear.) Use the carrot and zucchini slices as feathers. (See the illustration.) Stick three toothpicks into the body—two for legs (with carrot slices for feet), and one in back to steady the turkey.

· · · · · · · · · · · · · · · · · · ·

Make cut vegetable turkeys the morning of Thanksgiving Day, so they'll look their freshest.

26

Honor the turkey on Thanksgiving Day.

What would Thanksgiving be like without turkey? Millions of Americans sit down to a table laden with food. And the star of the day? The turkey! (Not everyone eats turkey, of course, but most do!)

There's still some question whether turkey was actually on the menu that first Thanksgiving in 1622. It probably was, since wild turkeys were plentiful (and much loved by the Indians) and already known to the Pilgrims. Even though they are New World natives, wild turkeys had been introduced in Europe at least a full century earlier. (The Spanish knew a good thing when they saw it, and took some back with them.)

Wild turkeys were once hunted almost to extinction, but their numbers have grown in recent years. They have a gamier taste than their commercially-raised cousins. Have you ever tasted wild turkey?

You've probably heard that Benjamin Franklin thought that the turkey would be a better choice as a symbol for this country than the eagle. He thought the eagle was "a bird of poor moral character" and the turkey much more respectable. What do you think? Would we be eating eagle on Thanksgiving Day instead?

27

Read a story or poem about thanking nature.

The Pilgrims knew it, and we should remember it. We owe so much to nature for making our lives so rich. Start a new tradition! Include a story or poem in your thanksgiving.

Child's Grace
Frances Frost *(poem)*

Hard Scrabble Harvest
Dahlov Ipcar *(story)*

Thanksgiving
Ivy O. Eastwick *(poem)*

Chill December brings the sleet,
Blazing fire, and Christmas treat.

December

28

Look for the natural origins of everyday objects.

We certainly do owe a lot to nature if you stop and think that almost everything we eat, wear, live in, and play with has natural origins.

Take any object in your house. Your bed, for instance. Its frame is probably made of wood or metal; its mattress is probably stuffed with natural fibers of some sort (in conjunction with man-made fibers, many of which have natural origins themselves). Your pillow may be stuffed with feathers, and your sheets are probably woven from cotton.

You can do this with anything in your house (or school or your mom's or dad's workplace). Are you surprised to discover how many objects have natural origins? Do some things seem more "natural" than others?

29

Play Animal, Vegetable, Mineral.

Have you ever played this guessing game? You may know it by another name, *Twenty Questions,* because that's how many questions you get to ask before you give up. Here's how the game, for two or more players, goes:

One person secretly chooses a common object (let's say "milk") and announces to all what category the object falls under. The choices are animal, vegetable and mineral, of course. (Milk is "animal.") The guessing players try to discover what the secret object is by asking questions that can be answered with either "yes" or "no." Someone might ask, "Is the object an animal product?" The answer would be "yes." Someone else might add, "Is this something people eat?" "Yes" again. With this information, someone else might ask, "Do we have this product in our house?" And so on. By process of elimination, the guessing players must learn the identity of the object before they run out of their twenty questions.

To make things a little easier, you can keep guessing until the answer is found (not stopping at twenty questions). Or you can narrow the field by insisting that only objects visible in a given area be chosen. To make the game harder. . . . well, all's fair!

30

Send for gardening catalogues.

If you discovered the joys of gardening this year, you are probably already looking forward to next year's garden! What do you think you'd like to plant this coming spring?

There's so much to choose from, it's hard to know where to begin. To give yourself plenty of planning time, why not send for seed and nursery catalogues this year? Most of them are free! And they are full of helpful hints, inspiration and gorgeous photographs of flowers and vegetables you can grow yourself.

You'll find the names and addresses of some of the better known seed purveyors in the Appendix under *Where to purchase supplies.* But don't stop there! Check your newsstand or library for a current issue of one of the gardening or country living magazines. Lots of seed and plant sellers advertise in these publications, and you can copy down their addresses and send for their catalogues.

1

Stuff a pillow with cattail fluff.

Around this time of year, the cattails bordering ponds and swampy areas are ready to disperse their seeds. On windy days, you can see the cigar-shaped tops of the plants bursting at the seams, sending seeds into the air. Doesn't it look a little like the stuffing coming out of a pillow?

You can gather a few handfuls of these seeds and actually stuff a pillow with them! Dress for wading (wear your waterproof boots), and bring along a bag to hold the fluff. When you get home, make a small pillow from tightly-woven fabric just large enough to be puffy when stuffed. Cut two pieces of fabric the same size and place them together, with the "right" side of the fabric to the inside. Stitch along three sides of the pillow; turn the pillow right-side out. Stuff with the cattail fluff and sew the opening closed.

It's amazing how many parts of the cattail plant can be used. Much of it is edible (see *September 5*). Even the leaves can be put to use. They can be woven into mats and baskets, and chair seats.

December

2

Make some note cards.

It's nice to stay in touch with friends and family living far from home, and what better way than with a homemade greeting card? Cards that have a nature theme are especially nice.

If you would like to make a lot of cards all at once, you can speed things up by printing with vegetables (see *September 12*). Cut some simple shapes from potatoes. Use them to print patterns on folded note cards, or compose a landscape with a couple of different shapes.

You can make cards with cut and torn paper, too. Make a winter scene with some pale blue for the sky, a torn strip of tan for some hills in the distance, and leave the rest of the card white, like a snow-covered field. Combine cut paper and potato printing for even more possibilities. You can also make your own thank-you notes with a special theme or symbol that is important to you.

To simplify your card-making, complete one step on all the cards before going on to the next.

3

Create pressed flower pictures.

With the flowers and leaves you pressed during the year, you can create some delightful artwork. Framed pictures, bookmarks, and note cards are fun to make.

Gather together all your pressed plants to see what you have. You'll also need paper (or folded notes), white glue, and clear adhesive-backed vinyl (for the notecards and bookmarks). Practice arranging some blossoms and leaves. When you are happy with your design, glue the plants in place with a spot of glue.

If you are framing your pictures, make them in standard sizes (5″ × 7″ and 8″ × 10″ for instance) so that you'll be able to find frames for them easily. Protect those arrangements on note cards and bookmarks with the clear vinyl. Cut a piece slightly larger than your artwork and press it down carefully. Trim off the extra around the edges. Place the artwork between two sheets of paper and press with an iron set on the cotton setting, for 2 to 3 minutes. (Have your parents help you with the iron.)

4

Make decorations from natural materials.

Decorations you craft from natural materials can be given as gifts, or hung in your own home. There are so many lovely things to make. Here are a few ideas to get you started.

Decorate pinecones with sequins and gold and silver balls glued to the scales. Make miniature wreaths from tiny hemlock cones glued to cardboard shapes. Tie bundles of cinnamon sticks (mmm . . . smells good!) with velvet ribbon. Add sprigs of dried herbs for an extra nice touch. Make tiny pomanders from limes!

Make some festive "snow"-covered cones to hang or wire to wreaths. Wind some wire around the cones and dip them into wallpaper paste. When the paste feels tacky, dip the cones into white laundry powder. Shake off the excess. Let dry before you decorate them with some ribbon.

Everyone loves to string popcorn and cranberries, but have you ever made a garland from strawflowers (an everlasting annual)? String the blossoms on strong thread one after another, making sure they all face the same way for an even look. What other ideas can you come up with?

Cone crafting

Cones lend themselves to a number of uses. With a little glue and imagination, you can turn them into all sorts of comical figures.

Make a jolly woodland clan. You can hang these people, or make them stand. (To keep the cones upright, glue the fat ends of the cones to small circles cut from cardboard, or make bases from modelling clay.) Make heads from acorns (the tops make good hats!), chestnuts and wooden beads. Fashion arms from pipe cleaners. Clothe your people in bits of felt and paper.

You can make some fanciful birds from cones, too. Different shaped cones will suggest different birds. Add real feathers to the cones, or make some from tissue, crepe and construction papers. Hang some birds horizontally (they're flying!); others can be made to perch.

5

Make a cone wreath.

Cone wreaths are a lot of fun to make, especially if you have collected some different types of cones. Handled with care, the wreaths will last for years.

You can either wire or glue your cones to wreath forms. Wiring works best with specially constructed wire forms. You need bendable wire, cutters, and a pair of pliers. Gluing is done with hot glue (so have your parents help you). The nice thing about glued wreaths is that you can make the forms out of cardboard cut into any shape. Go with a donut, or make a heart, or any shape you like.

Spray the cones with water several hours before you begin. They will close up, making them easier to work with. Start with the largest cones and place them evenly around the wreath. Fill in the empty spots with more cones, using smaller ones to make the wreath three-dimensional. Add nuts and pods as accents. Let the wreath dry completely (the cones will all open); spray with a coat of clear lacquer.

6

Bring potted bulbs indoors.

The bulbs you potted for indoor blooms (see *September 18*), should be ready to come indoors now. Place the bulbs in a bright, but cool (45° to 60°F) location. Avoid putting them in direct sunlight. Water them well.

When some green growth appears, move the pots to a sunny location (still cool, if possible). They will begin to bud and show a little color. When this happens, place the plants where they can best be enjoyed. The blooms will last longest if the plants are kept out of the sun.

· · · · · · · · · · · · · · · · · · · ·

To get the sticky pitch off cones, place them in a warm oven until the pitch melts. Rub the cones with a cloth.

7

Tie up pomanders.

By now, the pomanders you made earlier (see *November 2*) should be dry and properly cured. Take them out of their tissue wrapping and shake the excess orris root/spice mixture off.

Cut a piece of ribbon narrow enough for the space left by the masking tape. Choose satin or velvet ribbon for a rich look. (Select a dark color if the pomander will be a gift for a man.) Wrap the ribbon around the pomander like you wrap a package, crossing the ribbon at the bottom. Tie a bow with a double knot.

The pomanders you don't wish to hang, can be arranged in a pretty bowl or basket.

· · · · · · · · · · · · · · · · · · · ·

Include gift cards with your pomanders. Write down that they should be hung in closets or put in dresser drawers to give clothing a pleasant scent.

8

Package your potpourri.

Making your potpourri (see *October 23*) is only half the fun. Packaging it creatively is great fun, too!

There are all sorts of containers you can use for your potpourri. Clear glass jars filled to the brim are especially nice. The potpourri really stands out—you hardly have to do more than tie a ribbon around the lid and add some dried herb and flower sprigs (add some whole rose buds when you're packaging *Rambling Rose*). Or look for a small basket with a lid. Weave some dried flower stems in and out of the lid. (Make a handle for the basket from a bundle of cinnamon sticks for *Spice Delight*.)

Be creative with other potpourri blends, too. A coconut shell half could be filled with a tropical blend; a balsamy scent would look nice in a lidded basket decorated with greens or stenciled. Shells, cones, seed pods, and dried flowers and grasses of all sorts can be used to decorate lidded boxes, baskets, and jars.

December

9

Examine frost on a window.

Have you ever looked closely at the frost on a window? Frost forms in beautiful fern and feather-like patterns. Do you know what causes it to form?

When the cold outside air comes in contact with the warm inside air, at the glass itself, it freezes. This once common occurrence is seldom seen nowadays because most windows have double panes of glass, or are protected with storm windows. You can encourage frost to form by leaving a storm window up a bit and making sure that your windows aren't scrupulously clean! Frost patterns usually start around an irregularity on the surface of the glass and spread outwards.

Another place to look at frost patterns is on the windows of your car (if it's kept outside, and not in a garage). Look closely at the patterns before you scrape the frost off.

10

Be aware of wind chill.

You've probably heard someone warn, "You can't always believe what you read!" Well, that goes for the temperature, as well. You can't always believe what the thermometer reads!

Thermometers can't measure one factor that contributes greatly to the cold, and that is wind. As you can see in the box below, cold temperatures plus wind equal even colder temperatures! During the winter months, many weather forecasters warn of the dangers of wind chill. And right they are. While an outside temperature of 30°F is tolerable, that combined with a brisk wind of 25 miles per hour would make the perceived temperature more like 0°F. Brrr!

Remember to keep the wind chill in mind, and dress accordingly.

Keep this in mind

Tack a copy of this chart up by the coat rack as a reminder to button up when there's a breeze!

Wind Chill Factor Chart

Wind speed in mph	Air Temperature in °F									
	35	30	25	20	15	10	5	0	−5	−10
5	33	26	21	16	12	7	1	−6	−11	−15
10	21	16	9	2	−2	−9	−15	−22	−27	−31
15	16	11	1	−6	−11	−18	−25	−33	−40	−45
20	12	3	−4	−9	−17	−24	−32	−40	−46	−52
25	7	0	−7	−15	−22	−29	−37	−45	−52	−58
30	5	−2	−11	−18	−26	−33	−41	−29	−56	−63

11

Put on some warm natural fibers.

For warmth and comfort, clothing made from natural fibers, such as wool and cotton, can't be beat. Natural fibers let your skin breathe, but they are also good at trapping warm air close to your body.

Wool does this especially well. Take a close look at some wool yarn. Each fuzzy strand helps create a barrier to trap your body heat. Cotton can be made warmer in this way, too. Have you ever noticed how warm cotton flannel is?

The more layers you put on, the warmer you get. But too many layers . . . and you can hardly move around! This is where down comes in handy. The downy feathers used to stuff outerwear (and comforters and pillows) trap a lot of air without much weight.

So dress warmly when you go out to play. And keep in mind that more than 50% of human body heat is lost through the head, so wear a hat!

Wear a layer of cotton under wool if you find the wool too itchy.

12

Brew some birch tea.

How about a nice cup of tea to warm you up? Did you know that you can brew a delicious tea from the twigs of the birch tree?

The sweet birch (also known as the black or cherry birch) makes the best tea. Its crushed twigs (and leaves) give off a strong wintergreen scent. Wash and break a handful of twigs and steep them in boiling water for about five minutes. Strain the tea through a fine-mesh strainer. Sweeten with honey, if you like, and enjoy one of nature's warming treats.

If there aren't any sweet birch trees growing near you, brew up some tea with wintergreen leaves themselves. The wintergreens include a number of different plant species. (All, as you probably guessed, stay green year-round.) Look for checkerberries, the low-growing plants found in sandy woods and clearings, that bear red berries. You'll know you've found the right plant when you crush a leaf between your fingers. What a delightful smell!

Or look for the spotted wintergreen. Its mottled leaves have a pronounced white stripe along the mid-vein. A closely related plant that has plain green leaves is known as pipsissewa. This is a Cree Indian word that means "it-breaks-into-small-pieces," which refers to the Indian belief that the plants help break down kidney and gallstones.

13

Make a cloud with your breath.

Did you know that when you see your breath on a chilly day you are making clouds? Short-lived clouds, certainly, but clouds none-the-less!

The warm vapor coming from your nose and mouth condenses quickly when it hits the cold air around you. It's momentarily visible before it breaks apart. (For more on clouds, see the week of *August 12–18*.)

14

Make a draft dodger.

Brrr! Some days it's too cold to spend much time outdoors. Luckily, it's nice and cozy inside your house. But keeping your house warm takes a lot of fuel. What can you do to help conserve heat? Make a draft dodger!

A draft dodger (or stopper) will keep warm air from leaking out of heated rooms. (Warm air is constantly being drawn towards cold air. When your parents shout, "Don't let all that cold air in!" they really mean "Don't let all that warm air out!") Make a draft dodger to place across thresholds and window sills that lose a lot of heat.

Choose some tightly-woven fabric. Cut a piece 6″ wide by at least 4″ longer than the threshold or sill it will span. With the right side of fabric folded to the inside, stitch the fabric lengthwise, and across one end. (See the illustration.) Turn the fabric right side out and fill with sand. Sew up the open end. There you have it! Put your draft dodger in place. No more draft!

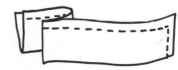

15

See if any animals have moved into your house.

Your nice, warm house is an open invitation to various small animals that neither migrate nor hibernate. Do you suspect that any have moved in?

Mice are the most common uninvited house guests. Depending on where you live, you might find shrews, rats, bats, and even squirrels moving right on in! These creatures seem capable of entering homes through the tiniest cracks. Some make themselves right at home within walls and ceilings. Have you ever heard them chattering and running about late at night?

The patter of little tiny feet isn't too much of a bother, but when mice start spoiling food and leaving their droppings as they go, something has to be done. Use humane traps to capture these wily critters. Peanut butter works well as bait. Keep the animals for a day or so before returning them to the wild. Let them go far away from your home (or anyone else's!); otherwise they'll be back in your house before you know it.

December

16

Participate in the Christmas bird count.

In late December every year, bird lovers of all ages pool their efforts and count all the birds they can find throughout the United States (and parts of Central and South America).

This event is known as the Christmas Count, and thousands of people participate. Small groups are assigned a circular area 15 miles in diameter (177 square miles). On a single day of their choosing (within a sixteen day period), the groups note how many birds are living in their prescribed circle. This information makes its way back to the National Audubon Society, which hopes to learn as much as it can about birds.

Ask at a local nature center or science museum if there are any groups you might join. Even if you don't know all the birds by sight and sound, you may be able to help in other ways. A birding event such as this is quite an experience!

17

Make a gingerbread forest.

'Tis the season to be baking . . . ! And nothing smells more inviting than gingerbread. This year, bake a gingerbread forest scene, complete with trees, flowers, and woodland animals!

You need a batch of gingerbread (have your mother help you find a recipe), some royal icing (this is the hard kind that cements the pieces together), and an assortment of candies that can be made into flowers. Shredded wheat and flaked coconut also come in handy.

Cut animals out of the dough using cookie cutters, or trace around basic shapes you've cut out of cardboard. Trees can be cut out, or three-dimensional ones can be made by cutting smaller and smaller circles of dough. Stack the baked circles one atop the other, separating them with a spot of icing or a small gumdrop. Spread slightly thinned icing like snow, adding coconut for texture. Make some fanciful flowers sticking out of the snow; shredded wheat looks like dried grass! Let your imagination run wild, and have fun!

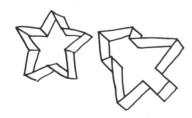

18

Gather some greenery.

Ancient people held evergreens in high esteem. To them, these plants (just by being green during the winter) held the promise of spring renewal, and were considered very special.

You can gather your own greenery to carry on the tradition. Depending on where you live, you can gather balsam fir, pine and hemlock boughs. Avoid spruce boughs because the needles are painfully sharp. You may also come across some holly if you live in the southern part of the United States.

Keep your greenery outdoors until the last minute, if possible. Spray the boughs with water now and again to keep them looking their freshest. You don't need much to make your house look festive. Use some to make wreaths (see *December 19*); use the rest in a number of creative ways. See the box below for some ideas.

Green magic

Decorating with evergreens can be as simple as dumping an armload of boughs in a big basket! You can use even little pieces in some surprising ways.

Help make your house look festive by tucking greenery in all sorts of places. Slip a few pieces behind mirrors and paintings on the walls; gather up some handfuls and hang them from the catches of all your windows. Don't forget to add some greenery to your room, and the bathroom! The high moisture level will keep the greens looking fresh for weeks.

Make lots of little wreaths to hold back curtains (slip the curtains right through the holes). Make an arrangement to put on the dinner table. What other ways can you think of using ev-ergreens to bring the sight and smell of nature indoors in winter?

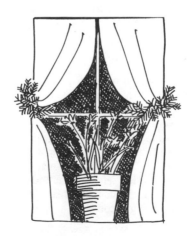

December

19

Make an evergreen wreath.

Evergreen wreaths are a traditional wintertime decoration. You can easily make your own! You need some evergreen boughs, a wire coat hanger and a roll of fine gauge wire.

Untwist the coat hanger and form it into a circle. (You can make a smaller wreath by scrunching down the hanger and forming a double-wire circle.) Cut the evergreen boughs into uniform lengths. Gather two or three pieces together. Place them on the wire circle, and wrap some wire around one end. Flip the wreath over and wrap another bundle on the other side. Continue wiring bundles of greenery to first one side and then the other. (Don't cut the wire between bundles.) Work around the circle until you reach the beginning. Tuck the last bundle under the bushy part of the very first bundle you put on.

This makes a full wreath that can be hung from either side. Add some cones, if you like, and a bright bow!

20

Look for some mistletoe.

Mistletoe can be found growing throughout the entire United States. It's a parasitic plant (one that gets its nourishment from another plant) that grows in rounded clumps on tree branches. Fortunately it doesn't harm the trees it grows on.

Mistletoe is usually only hung up at Christmastime (watch out, someone might try to kiss you!), but long ago it hung in homes all year long. It was thought to ward off evil spirits, and bring good luck to friends, and peace with enemies. The plant figures in many Norse legends, Greek and Roman myths and Druid rituals. Most likely all these stories served to explain why the plant flourished in the dead of winter when so many other plants appeared lifeless.

Look for mistletoe growing on the branches of deciduous trees that get full sun. The white berrylike fruits are covered with a sticky substance that is poisonous to people, but that doesn't bother the birds in the least. Cedar waxwings and bluebirds are among the birds that eat the fruits.

. . . .

The seven days before and after the winter solstice are known as the Halcyon Days. Long ago it was thought to be a time of peace and quiet in nature, when animals and birds stayed in their dens and nests.

21

First day of winter!

The first day of winter falls on or about the 21st of December. It is, in our hemisphere, the shortest day of the year. It is also known as the winter solstice, a day when the sun seems to stand still in the sky. (The summer solstice is its opposite, falling on or about June 21.)

For many people, this is a welcome day. Little by little they will watch the days lengthen, bringing spring! But that's a long way off, and winter is a wonderful season. Familiar landscapes take on a magical quality when they are blanketed in snow. If you dress properly, there's nothing to prevent you from spending time outdoors, playing and exploring.

Ancient peoples made huge bonfires on this day to encourage the sun to shine throughout the long winter months. You can honor the solstice this way, too. Ask your parents if you can have an outdoor fire tonight; or one in a fireplace indoors. Or at least light some candles!

Draw up near the fire and read one of the winter stories or poems (see *December 22*). Winter is full of wonders!

22

Read a story or poem about winter.

What is your favorite thing about winter? Do you like the quiet that descends with the snow? Or do you like the challenges the season presents?

The Guest from **Owl at Home**
Arnold Lobel *(story)*

I Heard a Bird Sing
Oliver Herford *(poem)*

Up North in Winter
Deborah Hartley *(story)*

Winter from **The Four Seasons**
Jack Prelutsky *(poem)*

Winter Clothes
Karla Kuskin *(poem)*

Winter Harvest
Jane Chelsea Aragon *(story)*

December

On Christmas Eve, it is said that farm animals are given the gift of human speech.

23

See how nature figures in Christmas customs.

Many Christmas customs pay tribute to plants and animals and nature in general.

Animals are given special privileges during the holiday season. Farm animals all over the world are given extra rations—in Czechoslovakia, a part of each course of the Christmas dinner is shared with the animals. In Denmark, suet and bread are hung from the trees for the birds; in rural areas sheaves of grain are lashed to poles.

Plants also figure in many customs. In some countries, trees are sprinkled with food to insure a good harvest the following year. In Costa Rica, the Christmas season begins with the orchid harvest; in Mexico the poinsettia figures in many celebrations.

In many countries the appearance of the evening star on Christmas Eve signals the start of the festivities, in honor of the star that guided the three wise men to the stable in Bethlehem. Light itself is important, symbolizing the light of warming fires, and welcoming lanterns. The Yule log, set ablaze on Christmas Eve (from the remains of last year's log) dates way back in time when bonfires were lit to encourage the sun to overcome the powers of darkness.

Some people celebrate . . .

Not everyone celebrates Christmas, of course. Hanukkah is a Jewish holiday that takes place every year some time during November or December. Hanukkah, also known as the Feast of Dedication and the Festival of Lights, commemorates the victory of the Jews over the Syrians over 2,000 years ago.

For each of the eight days of the celebration, candles are lit in memory of the sacred oil in the Palestinian temple that miraculously burned for eight days (even though there was only enough oil to burn for one day).

The candles are held in a candelabra called a menorah that has nine candle holders—one for each night, plus one for the Shammash ("servant candle") which is used to light the others. There is much feasting during Hanukkah, as well as game playing and an exchange of presents.

Less widely known is a new holiday started by some black communities in the 1970s. It is called Kwanza, and is based on African harvest celebrations. The holiday runs for seven days, from December 26 to January 1.

24

Make a straw star.

The wise men who journeyed to Bethlehem were supposedly guided by a star that mysteriously appeared in the sky. Astronomers have puzzled over what star this could possibly have been. They have reached no conclusions, but that hardly matters! The star will always be an important symbol.

You can cut stars from paper (see *Snip a star* on page 34), or you can make some six-pointed stars from straw (thought to have magical powers of its own!). You can also use slender twigs. Cut three pieces of straw the same length (4″ to 6″ is good), and cross one piece over another in the middle. With some colorful yarn or string, wrap these two straws together; then add the third (see the illustration). With a different colored yarn, wrap around each of the six spokes in turn, going completely around each straw before continuing on to the next. Continue wrapping the spokes until each is wrapped about 6 to 8 times. Tie the yarn on the back of the star, making a loop to hang the star from a window or ceiling.

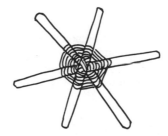

25

Merry Christmas!

This is a joyous time of year for a lot of people. Traditions that have been passed down for centuries add meaning to a special time for sharing.

Start your own family traditions that include activities everyone can join in. Adopt some of the customs that include nature and wildlife, too.

Sing carols that celebrate nature. *The Holly and the Ivy* and *The Friendly Beasts* are two traditional English carols you may know. *O Tannenbaum (O Christmas Tree)* is a German carol about a very special tree!

Set the dinner table in an unusual way. Do what's done in Poland and Czechoslovakia, and spread some hay on the floor and even under the tablecloth, like a stable.

Make sure to get outdoors at some point. Bring some scraps from the table for the birds. Warm up by the fire with a cup of herb tea (see *December 26*). Offer to feed the animals at a nature center (see *December 28*). The little things you do together, and for others, will make the day a very memorable one.

26

Warm up with some herb tea.

A nice cup of herb tea is just the thing after an outing on a cold winter's day. Herbs have been steeped in water and savored for centuries—often for their medicinal value. Nowadays, most people drink herb teas because they are simply delicious!

You can find all sorts of herbal teas in the supermarket, but you can easily brew your own teas from herbs you have grown and harvested yourself (see *Let's hear it for herbs!* on page 60). Many herb teas are a blend of two or more dried herbs, but some of the best teas are made from just one herb, such as mint or chamomile. Add a spoonful of dried leaves (or flowers, in the case of chamomile) to a cup of boiling water. Let steep for about five minutes, then strain through a fine-mesh sieve. Sweeten with a bit of honey, if you like.

Experiment with blending different herbs (and spices) to make other teas. Check the labels of herbal teas in your supermarket for the ingredients that make up some of the commercial blends. And don't forget another natural treat, birch tea (see *December 12*).

27

Trim a tree for the birds.

Carry on a centuries-old tradition and put out some special treats for the birds! Decorate a tree in your yard with edible ornaments.

Make the tree especially festive for the holiday season. Use cookie cutters to cut out shapes from stale bread, and spread them with peanut butter. Hang them from the tree with cotton or wool yarn (it will eventually decompose, or be used by the birds to build their nest come spring). Hang pretzels from the branches, or even donuts! Scooped-out orange halves can be filled with seed or suet and hung. When you take down your indoor Christmas tree, remember to save any edible decorations to add to the birds' tree.

What other ways can you think of sharing the holiday spirit with wildlife?

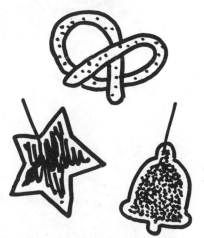

28

Donate some time or money to help nature.

Would you like to give a lasting gift to nature? You can! You can spend some of your time, and some of your allowance, helping support groups that are concerned with wildlife and the environment.

This is a good time of year to give both time and money. Many nature centers and zoos have small staffs that care for all the animals. They only get time off if volunteers offer to help feed the animals and keep an eye on things (especially over the holidays).

All the efforts made toward preserving land, saving endangered species and promoting an understanding of nature take money. Millions of Americans donate money each year to pay for these projects, but more is always needed. Donations are usually tax-deductible—your parents will know how that affects them. See *Nature conservancy groups* in the Appendix for the names and addresses of some of the better known organizations.

This may be the best tradition you and your family can adopt—giving what you can to the groups that are working so hard to protect our earth and all its inhabitants for generations to come.

29

Recycle your Christmas tree.

Don't forget that you can recycle your or your neighbor's tree in a number of ways.

First off, put any edible ornaments (cranberry and popcorn garlands, and cookie ornaments) outdoors for birds. Then decide what you want to do with the tree itself. The simplest thing is to set it in a corner of your property. Many animals and birds will use it for shelter. (Point this out to your parents if they object!) You can also strip the branches from the tree and use them to protect your garden plants.

If you haven't had a chance to count the rings of a tree yet, do so now. Saw the trunk straight across for a clear view. Most conifers are 8 to 10 years old when they are felled and sold as Christmas trees. How old is this tree?

December

30

Look back at your nature discoveries.

Now is a good time to look back (with the help of this book) to see what you've learned about nature this past year. Can you believe all the things you did? What were some of your favorite projects? Where did you enjoy exploring the most?

If you weren't able to finish some of the projects suggested throughout the year, maybe you can finish them now. If you didn't get a chance to get to the beach, or to the mountains, ask your parents if you can plan a trip to one of these places next year. All of these excursions make good family outings.

What is the most important thing you've learned about nature this year? Are you still scared of snakes? Well, that's okay, as long as you know that you don't have to fear most of them! Do you see beauty in a spider's web? Do you see how everything in nature fits together like a jigsaw puzzle? Do you know that you are one of the most important pieces?

31

Make a New Year's resolution.

Do you make New Year's resolutions every year? And do you keep them? Well, this year you can make a resolution that you *can* keep. Resolve to respect and enjoy nature in the years to come!

The fate of the earth, and all living things on it, is in human hands. Your hands! You and your family, and all your friends and their families, must do your part to keep the earth a healthy place to live. But the rewards for your hard work and care are great. The enjoyment you've gotten from discovering plants and animals you never knew existed is yours forever! The pleasure of drinking from a bubbling brook, or smelling a rose, is one you can have year after year.

Whether you live out in the country or in a city, every morning the sun is there to greet you. Every night the stars come out to shine. Every spring the flowers burst into bloom. There's magic everywhere! Each new day when you step outside your door, look around you and say, "This is my home!"

Growing up with nature

This book is just a beginning. There's more to nature than could possibly be written in just one book. But hopefully, this one has opened your eyes to some of the wonders of the natural world. Nature is all around you, in your backyard, down the street, everywhere you turn.

You can use this book again next year. You'll recognize and remember some of the suggestions, but you'll be a year older, and a year wiser. You may want to repeat some of the projects; others you'll skip over. Some you may want to expand upon and use as the basis for science projects in school. Some of the activities in this book may be the start of a pleasurable hobby.

And you can use this book the year after that! It is said that learning is a lifelong process. You may never outgrow this book. But when you do, be sure to pass it on to your grandchildren.

Additional Information

The greater outdoors

Many of the activities in this book take place out-of-doors, mostly in your own backyard or some place close to home. Some activities suggest you explore other habitats, from wooded spots to seaside stretches. While some people have such a variety of landscapes close at hand, few of us are that lucky. Even meadows to meander through and streams to walk beside are getting harder to find. At some point, you may want to plan a family trip farther from home. You may even be ready to take a long hike into a wilderness area, or camp out for a night or two.

It is beyond the scope of this book to provide details on hiking, backpacking, and camping (not to mention canoeing, cross-country skiing, and other outdoor recreation). If your parents have taken part in some of these activities, there is much you can learn from them. You may even have some of the equipment that you need to get started. But there are plenty of other ways to get a taste of

outdoor life. There are clubs specifically for children, such as the Boy Scouts and Girl Scouts, that teach outdoor skills and sponsor trips of various types. Some schools are equipped to offer outdoor experiences. Many summer camps concentrate on nature studies and self-sufficiency in the wilds. And then there are nature clubs and organizations that frequently sponsor excursions that are family-oriented, from day hikes to canoe trips that span several days.

In the comfort of your own backyard, you can practice lots of skills that will come in handy when you venture farther from home. With your parents' supervision, learn to build a campfire (and use it, instead of your grill, to cook dinner outdoors some evening). Practice setting up a tent on your own property, even spending the night in it to get used to sleeping out in the open. (Where insects are not a problem, you don't even need a tent. Snuggle up in your bedroll and gaze up at the star-filled sky before dropping off to sleep.) Learn how to use a compass and to read a topographical map, both of which are skills you should have before heading into unmarked areas. Once you are comfortable with finding your way, putting up shelter and providing food, away from the comforts of home, you'll have great fun "roughing it."

You can also read up on those outdoor skills that you would like to learn. Take a look at:

Camping and Walking
David Watkins and Meike Dalal
(Usborne Publishing, Ltd., 1987)
juvenile

The Official Boy Scout Handbook
(Boy Scouts of America, 1979)
juvenile

Starting Small in the Wilderness: The Sierra Club Outdoors Guide for Families
Marlyn Doan
(Sierra Club Books, 1979)
adult

Staying on track

Even if you don't wander far from home, you may wander off the beaten path now and again, and there are some things to keep in mind. Getting lost can happen to anyone, but not if you take some precautions and play it safe. Firstly, ALWAYS let someone know where you are headed and when you expect to return. That way help can be sent in the rare event that you lose your way or something happens to you. Secondly, take a map and compass with you, and use them! What you want here are the topographical maps published by the U.S. Geological Survey. Those for your area can be found at sporting goods stores and the like (or send for maps directly from the governent office—the address can be found under *Where to purchase supplies*). These maps are

Additional information

great fun, and, depending on the scale of the map, you may even find the street on which you live, sometimes even your own house! Experienced backpackers claim that orienteering compasses are the type to own for use in the wilds. If you already have a basic compass at home, it will probably do for those short trips you take in a relatively confined area. The books mentioned above outline the steps to take to learn how to use a map and compass. Read them or seek the help of someone who can explain the workings of these valuable exploration tools.

There really is no substitute for the map and compass, but you may only be wandering into an area already criss-crossed with trails. If they are well marked (with different colors, for instance) all you'll need to remember is which trail you are on and stick with it. If you plan on returning the way you came, you will have to mark the trails in some way (with a pile of rocks or an obvious bundle of sticks).

In any case, it's always a good idea to look behind you often as you are walking, in order to familiarize yourself with the way as seen from the opposite direction.

You can use the sun to help you head in the right direction, either by just looking for it in the sky and guessing where it is at that particular time, or by using the sun in conjunction with a watch to give you a primitive bearing. Holding your watch flat in your hand, point the hour hand towards the sun. The point mid-way between 12 and the hour hand will be south (the other directions will line up with other points of your watch accordingly). This works on standard time—if it's day-light saving time, the point between the hour hand and *1* is south. Before noon, you'll have to read backwards around the dial to determine south; after 12 noon, read clockwise.

· · · · · · · · · · · · · · · · · · ·

Have you ever seen colored bands and flashes of light in the sky? You probably witnessed the northern lights, or aurora borealis. Solar winds are responsible for large amounts of electrically-charged particles that are somehow deflected by the earth's magnetic shield, resulting in this display.

· · · · · · · · · · · · · · · · · · ·

Many cultures throughout history have worshipped the sun. In the United States certain Plains Indians, such as the Arapaho, Cheyenne, and Oglala Sioux, put on a spectacular religious ceremony known as the Sun Dance once a year in early summer.

The right stuff

You'll always want to travel as lightly as possible, but don't forget to bring along some essentials. Remember to wear the proper clothing (and pack anything you might need, such as rain-gear and repellent and an extra layer, if it will be getting cooler). Your foot-wear should be sturdy (and already broken in) and you should have a hat, not only to keep your head warm, but to shade you from the sun. Neutral colors are the best for clothing, because they blend in with the surroundings. You are less likely to startle some wildlife if you dress in the colors of nature. Closely woven fabrics are often chosen by outdoorsmen because they are not easily penetrated by biting or stinging insects.

Bring along anything you think you might need to study nature. You'll probably want to tote a magnifying glass, even a light-weight field guide. Depending on the nature of your trip, you may want to bring along a portable plant press, or small jars and plastic bags for collecting. Don't forget to bring something to eat, such as quick-energy snacks like candy bars or trail mix, for when energies flag. A canteen of water is always a good idea, as well.

Treading lightly

Once you take to the wilds, hiking through unspoiled areas and camping alongside untamed mountain streams that still dot this country, you will be joining a growing number of people who seek recreation out in the open air. There was a time (and your parents may remember it if they did any camping when they were younger) when it was acceptable to cut evergreen boughs to sleep on, and chop down young trees to construct shelters with. It was even okay to bury any trash that could not be burned in a campfire. There were so few people doing this, in such a seemingly vast wilderness, it was thought that little harm was being done. We know differently now, however, and because there are so many of us hiking and backpacking and canoeing and camping, we must change our habits.

Campfires are actually not allowed in many areas, as the risk of forest fires is too great, and the taking of firewood disturbs the habitat. Use a portable cook stove instead. You must also take out of an area everything you take into it (including all your trash) and you must make sure that nothing you do will foul a water source (such as dish soap and human wastes). Treat the wilderness like you would your own property; it is your property, in a way, because the land has been set aside for your enjoyment, especially in the case of state and national forests and you will always be welcome to make yourself at home there.

Treating poison plant rashes

The best way to deal with plants that cause an allergic reaction, such as poison ivy and nettles, is to avoid them. Learn what they look like (see *May 15*) and stay clear of them. But if, in the excitement of exploring an area, you forget to keep an eye out for these plants, there are a number of things you can do.

You know you have touched a stinging nettle the minute you brush against one. A fiery stinging sensation takes place, but luckily it lasts only about 10 minutes. Some people say you can "cool" your skin by rubbing it with the bruised leaves of the jewelweed, a plant often growing near nettles and poison ivy.

Poison ivy (and poison oak and poison sumac) is sneakier. Some people react instantly when they come in contact with the oily leaves or even the smoke from burning poison ivy, but others don't break out into a rash for as long as a week! Then they have to think back to where they were as many as seven days earlier. Once your skin has broken out into a rash there

Leaves of three, let it be.

Additional information

is little you can do but try to make yourself more comfortable. Calamine lotion helps, as do some other ointments. See a doctor if you are really troubled by the rash. It should completely disappear within a week or so.

Contrary to popular belief, poison ivy rash is not contagious, nor does it spread. It just seems to be spreading as the rash gradually develops. If you think you have brushed against some poison ivy, wash the area with soap and water within half an hour, and you may be able to get rid of the oils that contain the irritants. A product known as Poison Oak-N-Ivy Cleanser works for many people if used within 4 to 8 hours after exposure. Both of these measures are certainly worth a try. Otherwise, just grin and bear it!

Dealing with animal bites and stings

What would summer be without mosquitos? Well, if you are like most people, you probably don't have many kind things to say about mosquitos, especially when they are making a meal out of you, but you have to admit . . . they are part of nature! So what can you do about them, and some of the other creatures that occasionally bite and sting?

You can avoid them, for one. Many biting insects come out in full force after sundown (or on overcast days) so stay indoors when they are particularly bad. Many of these same insects can be kept at bay with repellents, especially those containing "deet" (a chemical properly known as N,N, diethyl-meta-toluamide). There are even some hand creams that seem effective against warding off these pesky critters, although it should be noted that many perfumes and scented hand creams and shampoos actually draw insects to you. These measures generally work for mosquitos, no-see-ums, blackflies, and some of the larger biters such as horseflies and deerflies.

What about bees and wasps? Luckily these insects only sting as a last resort. To avoid inciting these insects, look carefully where you are going and don't provoke a bee or wasp that is busy going about its business. Some stinging insects are plainly aggressive, however, so you may have to move away from them, and pack up the picnic lunch that might have attracted them in the first place.

Some people experience an allergic reaction when they are stung by bees and wasps. A sting victim showing signs of shortness of breath, dizziness, and whose skin feels cool and moist, should be treated immediately. Take that person to an emergency room right away. There *is* something that can be prescribed and taken with you on outdoor excursions, so ask you doctor for his advice, if you think you may be allergic.

If you are stung and are showing no adverse reaction, scrape the stinger off with the blade of a knife, rather than trying to pull it out with your fingernails or tweezers. Pulling the stinger only pushes more venom into your skin. Wash the spot with soap and water and cover with a bandage.

Ticks are annoying creatures that attach themselves to bare skin. They, too, can be repelled with repellents and clothing. If you do get a tick on you, remove it by covering it with oil (any type will do) and wait for half an hour or so until the tick lets go. Some people claim that a spot of kerosene or some other fuel works well. If neither of these tricks work, pull the tick

off with a pair of tweezers, wash the wound well, and cover it with a bandage.

Larger animals, from snakes to mammals, rarely bite, unless they are unable to defend themselves. Most will run from you first, or make threatening gestures before they bite as a last resort. You can avoid bites from frightened animals by never putting your hand into a hole in the ground (or in a tree) and wearing thick gloves when you must handle them (for more on capturing wild animals, see pages 13 and 14).

You should NEVER approach a wild animal that is acting tame. (Squirrels and pigeons in the park are an exception. They have become used to people throwing them scraps of food. A truly wild animal that is showing no fear is another matter.) This odd behavior often accompanies rabies, a potentially dangerous disease. While it is tempting to pet those animals that seem so friendly (raccoons, skunks, and bats are all occasionally rabid), do not do so. Tell your parents about any animals that are acting strangely. They should call a vet, or a nature center and ask for advice.

Preserving flowers with chemical desiccants

There are a number of substances that can be used in addition to sand for drying flower blossoms and foliage. The most popular desiccants, as these are called, include powdered borax (which is usually mixed with an equal amount of alum, or with two parts corn meal to one of borax) and silica gel crystals. These desiccants are used just like sand, so review the general instructions given on *July 24* for preserving blossoms in sand. For best results, heat your desiccant in the oven (with your parents' help) to completely dry it out. Silica gel crystals turn from blue to pink as they absorb moisture, so make sure they are blue when you are starting out. Generally, the chemical desiccants require less drying time than sand, but you'll still need to check a blossom to see if it is crackly dry and brittle. Recover the blossoms if they need more drying time.

A microwave oven can be used to speed the drying even more. Bury your blossoms in silica gel in a plastic, glass, or paper container (large enough to hold the gel when it expands). Do not cover this container, but place it carefully in the oven. Put a separate cup of water in one corner of the oven. The oven will need to be turned on for as few as 45 seconds for delicate and flat blossoms to as many as 2 minutes for heftier blooms such as roses, zinnias, and most foliage. Remove the container from the oven, but do not touch the gel for another 20 minutes, until it's cool. Carefully remove the blossoms from the gel, but let them cool for another 15 minutes before brushing them gently to get rid of all the desiccant. Wait until the next day before attaching any flowers or foliage to wires and arranging them.

Note: Always check the instructions that come with prepackaged desiccants. The instructions may vary somewhat.

Additional information

On a scale of 1 to 10

The hardness of a mineral provides clues to its identity. A hardness scale devised in 1822 by a German mineralogist named Friedrich Mohs is based on the relative hardness of minerals. The mineral in question is given a rating that is one number higher than a mineral it can scratch. For instance, quartz, with a rating of 7 will scratch all the minerals that have a lower rating. Diamonds are the hardest natural substance and will scratch any other mineral.

Fractions are often used to make the scale even more precise. The basic scale goes like this:

Mohs' Scale
1 Talc
2 Gypsum
3 Calcite
4 Fluorite
5 Apatite
6 Feldspar
7 Quartz
8 Topaz
9 Corundum
10 Diamond

The magnitude of an earthquake is also measured on a scale of 1 to 10. C.F. Richter developed a scale in 1935 that bears his name. Small tremors

. . . .

Seismology is the study of earthquakes.

measure about 2.5 on the Richter scale (this would be something like the rumble of a passing train). Minor earthquakes measure about 5.7; major quakes are about 7.8 on the scale. Anything over 8 is considered disastrous. The worst earthquake ever measured was 8.9 on the Richter scale.

Honor thy wildlife

The following chart includes all the birds, flowers and trees that the fifty states have designated as their "own." You'll notice that several species are shared by a number of states. Six states honor the Western meadowlark; four states hold the sugar maple in high esteem! Not surprisingly, Hawaii has chosen three distinctive native species.

Check in an atlas or encyclopedia to learn what other natural resources your own state has chosen to honor, from minerals to mushrooms.

State	Bird	Flower	Tree
Alabama	Yellowhammer	Camellia	Longleaf pine
Alaska	Willow ptarmigan	Forget-me-not	Sitka spruce
Arizona	Cactus wren	Saguaro cactus	Paloverde
Arkansas	Mockingbird	Apple blossom	Shortleaf pine
California	California valley quail	Golden poppy	California redwood
Colorado	Lark bunting	Rocky Mountain columbine	Colorado blue spruce
Connecticut	American robin	Mountain laurel	White oak
Delaware	Blue hen chicken	Peach blossom	American holly
Florida	Mockingbird	Orange blossom	Cabbage palmetto
Georgia	Brown thrasher	Cherokee rose	Live oak
Hawaii	Nene (Hawaiian goose)	Red hibiscus	Kukui (candlenut tree)
Idaho	Mountain bluebird	Syringa	Western white pine
Illinois	Cardinal	Violet	White oak
Indiana	Cardinal	Peony	Tulip tree
Iowa	Eastern goldfinch	Wild rose	Oak
Kansas	Western meadowlark	Sunflower	Cottonwood
Kentucky	Cardinal	Goldenrod	Coffee tree
Louisiana	Eastern brown pelican	Magnolia	Bald cypress
Maine	Chickadee	Eastern white pine cone and tassel	Eastern white pine
Maryland	Baltimore oriole	Black-eyed Susan	White oak
Massachusetts	Chickadee	Mayflower	American elm
Michigan	Robin	Apple blossom	Eastern white pine
Minnesota	Loon	Showy lady's slipper	Red pine
Mississippi	Mockingbird	Magnolia	Southern magnolia
Missouri	Bluebird	Hawthorn	Flowering dogwood

State	Bird	Flower	Tree
Montana	Western meadowlark	Bitterroot	Ponderosa pine
Nebraska	Western meadowlark	Goldenrod	Cottonwood
Nevada	Mountain bluebird	Sagebrush	Single-leaf pinyon
New Hampshire	Purple finch	Purple lilac	Paper birch
New Jersey	Eastern goldfinch	Purple violet	Red oak
New Mexico	Roadrunner	Yucca	Pinyon
New York	Bluebird	Rose	Sugar maple
North Carolina	Cardinal	Dogwood Pine	Pine
North Dakota	Western meadowlark	Wild prairie rose	American elm
Ohio	Cardinal	Scarlet carnation	Ohio buckeye
Oklahoma	Scissor-tailed flycatcher	Mistletoe	Redbud
Oregon	Western meadowlark	Oregon grape	Douglas fir
Pennsylvania	Ruffed grouse	Mountain laurel	Eastern hemlock
Rhode Island	Rhode Island Red	Violet	Red maple
South Carolina	Carolina wren	Yellow jasmine	Palmetto
South Dakota	Ring-necked pheasant	Pasqueflower	White spruce
Tennessee	Mockingbird	Iris	Yellow poplar
Texas	Mockingbird	Bluebonnet	Pecan
Utah	Sea gull	Sego lily	Blue spruce
Vermont	Hermit thrush	Red clover	Sugar maple
Virginia	Cardinal	Flowering dogwood	—
Washington	Willow goldfinch	Coast rhododendron	Western hemlock
West Virginia	Cardinal	Great rhododendron	Sugar maple
Wisconsin	Robin	Wood violet	Sugar maple
Wyoming	Western meadowlark	Indian paintbrush	Cottonwood

Where to purchase supplies

As mentioned in *How to use this book,* you might want to round up some tools and other gear in order to make the most of your nature explorations. What you don't already have at home, you can make in many cases, or buy with your allowance. Check out those businesses close to home, from gift shops at nature centers and science museums to toy and hobby shops. If you don't see what you are after, ask. Many shop owners are happy to order something special for you if they can. Otherwise look into ordering from those companies that offer their goods through the mail.

The businesses listed here sell articles relating to nature (or at least to the nature activities outlined in this book), from compasses to cloud charts. Write and ask for a catalogue (most are free of charge). Happy browsing!

Animal Town Game Company
P.O. Box 2002
Santa Barbara, CA 93120
(games on nature themes)

Aphrodisia
282 Bleeker Street
New York, NY 10014
(dried herbs and other potpourri ingredients)

W. Atlee Burpee & Company
300 Park Avenue
Warminster, PA 18974
(seeds and gardening supplies)

Dover Publications, Inc.
31 East 2nd Street
Mineola, NY 11501
(nature books and posters—request their Nature Book catalogue)

Duncraft
Penacook, NH 03303-9020
(bird watching and feeding supplies)

Into the Wind
1408 Pearl Street
Boulder, CO 80302
(kites)

Music for Little People
Box 1460
Redway, CA 95560
(audio and video tapes on nature themes, especially for children)

· · · · · · · · · · · · · · · · · · · ·

The kite—a graceful, gliding bird—has given its name to paper kites.

The Nature Company
P.O. Box 2310
Berkeley, CA 94702
(nature gift items)

Nature's Herb Company
281 Ellis Street
San Fransisco, CA 94102
(dried herbs and other potpourri ingredients)

Smith & Hawken
25 Corte Madera
Mill Valley, CA 94941
(gardening paraphernalia plus some nature gifts)

Three Rivers Amphibian, Inc.
30 Broadway
Massapequa, NY 11758
(Grow-a-Frog kit)

Tomahawk Live Trap Company
P.O. Box 323
Tomahawk, WI 54487
(humane animal traps)

Where to purchase supplies

U.S. Geological Survey
Map Distribution Center
1200 South Eads Street
Arlington, VA 22202
(U.S. east of the Mississippi River)

U.S. Geological Survey
Map Distribution Center
Federal Center, Building 41
Denver, CO 80225
(U.S. west of the Mississippi River)

Whale Gifts—Center for Environmental Education
Catalogue Order Department
P.O. Box 810
Old Saybrook, CT 06475-0810
(nature gift items)

Wild Bird Supplies
4815 Oak Street
Crystal Lake, IL 60012
(bird watching and feeding supplies)

. . . .

Make sun tea by placing two tea bags in a gallon jar filled with water. Cover and set it outside in full sunlight until the tea is as dark as you like it. Mix it up with sugar or honey and lemon and pour over ice.

Send for catalogues from the following museums. You'll find picture postcards, posters, books and lots of gift items, many celebrating nature.

The Art Institute of Chicago
Michigan Avenue at Adams Street
Chicago, IL 60603

The Metropolitan Museum of Art
255 Gracie Station
New York, NY 10028

Museum of Fine Arts, Boston
Catalogue Sales Department
P.O. Box 1044
Boston, MA 02120

San Francisco Museum of Modern Art
MuseumBooks—Mail Order
P.O. Box 182203
Chattanooga, TN 37422

The Smithsonian Institution
Department 0006
Washington, DC 20073-0006

Zoological Society of San Diego
P.O. Box 551
San Diego, CA 92112

Lastly, here are the names and addresses of three companies that stock almost everything you could possibly want for nature studies and other branches of science. These companies serve schools and other educational institutions, but will fill orders placed by individuals. The catch: their huge catalogues are very expensive. There are a number of ways to get around this. Your best bet is to ask a science teacher at your school if you may borrow a copy of one of these catalogues (be sure to return it!). Or see if you can have one of the previous year's editions. New catalogues are issued each year, and the old ones are usually thrown out. The items in the catalogues change very little from year to year.

Or write directly to one of these companies with a specific question or request. They will happily answer your letter. Note: These companies all have East and West Coast facilities.

Carolina Biological Supply Company
2700 York Road
Burlington, NC 27215
(East Coast)
Box 187
Gladstone, OR 97027
(West Coast)

Science Kit & Boreal Laboratories
777 East Park Drive
Tonawanda, NY 14150-6782
(East Coast)
P.O. Box 2726
Santa Fe Springs, CA 90670-4490
(West Coast)

Ward's Natural Science Establishment, Inc.
5100 West Henrietta Road
P.O. Box 92912
Rochester, NY 14692-9012
(East Coast)
11850 East Florence Avenue
Santa Fe Springs, CA 90670-4490
(West Coast)

. . . .

Have you ever heard of leap seconds? As of January 1988, 14 seconds have been added to "time" since 1972 when the idea was first proposed. Because the earth's rotation has slowed, and we have a need for very precise time measurement, we have added seconds so that clocks will coordinate with astronomical time.

Nature conservancy groups

The following organizations are some of the better known groups that have done much to promote our understanding of the natural world. Their work is not done yet. If you would like to know more, write these groups for more information. (Many publish wonderful magazines for their members, and these are noted in each entry.) For a complete list of all the conservation organizations in this country (many of which do work worldwide) look for *The Conservation Directory*, a publication put out by the National Wildlife Federation each year. Your local library should have a copy of it.

American Museum of Natural History
Central Park West at 79th Street
New York, NY 10024

Natural History (monthly, adult readers)

Center for Environmental Education, Inc.
1725 DeSales Street, NW
Suite 500
Washington, DC 20036

The Cousteau Society, Inc.
930 West 21st Street
Norfolk, VA 23517

Calypso Log (bi-monthly, adult readers)
Dolphin Log (bi-monthly, ages 7-15)

Defenders of Wildlife
1244 19th Street, NW
Washington, DC 20036

Defenders (bi-monthly, adult readers)

Friends of the Earth
530 7th Street, SE
Washington, DC 20003

The Fund for Animals, Inc.
200 West 57th Street
New York, NY 10019

Greenpeace USA, Inc.
1436 U Street, NW
Washington, DC 20007

The Greenpeace Magazine (bi-monthly, adult readers)

National Arbor Day Foundation
100 Arbor Avenue
Nebraska City, NE 68410

Arbor Day (bi-monthly, adult readers)

National Audubon Society
950 Third Avenue
New York, NY 10022

Audubon (monthly, adult readers)

National Geographic Society
17th and M Streets, NW
Washington, DC 20036

National Geographic (monthly, adult readers)
National Geographic World (monthly, ages 8 and up)

National Wildlife Federation
1400 16th Street, NW
Washington, DC 20036-2266

National Wildlife (bi-monthly, adult readers)
International Wildlife (bi-monthly, adult readers)
Your Big Backyard (monthly, ages 3-5)
Ranger Rick (monthly, ages 6-12)

The Nature Conservancy
1815 North Lynn Street
Arlington, VA 22209

The Nature Conservancy Magazine (bi-monthly, adult readers)

Sierra Club
730 Polk Street
San Francisco, CA 94109

Sierra (bi-monthly, adult readers)

The Wilderness Society
1400 I Street, NW
Washington, DC 20005

Wilderness (quarterly, adult readers)

World Wildlife Fund—US
1250 24th Street, NW
Washington, DC 20037

· · · · · · · · · · · · · · · · · ·

Don't forget nature's clean-up crews—the scavengers. These animals (ranging from microscopic creatures to vultures) eat only dead flesh or decaying plant material, as the case may be. They keep things tidy, and see that everything in nature is put to further use.

Other books you might enjoy reading

While this book has given you a taste of many of the wonders of the natural world, you may want to read more about certain aspects of nature that interest you. You'll probably also want to identify some of the plants, animals and rocks that you find. There are hundreds of wonderful books you can pick up, from field guides to craft books full of creative ways to use nature's treasures. They are as close as your local library!

The following list is by no means complete (some of your own favorites may be missing), but you'll find all sorts of helpful titles here. Generally, the books listed are rather comprehensive—they are fat volumes that cover a lot of ground. (Ask your librarian to help you find those books that concentrate on a particular species or habitat, for instance, if you'd like a more in-depth look.) Some of

these books have been written for younger readers, others specifically for adults. Many of the books fall somewhere in between. You'll notice that each book is given a "juvenile" or "adult" rating. This is simply a device to help you find the books you want. The juvenile books can be found in the children's departments of libraries and bookstores; the adult books will generally be on the adult shelves. Books marked "juvenile/adult" are just as likely to be found in one place as the other.

Grouping books that cover so many different topics isn't easy, but you'll notice that there are six basic categories. The first, *Nature—A many splendored thing,* lists books that are broad in scope, and that treat many aspects of nature much as this book does. The categories *Animal, Vegetable* and *Mineral* follow, each containing books that have something to do with these three divisions of nature. For more about habitats in general, and weather in particular, check the next category *Earth.* This is followed by *Nature and culture,* which includes books about crafting with natural materials as well as books examining nature lore.

Nature—A many splendored thing

FOR THE AMATEUR NATURALIST

ABC's of Nature: A Family Answer Book (The Reader's Digest Association, Inc., 1984) *juvenile/adult*

The Amateur Naturalist's Handbook by Vinson Brown (Prentice-Hall, Inc., 1980) *adult*

The Backyard Naturalist by Craig Tufts (National Wildlife Federation, 1988) *adult*

The Curious Naturalist by John Mitchell and the Massachusetts Audubon Society (Prentice-Hall, Inc., 1980) *juvenile/adult*

Enjoying Nature With Your Family by Micheal Chinery (Crown Publishers, Inc., 1977) *adult*

A Field Guide to Your Own Back Yard by John Hanson Mitchell (W.W. Norton and Company, 1985) *adult*

Joy of Nature: How to Observe and Appreciate the Great Outdoors (The Reader's Digest Association, Inc., 1977) *adult*

A Naturalist's Guide to the Year by Howard Smith (E.P. Dutton, Inc., 1985) *adult*

The Nature Book by Midas Dekkers (Macmillan Publishing Company, 1988) *juvenile*

North American Wildlife (The Reader's Digest Association, Inc., 1982) *adult*

A Practical Guide for the Amateur Naturalist by Gerald Durrell (Alfred A. Knopf, 1983) *adult*

The Young Naturalist: An Introduction to Nature Studies by Andrew Mitchell (Usborne Publishing, 1982) *juvenile*

MORE BOOKS WITH NATURAL SCIENCE ACTIVITIES

The Evolution Book by Sara Stein (Workman Publishing, 1986) *juvenile*

Reasons for the Seasons by Linda Allison (Little, Brown and Company, 1975) *juvenile*

The Science Book by Sara Stein (Workman Publishing, Inc., 1979) *juvenile*

Scienceworks from The Ontario Science Centre (Addison-Wesley, 1988) *juvenile*

This Book is About Time by Marilyn Burns (Little, Brown and Company, 1978) *juvenile*

The Wild Inside: Sierra Club's Guide to the Great Indoors by Linda Allison (Little, Brown and Company, 1979) *juvenile*

Other books you might enjoy reading

Animal

TRACKING & WATCHING ANIMALS

America's Favorite Backyard Wildlife by Kit Harrison and George H. Harrison (Simon & Schuster, 1987) *adult*

Beastly Neighbors by Mollie Rights (Little, Brown and Company, 1981) *juvenile*

Crinkleroot's Book of Animal Tracks and Wildlife Signs by Jim Arnosky (G.P. Putnam's Sons, 1979) *juvenile*

The North American Animal Almanac by Darryl Stewart (Stewart, Tabori and Chang, 1984) *adult*

Secrets of a Wildlife Watcher by Jim Arnosky (Lothrop, Lee & Shepard, 1983) *juvenile*

Suburban Wildlife: An Introduction to the Common Animals of Your Back Yard by Richard Headstrom (Prentice-Hall, Inc., 1984) *adult*

MAMMALS

The Audubon Society Field Guide to North American Mammals by John O. Whitaker, Jr. (Alfred A. Knopf, 1980) *adult*

A Field Guide to the Mammals by William H. Burt and Richard P. Grossenheider (Houghton Mifflin Company, 1976) *adult*

Mammals by Tessa Board (Franklin Watts, 1983) *juvenile*

BIRDS

America's Favorite Backyard Birds by Kit Harrison and George H. Harrison (Simon & Schuster, 1983) *adult*

The Audubon Society Field Guide to North American Birds by John Bull and John Farrand, Jr. (Alfred A. Knopf, 1977) *adult*

Bird by David Burnie (Alfred A. Knopf, 1988) *juvenile/adult*

Birds by Carolyn Boulton (Franklin Watts, 1984) *juvenile*

Birds by Herbert S. Zim and Ira W. Gabrielson (Golden Press, 1956) *juvenile/adult*

The Birds Around Us edited by Alice E. Mace (Ortho Books, 1986) *adult*

The Country Journal Book of Birding and Bird Attraction by Alan Pistorius (W.W. Norton & Company, 1981) *adult*

A Field Guide to the Birds by Roger Tory Peterson (Houghton Mifflin Company, 1980) *adult*

Garden Birds: How to Attract Birds to Your Garden by Dr. Noble Proctor (Rodale Press, 1985) *adult*

A Guide to the Behavior of Common Birds by Donald W. Stokes (Little, Brown and Company, 1983) *adult*

Invite a Bird to Dinner: Simple Feeders You Can Make by Beverly Courtney Crook (Lothrop, Lee & Shepard, 1978) *juvenile*

Making Birdhouses and Feeders by Charles R. Self (Sterling Publishing Company, 1985) *adult*

REPTILES AND AMPHIBIANS

The Audubon Society Field Guide to North American Reptiles and Amphibians by John L. Behler and F. Wayne King (Alfred A. Knopf, 1979) *adult*

A Field Guide to Reptiles and Amphibians by Roger Conant (Houghton Mifflin Company, 1975) *adult*

Reptiles and Amphibians by Herbert S. Zim and Hobart M. Smith (Golden Press, 1956) *juvenile/adult*

INSECTS

The Audubon Society Field Guide to North American Butterflies by Robert Michael Pyle (Alfred A. Knopf, 1981) *adult*

The Audubon Society Field Guide to North American Insects and Spiders by Lorus Milne (Alfred A. Knopf, 1980) *adult*

Butterflies and Moths by Robert Mitchell and Herbert Zim (Golden Press, 1964) *juvenile/adult*

Butterfly & Moth by Paul Whalley (Alfred A. Knopf, 1988) *juvenile/adult*

Discovering Butterflies by Douglas Florian (Charles Scribner's Sons, 1986) *juvenile*

A Field Guide to Insects by Donald J. Borror and Richard E. White (Houghton Mifflin Company, 1970) *adult*

Other books you might enjoy reading

A Guide to Observing Insect Lives by Donald W. Stokes (Little, Brown and Company, 1983) *adult*

Insects by Herbert Zim and Clarence Cottam (Golden Press, 1956) *juvenile/adult*

Looking at Insects by David Suzuki (Warner Books, Inc., 1987) *juvenile*

MARINE LIFE

The Audubon Society Field Guide to North American Fishes, Whales and Dolphins by The Audubon Society Staff (Alfred A. Knopf, 1983) *adult*

The Audubon Society Field Guide to North American Seashells by Harald A. Rehder (Alfred A. Knopf, 1981) *adult*

The Audubon Society Field Guide to North American Seashore Creatures by Norman A. Meinkoth (Alfred A. Knopf, 1981) *adult*

Discovering Seashells by Douglas Florian (Charles Scribner's Sons, 1986) *juvenile*

A Field Guide to Shells by Percy A. Morris (Houghton Mifflin Company, 1975) *adult*

Fishes by Herbert S. Zim and Hurst H. Shoemaker (Golden Press, 1987) *juvenile/adult*

The Whale Watcher's Handbook by Erich Hoyt (Doubleday & Company, Inc., 1984) *adult*

HOME ZOOS

The Aquarium Fish Survival Manual: A Comprehensive Guide to Keeping Freshwater and Marine Fish by Brian Ward (Barron's, 1985) *adult*

Care of the Wild Feathered and Furred: Treating and Feeding Injured Birds and Animals by Mae Hickman and Maxine Guy (Kesend Publishing, Ltd., 1983) *adult*

Care of Uncommon Pets by William J. Weber, DVM (Holt, Rinehart and Winston, 1979) *juvenile/adult*

Great Pets! by Sara Stein (Workman Publishing Company, 1976) *juvenile*

Pets in a Jar by Seymour Simon (The Viking Press, 1975) *juvenile*

A Zoo in Your Room by Roger Caras (Harcourt Brace Jovanovich, 1975) *juvenile*

Vegetable

TREES

The Audubon Society Field Guide to North American Trees by Elbert L. Little (Alfred A. Knopf, 1980) *adult*

A Field Guide to Trees and Shrubs by George A. Petrides (Houghton Mifflin Company, 1973) *adult*

Tree by David Burnie (Alfred A. Knopf, 1988) *juvenile/adult*

Trees by Carolyn Boulton (Franklin Watts, 1984) *juvenile*

Trees by Herbert S. Zim and Alexander C. Martin (Golden Press, 1987) *juvenile/adult*

WILDFLOWERS

The Audubon Society Field Guide to North American Wildflowers by William A. Niering (Alfred A. Knopf, 1979) *adult*

A Field Guide to Wildflowers by Roger Tory Peterson and Margaret McKenny (Houghton Mifflin Company, 1968) *adult*

Flowers by Herbert S. Zim and Alexander C. Martin (Golden Press, 1950) *juvenile/adult*

WILD FOODS

The Audubon Society Field Guide to North American Mushrooms by Gary H. Lincoff (Alfred A. Knopf, 1981) *adult*

A Field Guide to Edible Wild Plants by Lee Allen Peterson (Houghton Mifflin Company, 1977) *adult*

A Field Guide to Mushrooms by Kent H. McKnight and Vera B. McKnight (Houghton Mifflin Company, 1987) *adult*

Mushrooms: Wild and Edible   A Seasonal Guide to the Most Easily Recognized Mushrooms by Vincent Marteka (W.W. Norton & Company, 1980) *adult*

Stalking the Wild Asparagus by Euell Gibbons (David McKay Company, Inc., 1962) *adult*

Other books you might enjoy reading

Wild Foods by Lawrence Pringle (Four Winds Press, 1978) *juvenile*

The Wild, Wild Cookbook: A Guide for Young Wild-Food Foragers by Jean Craighead George (Thomas Y. Crowell, 1982) *juvenile*

GARDENING

The Butterfly Garden: Turning Your Window Box or Backyard into a Beautiful Home for Butterflies by Mathew Tekulsky (The Harvard Common Press, 1985) *adult*

The Country Diary Book of Creating a Wild Flower Garden by Jonathan Andrews (Henry Holt and Company, 1986) *adult*

Cucumbers in a Flowerpot by Alice Skelsey (Workman Publishing, 1984) *adult*

A Garden of Wildflowers: 101 Native Species and How to Grow Them by Henry W. Art (Storey Communication, Inc., 1986) *adult*

Growing Things by Angela Wilkes (Usborne Publishing, Ltd., 1984) *juvenile*

The Herb Growing Book by Rosemary Verey (Little, Brown and Company, 1980) *juvenile*

Let it Rot! The Gardener's Guide to Composting by Stu Campbell (Garden Way Publishing, 1975) *adult*

Looking at Plants by David Suzuki (Warner Books, Inc., 1987) *juvenile*

The Naturalist's Garden by Ruth S. Ernest (Rodale Press, 1987) *adult*

The Victory Garden Kids' Book by Marjorie Waters (Houghton Mifflin Company, 1988) *juvenile*

Your First Garden Book by Marc Brown (Little, Brown and Company, 1981) *juvenile*

Mineral

ROCKS AND MINERALS

The Audubon Society Field Guide to North American Fossils by Ida Thompson (Alfred A. Knopf, 1982) *adult*

The Audubon Society Field Guide to North American Rocks and Minerals by Charles W. Chesterman (Alfred A. Knopf, 1979) *adult*

A Field Guide to Rocks and Minerals by Frederick H. Pough (Houghton Mifflin Company, 1983) *adult*

Fossils by Frank Rhodes, Herbert Zim and Paul Schaffer (Golden Press, 1962) *juvenile/adult*

Geology by Frank H.T. Rhodes (Golden Press, 1972) *juvenile/adult*

Rocks and Minerals by Herbert S. Zim and Paul R. Schaffer (Golden Press, 1957) *juvenile/adult*

Rocks & Minerals by The Natural History Museum Staff (Alfred A. Knopf, 1988) *juvenile/adult*

Start Collecting Fossils by Ted Daeschler (Running Press, 1988) *juvenile*

Earth

SALTWATER HABITATS

At the Sea's Edge: An Introduction to Coastal Oceanography for the Amateur Naturalist by William T. Fox (Prentice-Hall, 1983) *adult*

The Beachcomber's Book by Bernice Kohn (The Viking Press, 1970) *juvenile*

The Rock Pool by David Bellamy (Clarkson N. Potter, Inc., 1988) *juvenile*

The Seashore by Joyce Pope (Franklin Watts, 1985) *juvenile*

Secrets of the Sea by Brian Williams (Ray Rourke Publishing Company, Inc., 1981) *juvenile*

Other books you might enjoy reading

FRESHWATER HABITATS

Pond Life by George Reid (Golden Press, 1967) *juvenile/adult*

Pond & River by Steve Parker (Alfred A. Knopf, 1988) *juvenile/adult*

The River by David Bellamy (Clarkson N. Potter, Inc., 1988) *juvenile*

FIELDS AND FORESTS

Exploring Fields and Lots by Seymour Simon (Garrard Publishing Company, 1978) *juvenile*

The Forest by David Bellamy (Clarkson N. Potter, Inc., 1988) *juvenile*

Oak & Company by Richard Mabey (Greenwillow Books, 1983) *juvenile*

The Roadside by David Bellamy (Clarkson N. Potter, Inc., 1988) *juvenile*

A View from the Oak by Judith and Herbert Kohl (Sierra Club Books/ Charles Scribner's Sons, 1977) *juvenile*

WEATHER

Nature's Weather Forecasters by Helen R. Sattler (Thomas Nelson, Inc., Publishers, 1978) *juvenile*

The Old Farmer's Almanac Book of Weather Lore by Edward F. Dolan (Yankee Books, 1988) *adult*

Questions and Answers about Weather by M. Jean Craig (Four Winds Press, 1969) *juvenile*

Weather by Paul E. Lehr (Golden Press, 1965) *juvenile/adult*

NATURE IN WINTER

Exploring Winter by Sandra Markle (Macmillan Publishing Company, 1984) *juvenile*

A Guide to Nature in Winter by Donald W. Stokes (Little, Brown and Company, 1976) *adult*

Into Winter: Discovering a Season by William P. Nestor (Houghton Mifflin Company, 1982) *juvenile*

Snow Crystals by Wilson Bentley and W.J. Humphreys (Dover Publications, Inc., 1931) *adult*

Winter Book by Harriet Webster (Macmillan Publishing Company, 1988) *juvenile*

LIVING WITH THE EARTH

As We Live and Breathe: The Challenge of Our Environment edited by Donald J. Crump (National Geographic Society, 1971) *adult*

The Endangered Species Handbook by Greta Nilsson (The Animal Welfare Institute, 1983) *adult*

Guide to the National Wildlife Refuges: How to Get There, What to See and Do by Laura and William Riley (Doubleday & Company, Inc., 1979) *adult*

It's Your Environment: Things to Think About, Things to Do from The Environmental Action Coalition (Charles Scribner's Sons, 1976) *juvenile*

Tom Brown's Guide to Living with the Earth by Tom Brown, Jr. (Berkley Publishing, 1984) *adult*

STARS AND PLANETS

A Field Guide to Stars and Planets by Donald H. Menzel and Jay M. Pasachoff (Houghton Mifflin Company, 1983) *adult*

The Glow-in-the-Dark Night Sky Book by Clint Hatchett (Random House, 1988) *juvenile*

The Night Sky Book: An Everyday Guide to Every Night by Jamie Jobb (Little, Brown and Company, 1977) *juvenile*

The Sky Observer's Guide by R. Newton Mayall, Margaret Mayall and Jerome Wyckoff (Golden Press, 1985) *juvenile/adult*

The Young Scientist Book of Stars & Planets by Christopher Maynard (Usborne Publishing Ltd., 1977) *juvenile*

Other books you might enjoy reading

Nature and culture

CRAFTING WITH NATURAL MATERIALS

A Book of Pot-pourri: New and Old Ideas for Fragrant Flowers and Herbs by Gail Duff (Beaufort Books, 1985) *adult*

A Book of Pressed Flowers: A Complete Guide to Pressing, Drying and Arranging by Penny Black (Simon & Schuster, 1988) *adult*

The Complete Book of Straw Craft and Corn Dollies by Doris Johnson and Alec Coker (Dover Publications, Inc., 1987) *adult*

Country Treasures edited by Louis Beetschen (Knopf/Pantheon, 1971) *juvenile*

Creative Shellcraft by Katherine N. Cutler (Lothrop, Lee & Shepard, 1971) *juvenile*

Decoration from Nature: Growing, Preserving and Arranging Materials by Linda Lee Lindgren (Chilton Book Company, 1986) *adult*

From Petals to Pinecones: A Nature Art and Craft Book by Katherine N. Cutler (Lothrop, Lee & Shepard, 1969) *juvenile*

Making Leaf Rubbings: A Hobby for the Entire Family by Mary Lou Burch (The Stephen Greene Press, 1979) *juvenile/adult*

Natural Dyes and Home Dyeing by Rita J. Androsko (Dover Publications, Inc., 1971) *adult*

Nature Crafts and Projects by Beverly Frazier (Price/Stern/Sloane Publishers, 1987) *juvenile*

Potpourri, Incense and Other Fragrant Concoctions by Ann Tucker Fettner (Workman Publishing, 1977) *adult*

Snips & Snails & Walnut Whales by Phyllis Fiarotta (Workman Publishing, 1975) *juvenile*

The Wreath Book by Rob Pulleyn (Sterling Publishing Company, 1988) *adult*

ART INFLUENCED BY NATURE

Art Forms in Nature by Ernst Haeckel (Dover Publications, Inc., 1974) *adult*

The Complete Book of Origami by Robert J. Lang (Dover Publications, Inc., 1989) *juvenile/adult*

Designing from Nature: A Source Book for Artists and Craftsmen by Esther W. Dendel (Taplinger Publishing Company, Inc., 1978) *adult*

Drawing from Nature by Jim Arnosky (Lothrop, Lee & Shepard, 1982) *juvenile*

Easy Origami by Dokuohtei Nakano (Viking Kestral, 1985) *juvenile*

Flights of Imagination by Wayne Hoskings (National Science Teachers Association, 1987) *juvenile*

Kites for Kids by Burton and Rita Marks (William Morrow, 1980) *juvenile*

NATURE LORE

The Earth Is on a Fish's Back: Tales of Beginnings by Natalia Belting (Holt, Rinehart and Winston, 1965) *juvenile*

Honeysuckle Sipping: The Plant Lore of Childhood by Jeanné R. Chesanow (Down East Books, 1987) *juvenile/adult*

A January Fog Will Freeze a Hog and Other Weather Folklore by Hubert Davis (Crown Publishers, Inc., 1977) *juvenile*

The Man in the Moon: Sky Tales from Many Lands by Alta Jablow and Carl Withers (Holt, Rinehart and Winston, 1969) *juvenile*

Midsummer Magic: A Garland of Stories, Charms and Recipes compiled by Elin Greene (Lothrop, Lee & Shepard, 1977) *juvenile*

Someone Saw a Spider: Spider Facts and Folktales by Shirley Climo (Harper & Row Junior Books, 1985) *juvenile*

Star Tales: North American Indian Stories about the Stars by Gretchen Will Mayo (Walker & Company, 1987) *juvenile*

Index

A

Acid rain, 46
Activities. *See also under* Arts and crafts
animal characteristics chart, 54
animal tracks, 24, 50
aquarium, 65
birds, 44, 45, 98-99
clouds, 84-85
in cold weather, 118-119
collections, 58, 67, 75, 76, 88, 91, 97, 98, 108, 112
storage and display, 20
edible roots, 90
exploring, 29, 37, 48, 64, 127-129
games, 26, 113, 115
gardening, 40, 41, 53, 59-61, 68, 94, 103, 107, 115, 134-135
ice, 28
insects, 67, 70-71
leaves, 100-101
make a pond, 65
mushroom hunting, 92
nature programs, 68
nighttime, 34, 82-83
ocean, 72-76
planetarium, 35
rain, 46
rocks and minerals, 86-89
sand, 77
snowflakes, 22
with the sun, 80-81
trees, 30-31, 36, 41, 52
weather, 84-85
wind, 38

Amphibians and reptiles
books about, 140
capture, 14-15, 65
eggs, 53
feeding, 70
Animals. *See also under* names of animals
behavior and habitat, 24, 32, 39, 55, 82
books about, 140-141
capture, 14-15
classification, 54
endangered species, 33
job opportunities with, 62
map of, 112
and people, 62, 63, 113, 131
as pets, 13, 63
predicting weather, 47
tracks, 24, 50, 140
in winter, 21, 24, 24, 119
Ants, 71, 90
Apples, 97, 106
Applesauce, 97
Aquariums, 59, 65, 75
Arbor Day, 52
Art, nature's influence on, 110
Arts and crafts. *See also under* Activities
books about, 144
books to make, 35, 58, 110
holiday decorations, 114-115

ideas for pictures, 23, 43, 48, 57, 72, 84
maps, charts, and diagrams, 32, 34, 72, 112
materials:
bark rubbings, 31
bottles, jars, and containers, 23, 48, 56, 70, 73, 77
cardboard boxes, 35, 41
clay, 89
cones, 116
corn, 93, 105
cotton balls, 84
fabric, 32, 119
flowers, 78, 79, 116
fruit, 106, 107
glass, 51, 71
gourds, 111
leaves, 58, 78, 100, 101
light bulbs, 40
light-sensitive paper, 81
milk cartons, 64
mushrooms, 92
paper and cardboard, 22, 27, 34, 38, 39, 49, 66, 106, 111
rocks, 89
sand, 77
seashells, 75
straw, 38, 122
straws, 71
various materials, 39, 60, 70, 110
vegetables, 92
vines, 105
wood, 36, 58, 98
storage and display, 20

Astronomy. *See under* stars
Autumn
first day (autumnal equinox), 95
first frost, 94
foliage, 100
stories and poems about, 95
wildflowers, 90
Autumnal equinox, 95
Avocado, 41

B

Beaches. *See under* Oceans; Sand
Bees, 51, 71, 102, 103
Bird blind, 44
Bird feeder, 98
Birdbath, 56
Birdhouse, 36
Birds. *See also under* names of birds
books about, 140
Christmas count, 120
feeding, 24, 27, 32, 98, 99, 123
flight, 56
migration, 95, 98, 99, 102
nests, 45, 108
physical characteristics, 56, 57
shore birds, 74
song, 37, 44
state birds, 132-133
stories and poems about, 57, 99
Birthstones, 86
Boats, 72, 105
Bread baking, 93
Bulbs, 36, 94, 102, 117
Burrs (burdock), 91
Butterflies, 69, 71, 94

147

Index

Index

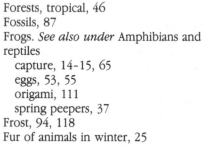

Index

Index

. . . .
The largest desert in the world is the
Sahara in northern Africa. The largest
desert in the United States is the Mo-
jave Desert.

Notes

. . . .
The sunniest city in the United States
is Las Vegas, Nevada, which isn't surprising since it averages only nine
inches of rain each year.

The Yellow Sea in China has a yellowish cast, due to yellow soil that has washed down to the sea over the years. The Red Sea is a reddish-brown, a color that comes from the tiny reddish plants that float on the surface. The White Sea, in northern Russia, is so named because for six to seven months of the year it is covered by ice and snow. The Black Sea, north of Turkey, seems black when heavy fogs hover over it.

Notes

A large oak tree is thought to transpire as many as 300 gallons of water each day.

. . . .

There is a rotating list of names for
potential hurricanes (alphabetized,
with the exception of Q,U,X,Y and Z)
that the U.S. Hurricane Bureau has
composed. Only since World War II
have names been given to these
storms, and then only since 1979 have
men's names been used. Hurricanes
were named for women before that!

Notes

. . . .
When salt water freezes, the ice contains little or no salt. Eskimos often melt ice and use it as fresh drinking water.

TO ORDER MORE GOOD BOOKS FROM WILLIAMSON PUBLISHING

To order additional copies of **The Kids' Nature Book,** please enclose $12.95 per copy plus $2.00 shipping and handling to Williamson Publishing Company at the address listed on the last page.

DOING CHILDREN'S MUSEUMS
A Guide to 225 Hands-On Museums
by Joanne Cleaver

Turn an ordinary day into a spontaneous "vacation" by taking a child to some of the 225 participatory children's museums, discovery rooms, and nature centers covered in this one-of-a-kind book. Filled with museum specifics describing age-appropriate exhibits, facilities, specialties, toddler playspaces, other nearby attractions and eateries. Cleaver has created a most valuable resource for anyone who loves kids!

224 pages, 6 X 9, illustrations
Quality paperback, $12.95

PARENTS ARE TEACHERS, TOO
Enriching Your Child's First Six Years
by Claudia Jones

Be the best teacher your child ever has. Jones shares hundreds of ways to help any child learn in playful home situations. Lots on developing reading, writing, math skills. Plenty on creative and critical thinking, too. A book you'll love using!

192 pages, 6 X 9, illustrations
Quality paperback, $9.95

PUBLIC SCHOOLS USA
A Comparative Guide to School Districts
by Charles Harrison

"How are the schools?" is the question most asked by families on the move whether its cross-town, cross-state or cross-country. Finally, here's the answer as over 500 school districts in major metropolitan areas nationwide are rated on everything from special programs for high-or-low achievers to SAT scores, to music and art programs, to drop-out rates. If your children's education matters to you, here's a book you'll want to own.

368 pages, 8½ X 11
Quality paperback, $17.95

BIKING THROUGH EUROPE
A Roadside Travel Guide with 17 Planned Cycle Tours
by Dennis & Tina Jaffe

Imagine the most idyllic biking vacation in Europe, winding your way through the Bordeaux region of France or on a 3-country (Germany, Austria, Switzerland) tour around Lake Constance, stopping at wonderful cafes and bakeries, picnicking at little known, out-of-the-way scenic treasures. All this and more can be your experience using the Jaffe's fabulous book jam-packed with detailed, specific information.

304 pages, 8 X 10, illustrated
Quality paperback, $13.95

GOLDE'S HOMEMADE COOKIES
by Golde Hoffman Soloway

"Cookies are her chosen realm and how sweet a world it is to visit."
Publishers Weekly

Over 100 treasured recipes that defy description. Suffice it to say that no one could walk away from Golde's cookies without asking for another . . . plus the recipe.

144 pages, 8¼ X 7¼, illustrated
Quality paperback, $8.95

THE BROWN BAG COOKBOOK
Nutritious Portable Lunches for Kids and Grown-Ups
by Sara Sloan

Here are more than 1,000 brown bag lunch ideas with 150 recipes for simple, quick, nutritious lunches that kids will love. Breakfast ideas, too!

192 pages, 8¼ X 7¼, illustrated
Quality paperback, $8.95

. . . .

Easy-to-Make
GIFTS FOR THE BABY
by Cindy Higgins

There's still nothing nicer than a home-crafted, straight from the heart, gift for babies and toddlers. Somehow store-bought just doesn't measure up. Here are 65 gifts-everything from practical carry-all totes to huggable bunnies and two-sided dolls to clever wooden toys, rocking chairs, clown book shelf, and toy soldier clothes racks. Plus quick and easy quilts, blankets, kids backpacks. Best of all—simple directions and many projects to make in an hour or less!

144 pages, 8 X 10, illustrated
Quality paperback, $8.95

. . . .

DINING ON DECK:
Fine Food for Sailing & Boating
by Linda Vail

For Linda Vail a perfect day's sail includes fine food-quickly and easily prepared. She offers here 225 outstanding recipes (casual yet elegant food) with over 90 menus for everything from elegant weekends to hearty breakfasts and suppers for cool weather sailing. Her recipes are so good and so varied you'll use her cookbook year-round for sure!

160 pages, 8 X 10, illustrated
Quality paperback, $10.95